THE SOUL
OF CHINA

Also by Amaury de Riencourt

ROOF OF THE WORLD
THE COMING CAESARS
THE SOUL OF INDIA

THE SOUL
OF CHINA

Revised Edition

Amaury de Riencourt

Harper Colophon Books
Harper & Row, Publishers
New York

THE SOUL OF CHINA
Revised Edition

Copyright © 1958, 1965 by Amaury de Riencourt

Printed in the United States of America. All rights reserved. No part of this book may be used or reproduced in any manner whatsoever without written permission except in the case of brief quotations embodied in critical articles and reviews. For information address Harper & Row, Publishers, Incorporated, 49 East 33rd Street, New York, N.Y. 10016.

This book was originally published by Coward-McCann, Inc., New York, New York, in 1958, and is here reprinted by arrangement.

First Harper Colophon edition published 1965 by
Harper & Row, Publishers, Incorporated
New York

Library of Congress Catalog Card Number: 58-5698

CONTENTS

2 The Spring and Autumn

3 The Twilight of Culture

part four
CHINA AND
THE WORLD

10 The Collapse of Chinese Civilization

11 In Search of a New Philosophy

INTRODUCTION

Few people would argue today that the fate of China is of primary importance to the world. What might seem to be quaint traditions and colorful oddities in small communities becomes a formidable fact when shared by more than six hundred million human beings. Revolutions can become major catastrophes of history when they overturn such immense masses as the Chinese people.

The history of China during the past half-century has been tragic for the Chinese and for their Western friends alike. A great many Western people who knew China well have been appalled by this hopeless unfolding of events, anguished by the endless tale of pathetic misunderstandings which perpetually garbled the relations between China and the West, and puzzled by seemingly irrational reactions on the part of Far Eastern friends of long standing. A great many more Westerners had fallen in love with China than ever did with Japan, India or the Arab world. The Chinese, the supreme humanists of all times, seemed closer to us than any other Asian people; their delicate civilization was utterly entrancing to the more discriminating type of Westerner. Their refined courtesy, their subtle humor, their profound art, their exquisite food, everything conspired to make of China the second homeland of most Europeans and Americans who had ever been to the Celestial Land.

And, suddenly, this fantastic revolution, this bold plunge into an inhuman form of totalitarianism, this sudden disclosure of an almost pathological hatred for the West! It seems utterly incomprehensible. Yet it is not through lack of authoritative books and comprehensive studies that the West has sinned. Centuries ago, Europe became fascinated by the remote Celestial Empire and all those who care to do so can still find on some dusty shelf a copy of a work entitled *Confucius, Sinarum Philosophus, sive Scientia Sinensis*, published in Paris in 1687. This remarkably thorough work was written by Jesuits who had spent a great part of their lives in China, and who had become thoroughly Chinese indeed. Every cultured European in the eighteenth century read this work and the countless works which followed on its heels. Such profound minds as Leibnitz and Voltaire were deeply influenced by Chinese thought. And generation after generation of Westerners studied Chinese affairs, then traveled to the Far East and became immersed in an "immemorial" China without noticing that, somehow, they had never really penetrated into the innermost recesses of the Chinese soul, had never grasped the essence of the Chinese mind.

There was, from the start, something wrong in the intellectual approach of the Westerners. Caught in the tight web of their own specific problems, trapped by their own intellectual snares, imprisoned within the narrow vista of their peculiar world-outlook, the Westerners saw of China only what they wanted to see. Quite unconsciously, they looked at

China in a subjective way and inevitably made two fundamental and related mistakes: on the one hand, they were unwilling to look for a comprehensive philosophy of history
which might determine the great similarities existing between
the historical evolutions of China and the West—and of all
other civilizations, for that matter. They were thus unable to
determine at what stage of their evolutions both China and
the West had arrived. Yet it was obvious that a China that
was old when Julius Caesar crossed the Rubicon had already
gone through the same stages of cultural development through
which the modern West was proceeding two thousand years
later, and in the same sequence. Thus, one aspect of the
Chinese problem which Westerners chose to ignore was the
point of intersection at which both China and the West, following their separate historical courses, were meeting. And
then, on the other hand, they refused to see the unique, original and utterly incomparable features of Chinese civilization.
Westerners, basically, saw only in the Chinese men like themselves, a little wiser, a little weaker, a little more mellow. Those
of definite religious bent saw in the Chinese a wonderful raw
material for conversion to Christianity; others, on the contrary, saw in them skeptics who had been able to do without
theological notions, men who were a living proof that morality
and lack of religion were perfectly compatible. Nowhere was
there an attempt to look at China from both angles at once,
to see objectively that Chinese history conformed to a definite
pattern of history but that, at the same time, Chinese civilization had a unique personality of its own and would one day
refuse to bow to a Western civilization that was wholly alien
to it. Westerners looked upon China as Herodotus had once
looked upon a petrified Pharaonic Egypt—baffled, awed and
totally unconscious of their respective positions in the development of history.

From this initial misconception sprang all the others. A
great myth arose among Westerners watching the oceanlike
uniformity of a static Chinese civilization which never seemed
to be stirred by the slightest breeze, whereas dynamic Europe

was in the throes of perpetual convulsions—the myth of the "timeless East," a motionless giant who was forever condemned to follow clumsily in the wake of Western progress. What the West failed to understand was that China had long since passed the point at which Western Europe was arriving in the nineteenth and twentieth centuries.[1]

As a self-contained, self-enclosed and autonomous civilization China had *completed* her historical cycle, whereas the West was not even halfway through. The disastrous encounte of the past century was the inevitable outcome of this mental blindness.

So long as the West itself refuses to revise its own philosophic approach to take into account all the other civilizations and, somehow, explain them all and relate them to some basic principle of historical evolution, there is no real possibility of understanding China. But if the reflective Westerner is willing to approach the study of historical development with a constructive and unbiased mind, if he is willing to attempt to make sense out of the universe of historical Time as he is attempting to make sense out of the physical universe of Space, a bright light will begin to shine where there was only darkness. If he undertakes a comparative study of all civilizations known to history, he will see that there is some mysterious inner reason for these analogous growths of social organisms, some spiritual plan which unfolds itself through the process of historical evolution. China then becomes understandable to him as it never could otherwise. Chinese evolution seen against the fluid background of world history acquires a remarkable relief, a distinctness of outline which projects itself into the future and illuminates the present in startling fashion. It then becomes clear that contemporary China is by no means emerging from some dark, medieval feudal age which happens to be centuries behind modern times—as characterized by the West—but, on the contrary, is historically 'way beyond. China does not suffer from *arrested* growth but from *terminated* growth—such a termination as the West might well experience in coming centuries if the lessons of the past are not heeded.

We therefore have to find some guide, some connecting thread which will show us both the similarities and the differences between China and the Western world. A philosophy of history is what we need—an effort to find trends and patterns which are as similar in all civilizations as physiological phenomena are similar in human individuals, however unique and wholly original they may be in other ways.*

The essence of history does not reside in recorded facts but in the thoughts, emotions, ideas and aspirations of the human beings who have made it. Facts are only the outer shell, the crystallization and materialization of ideas and emotions. History is life itself, and, like everything else that is alive, it has both a cyclical rhythm and a linear tension. This linear unfolding of history—the Industrial Revolution, scientific progress and such—is familiar to us because we keep our eyes glued to it; there is no need to go deeper into it at this stage. On the other hand, this cyclical rhythm, this pulse shows us a definite pattern of recurrences which is clearly visible in all human societies: they are born, they grow and they die—and often enough they are followed by other societies in formation who feed off their rotting corpses like maggots—the Persians in Babylon, the Classical Greeks in Egypt, the Germanic hordes in the Roman Empire. What we have to discover is the grand cycle of history, that which takes into account the whole of a particular society's life—its arts, sciences, religions, philosophies, politics, economics, all of which are intimately connected and interrelated. It has to be all-inclusive.

The great cycle which has been in evidence throughout history like a giant wheel of destiny revolves around the sequence leading from *Culture* to *Civilization*. Those two familiar words we are now going to use in an unfamiliar fashion: in the periodic sense of youth followed by maturity, in the sense of organic succession. Instead of coinciding in time, Civilization follows and fulfills the Culture which was tending toward it during the life span of a particular society. In this sense, each organic society has "its" own Culture and "its" own Civilization.

Culture is the state of being of a young society awakening to new life, a society which is often a result of the rape of old, decadent, overcivilized people by dynamic barbarians. This society is born when the fusion between the old and the primitive is more or less completed—as it was in Western Europe after the last Norse barbarians had been digested. The result is an entirely new outlook on the world and, therefore, original creation in every field of human activity—religious, artistic, intellectual, political. Culture is essentially trail-blazing.

Culture is a pulsating organism endowed with immense flexibility, in a state of constant, irrepressible growth. Civilization, on the other hand, is the rigid crystallization of a particular society; it is the unavoidable horizontal tread on history's stairway, the inevitable pause of a society whose creativity is exhausted by its cultural growth and seeks to digest, duplicate, spread and distribute mechanically the output of its parent culture. Culture lays the emphasis on the original and unique, Civilization on the common and general: they are respectively the Greek and the Roman ideals.

The following work will show how, under this new system of reference, the West came to collide with China and how Chinese civilization caved in under the impact. But it should be emphasized that, like wheels within wheels, smaller cycles operate within the broad cycle just outlined. This will illustrate more particularly a phenomenon which has struck every thoughtful observer of the recent events in China: the triumph of Marxism in China implies to a very great extent a return to the past; China experienced a minor but almost full cycle during the past half-century, the net result of which has been to substitute a new Marxist orthodoxy for the old Confucian one. And this, in turn, throws an entirely new light on the future of both China and the West.

Now, as to the structural form of this work. The application of this philosophy of history to China results in a thorough study of the two extremities of Chinese history's time span—of the formation and development of Chinese Culture before the Christian era, and of the convulsions of China under the impact of the West in the past hundred years. The two thousand years which stand between these two epochs—Chinese Civilization—are only briefly surveyed. This emphasis on the two extremities of Chinese history's time span underlines the twofold purpose of this volume: first, to illustrate with the help of a survey of ancient China the similarities existing between the development of all human Cultures, as well as the profound psychological differences which separate them (the fact that at one time or another all human societies have had to face, usually in the same ordered sequence, many of the problems which we face today, is of great interest to us—many of the solutions which they worked out could be applied to the contemporary world); and second, to explain modern China against the background of Chinese culture and psychology, to analyze the contemporary development of Chinese culture, society and political institutions within the framework of this philosophy of history.

This volume is divided into four parts, the first one of which presents the full and autonomous Chinese cycle as it evolved from Culture into Civilization. The titles of the other parts—China and Asia, China and the West, China and the World—illustrate the fact that history has a linear as well as a cyclical development—technological progress, which made possible the ever widening contacts between alien civilizations, which brought China into contact with India, Southeast Asia and the Arab world, then with Western Europe, and finally with America and the whole world.

If any geometrical figure can best illustrate the pattern of man's historical development, it is the *spiral*. Although separate human societies undergo similar growths in the same organic sequence, they do so on ever higher levels of cultural and technical development. They ascend a figurative spiral rather than follow a straight ascending line or run around in disconnected cycles. It is to this linear development that we owe the tragic clash between two autonomous cyclical developments—the Chinese and the Western—and it is to the higher stage of development reached by the West that we owe the collapse of the traditional Chinese structure.

A short introduction such as this one can barely outline a philosophy of history. A great deal more of it will become clear as the history of China unfolds.* All that can be done at this stage is to apply the system objectively and see whether it explains the Chinese enigma more satisfactorily than has been done so far. For all its drawbacks, the approach of a philosopher of history may have its advantages—perhaps in a better perspective of the whole problem. I have attempted to draw a sharply defined picture of China and I hope that the broad generalizations which follow will be forgiven for the sake of the clearer perspective which they offer. And so this work is presented with the hope that, through this new system of reference, a modest contribution will have been made to solve one of the most baffling problems of our times.

* I would like to mention the fact that the study of China which follows is only a fragment of a much larger work, of an all-inclusive philosophy of history in several volumes based on a comparative study of all cultures and civilizations. In another volume, *The Coming Caesars* (New York, Coward-McCann, 1957), I have already set forth the application of this philosophy of history to our modern world. I have repeated certain definitions and explanations in this introduction for the benefit of those readers who are not familiar with *The Coming Caesars*.

part one

THE MAKING
OF CHINA

1

"MEDIEVAL" CHINA

One of the presumed mysteries of history is the amazing durability of China's civilization through those thousands of years which saw the rise and fall of so many glorious civilizations in other parts of the world —Babylonia, Egypt, Persia, Rome, Islam. But there is no real mystery; geography explains it.

Far away from the other great centers of human population, beyond the highest and bulkiest mountains in the world, beyond eternal snows, steaming jungles, inaccessible swamps and parched deserts, China was essentially a self-enclosed area —an isolated subcontinent, at the far end of the known world beyond whose shores there was nothing but an infinitely vast ocean, leading nowhere, fading away into boundless space. For those who arrived in China, as guests or as invaders, there was no beyond, nowhere else to go—

and a great deal to learn and enjoy in its exquisite civilization. Protected from cultural drafts and cross-currents, invulnerable because of her sheer massiveness, China was able to preserve the basic forms of her civilization until the twentieth century, digesting, assimilating and absorbing into her vast structure all invaders, ideas as well as men.

Early in the second millennium B.C. a number of primitive cultures had already appeared in the valleys and plains centered around the Yellow River. A gradual interpenetration of these various cultures eventually gave rise to small tribal states, and the progressive integration of these states generated the first organized society on a civilized level, with which China leaves the fabulous world of prehistory to enter history proper. About the middle of the second millennium B.C., the Shang dynasty —the "Carlovingian" dynasty of China—originated the first elements of China's higher culture in northwest Honan, along the Shansi mountains. It was to China what the Homeric Age was to Greece or Charlemagne's to Western Europe, the typical "Heroic Age" which ministers to the birth of a new Culture.

The main social feature of a Heroic Age is the gradual collapse of the *tribal* organization through the emancipation of the chiefs of clan from all tribal obligations. This collapse of the type of organization which characterizes primitive societies everywhere is the first step in the rise of a higher culture. Tribal *chiefs* free themselves from public control by the tribes, become *princes* and commanders of war bands, surrounded no longer by their kindred but by chosen followers pledged to *personal* loyalty: *tribal* society metamorphoses itself into *feudal* society.[1]

But, as a rule, this disintegration of a tribal society (essentially "barbarian") takes place in the midst of an old "civilized" society, decadent and already conquered by the barbarian tribes. In Shang China we have a "Carlovingian" type of empire in which the two elements are clearly present. Shang society was far more civilized and sophisticated than the barbarian Chou who dwelt on the fringes of its geographical area. The rise of feudalism was made inevitable, as it always is in such cases, by the gradual collapse of the Shang empire, unable to protect its subjects against oppressors, military power falling into the hands of small groups of barbarians and economic unity breaking down. Political power, formerly concentrated, becomes diffuse. Feudalism is largely a backward step taken by a society in order to organize and protect itself on a *local* scale, since the collapse of its civilization makes it impossible on a large scale.

But this is anticipation. The Shang state was clearly a pre-feudal state, doomed, like Charlemagne's, to eventual dislocation because its primitive structure could not cope with its enemies on an empire-wide scale. Although this new society in formation enjoyed at first a purely agrarian economy, the rudiments of Chinese art made their appearance shortly after the foundation of the dynasty: bronze implements were cast and soon reached high artistic standards which have not been excelled since, as perfect in their way as Romanesque art during Europe's Dark Ages. Sericulture started also in early Shang days, and threads spun by every type of caterpillar were tested and eliminated for centuries until the silkworm triumphed for all time over its clumsier competitors. Weaving techniques progressed swiftly and, when communications were established with the rest of Asia, silk brocades became the first notable export of China.

Meanwhile the areas under cultivation were constantly expanded by the indomitable will and energy of the sturdy Chinese peasant who drove back the wild beasts by clearing jungles and dank undergrowth, draining swamps and marshes, destroying or absorbing aboriginal savages, annihilating insects, controlling floods and droughts, laying the basis of a complex irrigation network, building modest huts at first, more elaborate homes later on and finally mighty cities with multitudes of temples and palaces. This relentless, gigantic effort was carried out over a period of many centuries, and the quick multiplication of prolific human beings offered an expanding base on whose biological vitality one of the highest Cultures of the world was in the process of being built.

In the Shang era the first and most original element of that culture was born—a pictorial script which triumphed over every phonetic script that might have filtered in from the Middle East. Around 800 B.C. this pictorial writing, the ancestor of modérn Chinese characters, began to include a few phonetic signs for the sake of convenience. But it remained essentially visual and, as culture progressed with each new generation, new characters had to be created out of old ones. This script soon evolved into a strange but complicated writing system which possessed no grammar, no alphabet, no spelling, no inflections, no declensions, no conjugations nor tenses. Every word might be a noun, a verb or an adjective, depending on the context and on the tone.

Chinese psychology shaped this strange structure and was shaped by it in its turn over thousands of years. From the start, there was a definite lack of logic which a grammar using a phonetic script will automatically impart, even if it is as loose and plastic as the Sanskrit logic of India. Fundamentally, the Chinese remained staunch rationalists but lacked the feeling for logical sequence in any line of reasoning which is so familiar to Classical and Western thinking.

On the other hand, the great advantage of such a system lies in the depth of aesthetic appreciation developed by visual characters, each one of which requires all the qualities essential to a perfect drawing. A script which is visual instead of phonetic is bound to require a high degree of technical skill in the art of drawing, a powerful sense of form and line. Inevitably calligraphy and painting, shu-hua, became closely welded by the Chinese into a twin combination which made of both an indissoluble unit.

Calligraphy became the training ground of Chinese painters, the gospel of Chinese aestheticism. The greatest calligraphist of all times, Wang Hsi-chih, defined his art in the following terms: "Every horizontal stroke is like a mass of clouds in battle formation, every hook like a bent bow of the greatest strength, every dot like a falling rock from a high peak, every turning of the stroke like a brass hook, every drawn-out line like a dry vine of great old age and every swift and free stroke like a runner on his start." [2] Every artist had his own personal style of writing which he developed from his observations of nature: the bending of a reed under the wind, the struggle between a tiger and a powerful snake, a waterfall dissolving into a misty cloud.

Chinese literary style at first deliberately shunned theoretical abstractions. It became noted for its vivid, flashing and intensely concrete images: lightness of touch became the "method of dragonflies skimming the water surface," the direct opening was the "method of going straight into the fray with one knife," light raillery was depicted as the "method of side stabs and flanking attacks" and a mellow style translated itself as the "method of a light mist hanging over a gray lake."

Closely woven into each other, calligraphy, painting and poetry established the most exquisite channels through which a communion between nature and the cultivated Chinese could be established. Calligraphy, especially, became the most highly prized accomplishment resulting from many years of study. It is almost impossible for a foreigner to understand the immense poetic profundity of a script which is symbolic rather than factual, which always suggests but never defines rigidly and therefore never circumscribes thought and expression as sharply as a logical grammar with its mathematical rules.

As long as the ideograms represented concrete objects or movements, their shaping presented no difficulty. But abstract ideas soon appeared and their pictorial representation created an intricate problem. The Chinese solved it by using such characters as were already used to depict concrete objects, totally unrelated in the abstract but sounding similar in speech, and adding a distinctive sign, the "determinative." This new set of abstract characters became the "phonograms"; added to the ideograms, they expanded the entire Chinese script until it finally amounted to more than forty thousand characters.

It is easy to imagine how cramping such a complex system could become when it is remembered that ten thousand characters had to be mastered before a Chinese scholar could call himself truly literate. The social consequence was to restrict intellectual development to a small class of scholars who were destined to become a more or less fluid but exclusive ruling class.

A further but related difficulty was the monosyllabic nature of China's original languages. The Pekinese dialect knows only 420 primary monosyllables, so that one sound can express dozens of different ideas or objects. Each vocable can be read out loud in four to nine different tones—the context and gestures often help out where conversation has become hopelessly entangled in a multitude of homophones, for example because *shi* has fifty-nine different meanings. Chinese usually have to wait until the end of a whole sentence before they can understand the basic meaning of the speech, but the high-pitched tones of voice and accents which are an essential complement often vary from one province to another. In desperation, men from different parts of China often communicate with the help of signs drawn with a finger on the palm of the hand. Because of these difficulties, most of the characters were built on the concept of a phonetic combination with the help of thirteen hundred phonograms.

The Chinese ideographic system crystallized and became fixed during the early Han dynasty, the dawn of China's Civilization, to remain fairly static and immutable thereafter. No phonetic script could have remained as petrified as China's ideographic structure, and its immensely conservative influence can never be overestimated. Languages and dialects could change, the climate, politics, economic and social conditions could undergo complete revolutions—but as long as the ideograms remained intact, the Chinese mind revolved within the confines of a rigid mold. The monosyllabic structure of the spoken language, joined with the ideograms, gave to the literary achievements of the Chinese a remarkable brevity which is unparalleled in any other culture. The old characters, especially, being more visual than phonetic, had a monosyllabic terseness which was considerably weakened by the reforms introduced early in the twentieth century.

The ruler of the Shang state, surrounded by monks, was as much a high priest as he was a political sovereign. Under his rule, China enjoyed the same type of medieval unity as Europe's Christendom in the pre-Gothic Dark Ages under its Roman pope. In the already vast area of *Chung-Kuo* (the Middle Kingdom), which had come under the spell of this budding culture, society was still organized on a clan basis and apparently retained many features of the earlier tribal organization—as in early Vedic India or pre-Homeric Greece. But before it entered its true "medieval" era, a new and momentous invasion took place. Like the Normans in Europe or the Dorians in Greece, the barbaric and audacious Chou tribes invaded the Chinese world and put an end to the Shang dynasty in 1122 B.C.

This new dynasty—China's equivalent of France's Capetian —presided over the development of Chinese Culture proper over a period of seven centuries, and most of the traits which were to remain typical of the Chinese date from that trailblazing era. The first Chou ruler, Wu Wang (King Wu), injected rejuvenating elements borrowed from the surrounding barbarians into the bloodstream of the sedentary Chinese society. And it is under his rule that China saw the birth of feudalism. Most of the greater and lesser tribal chiefs who had helped him in overthrowing the Shang divided the spoils and were granted hereditary fiefs, like so many Frankish and Norman leaders in Western Europe. Whatever central power there had been before that time gradually disappeared and the same evolution which characterized feudalism everywhere took place in China between the eleventh and the seventh centuries B.C.: the rise of chivalry with its knights *(shih)* and code of ethics *(li)*, the gradual absorption of smaller fiefs *(fu-yung)* by larger ones *(kuo)*, the weakening of the personal allegiance from vassal to suzerain, the slow rise of the notion of state and nation, and eventually the metamorphosis of feudal lords (bearing one of the five titles of *kung, hou, po, tzu* and *nan*) into noble aristocrats (*chün-tzu*).

The social gap between the Chinese population—the "black-haired people"—and the ruling conquerors—the noble "hundred families"—remained considerable for centuries, only to disappear in the end. The same social evolution took place in all the other higher Cultures of the world. The Aryan feudalism in India, the Dorian feudal nobility of early Greece, the Visigothic, Frankish and Norman feudal lords of Western Europe, all of which were of barbarian descent, ended by merging with the conquered populations and transforming their autonomous *feudal* lords into *aristocratic* nobilities when organized states appeared at the close of their respective "medieval" ages. But the complete absorption of the Chou was the first dramatic example of that fabulous capacity for ethnic digestion which the Chinese have displayed repeatedly throughout their history and which defeated all their invaders in the long run. Racial differences between the Chinese and their barbarian neighbors were at all times slight, racial consciousness was nonexistent and no caste system ever arose. But as a compensation for social fluidity, cultural freedom was never as substantial as it was in India with its castes or in Greece with its slaves. Social absorption was purchased at the cost of a psychological "conformity" that was definitely consecrated when Chinese Civilization finally petrified.

Endowed with an irrepressible biological vitality, the Chinese started the long process of expansion and emigration over a large portion of the Far East which is still going on in our twentieth century. Along the valleys and around impenetrable mountains, across deserts or marshland, the Chinese peasant was ceaselessly penetrating into wild areas, turning over pastoral land into agricultural settlements, introducing the culture of cereals on a large scale. In the warm south there was little resistance, but in the frosty north barbarians were more hostile. In times of economic depression or political disorder in China the nomads had their supplies cut off, and hunger became telling. They were then constrained to turn to raiding, often to launch aggressive invasions. This process went on for thousands of years and, as the Chinese were prolific, every advance of the Chinese peasantry toward the north increased the dangers of nomad pressure on the frontiers of civilization. There was a sort of blind, instinctive rhythm in this alternation of attraction and repulsion which became the biological leitmotiv hidden behind Chinese history, behind invasions, dynastic cycles, alternating times of peace and war.

The developing *weltanschauung* of the Chinese had first expressed itself, as it did in every other culture, in their religious concepts. The primary goal of their ritual sacrifices was to make sure that the rhythm of man's life on Earth was in full concordance with the rhythm of Heaven. A specific theism proclaimed that the celestial order was minutely regulated by Shang-ti, the "Sovereign on High"; his human counterpart was the pope-king, *T'ien-tzu* ("Son of Heaven"), who was invested with the "Mandate of Heaven," *T'ien-ming*. The Son of Heaven's duty was to harmonize Heaven and Earth through appropriate sacrifices, fix the calendar, determine the appropriate dates for agricultural celebrations and the inauguration of the seasons.

As time went on, the anthropomorphic god Shang-ti began to fade away in favor of the more impersonal Heaven; this metamorphosis was considerably accelerated by the remarkable Duke of Chou, brother of the first ruler of China's "Capetian" dynasty and one of the most outstanding personalities in Chinese history. In fact, we can trace back to him the destruction of the Shang priesthood and the permanent establishment of *ancestor worship* as a substitute for the vanished *cults*. Family feeling invaded the sphere of religion; the ruler became the father of the Chinese people as well as the Son of Heaven.

A deep metaphysical structure was elaborated at the time. Most of it disappeared, along with many works of poetry and philosophy, in the destructive "epurations" and literary holocausts carried on centuries later by Confucianists and anti-Confucianists, but enough has come down to us through the famous *I-Ching*, the "Book of Changes." According to this remarkable work, all the laws of nature can be condensed into eight Kuas, mystic trigrams which consist of three lines each.

In this "shorthand" summary of metaphysical laws, continuous lines represent the *Yang* or male principle, the symbol of the positive, active, dynamic and spiritual elements of nature. Broken lines represent the *Yin* or female principle, which stands for the negative, passive, earthly element of nature. The trigram which stands for purely masculine Heaven consists of three straight lines and the purely feminine Earth is depicted by three broken lines, all other trigrams and elements being a combination of these two fundamental elements. They pictured the interplay between Yang and Yin, under its purely sexual aspect as well as on the highest metaphysical level, as regulating the whole cosmic life. To the earthy Chinese, endowed with immense vitality and a great love for life, the life-giving union of the two complementary sexes was the fundamental principle from which everything else—nature, man, thought, art, society—derived. And since the human mind had to remain in tune with nature in order to think correctly, human thought had to start from this basic principle. The *I-Ching* remained the metaphysical bible of China, a work of such fundamental importance that Confucius was obliged to stamp it with his grudging approval.

This anti-metaphysical bias which was beginning to make itself felt with increasing force, and which Confucius symbolized later on, resulted from one of the most remarkable traits of Chinese psychology. Whereas Indians were solely interested in the "spatial" world of nature, material and spiritual, physical and psychical, and disregarded *history* entirely, the Chinese had a strong chronological conception of Time, a deep feeling for historical sequence which Confucius eventually crystallized. One of the greatest symbols of a Culture's attitude

toward Time and Space lies in its disposal of the dead. The
Indians, unwilling to fight the inevitable corruption wrought
by years and centuries, burned their dead as if to obliterate
forever their duration in Time. The Homeric Greeks, turning their backs on the strong sense of historical preservation
of the Egyptians and the Mycenaeans, did likewise. Not so
the Chinese, who buried their dead almost as carefully as the
Egyptians in their sarcophagi and thus revealed their instinctive concern for *duration*.

The numerous gods of the Shang and pre-Shang epochs
represented forces of nature—the awesome "Lord of the
River," wind deities, waterfall deities, gods of the soil, sun-
gods. They were usually gods of fertility—first of Nature's fertility, then of Man's. Almost the same phallic symbols served
to designate *Shê*, god of the soil, and the term *ancestor*. These
mythical elements in *Space* were slowly transmuted into mythical ancestors in *Time*. Over a period of centuries, they became mythological emperors and kings, model rulers of an
imaginary Golden Age. One of the many reasons or pre-
texts was the strong desire of many feudal rulers to rival
the Chou king and claim descent from a mythical emperor whose name was already familiar to the Chinese
masses as a local deity. All such gods were thus withdrawn
from spatial nature and placed arbitrarily in mythical-histor-
ical perspective, later on methodically arranged and fitted
chronologically into dynasties for the sake of harmony. For
instance, Huang Ti, a local god of southern Shansi, became
officially the ancestor of all the feudal rulers of the area in
450 B.C. Another instance is the case of Yü the Great, originally a god who had raised the earth above the surface of the
water. Gradually, in late Chou times, he became a human
king, and finally, during the Warring States era, he ended by
being the acknowledged ancestor of the Hsia dynasty.[3] In
India, on the contrary, princes and rulers were inclined to
transmute their real, historical ancestors into transcendental
gods and goddesses, still alive in a timeless present beyond
form.

The psychological roots of these two opposed world-out-looks dig deep into one of man's primary instincts: the urge to survive beyond death. There are two ways in which such an urge can conceivably be satisfied: by personal survival in spiritual form (whether dwelling for eternity in a Christian paradise or undergoing the cycle of Hindu and Buddhist reincarnations) or by survival through descendants who perpetuate in this world one's own flesh and blood. In this latter outlook, which the Chinese adopted, the sense of survival can exist only to the extent that the descendants actually "remember" the ancestors by paying homage to them. The ancestors survive only to the extent that their own flesh and blood, extended in Time beyond their own death, think about them. This more earthy, less spiritual form of survival is at the root of *ancestor worship*. And the fact that memory becomes the essential part of this worship tends to promote a *historical*, Time-conscious outlook which is diametrically opposed to the Indian.

Chinese historiography, which seems fanciful to the Western historian, was molded to suit the growing ethical philosophy that Confucius summed up and dramatized. Every cultured Chinese was given such historical myths as examples and he was invited to keep an eye on the meaningful past for the sake of the present and future, as an inspiration fostering a moral life. It was a subjective rather than an objective view of the past, an ethical rather than a scientific one. What should be kept in mind, however, is that this historiography was a substitute for true religion. Every philosophical school had its own presiding deity, but this deity was never a spiritual god dwelling in some timeless heaven—it was a flesh-and-blood historical man who had lived in a more or less mythical past. "The Mohists emphasized the abdication-legends in the interests of peace and good government; Mencius emphasized the people's choice of Yü instead of the son of Shun on account of his democratic theories; the Taoists invented Huang Ti who governed through inactivity, and so on." [4]

This conception of Time and History became indelibly

woven into the cultural and psychological fabric of the Chinese people and to this day influences the subconscious thinking of every man of thought and action in China. The true goal of the higher type of Chinese man was not self-realization through mystical introspection, as in India, but the securing of an honored place in the harmonious procession of historical personages. Spiritual realization came from "duration," triumphing over the corrupting process of *Time* rather than escaping into *Eternity*; instead of spiritual self-realization we have "historical significance."

The emerging keystone of the Chinese world-outlook was no longer a waning *religion* centered around the worship of static deities manifesting themselves through Nature and Space but a rudimentary *philosophy of history* which claimed to see in the Time sequence the true manifestation of the supreme spiritual being. The Book of Changes could be considered in many ways the psychological watershed between those two opposed world-outlooks: its purpose is already to help men emancipate themselves from the tyranny of events by seeing into both the past and the future. The commentary on the first hexagram, Ch'ien, (the Creative) tells us that it "includes also the power of time and the power of persisting in time, that is, duration"; [5] and it adds: "Time is no longer a hindrance but the means of making actual what is potential." [6] In a sense, this was the hard core of Chinese metaphysics. The commentary added: "this duration in time is the image of the power inherent in the Creative." [7]

Consider the second hexagram, K'un (the Receptive); it is the complement of the first one (not the opposite, because the Chinese had substituted at an early date the concept of *co-operation* for that of *competition*). [8] The Receptive "represents nature in contrast to spirit, Earth in contrast to Heaven, Space as against Time, the female-maternal as against the male-paternal"; the primacy of Time (Heaven) over Space (Earth) is stoutly affirmed. [9]

This cardinal development in Chinese thinking—this sublimation of an awareness of the flow of Time, of memory and

anticipation, into a *philosophy of history* rather than the sublimation of Space into a static *religion* concerned with timeless and absolute spirituality—took place over a period of many
centuries, a purely instinctive development which gives us one
of the fundamental keys to Chinese psychology.

The decay of the Chou dynasty started about three centuries later, when the racial absorption of the Chou ruling class
by the Chinese population was completed. The growing
strength and independence of the various national states which
mushroomed out of the disintegrating feudalism put increasing limitations on the powers of the Chou ruler, who in
771 B.C. had been forcibly moved to Loyang, in the center
of the Chinese world. He became a sanctified overlord, an
ineffective religious symbol who lost whatever political authority he had ever had in the past, while the states assumed all
the trappings of national sovereignty, as in Europe after the
Renaissance.

This slow evolution put no brake on the ceaseless expansion of the Chinese world at the expense of the surrounding
barbarians. In those days of growing tension within the Chinese world, the most constructive work was done by the "Lords
Protectors," who assumed the new title of *pa*, strong personalities who exercised a semidictatorship over their respective
states, calling congresses of princes and rulers. They emerged
toward the close of China's "medieval" era like the typical
condottieri of Europe's Renaissance or the early tyrants of
Classical Greece, representatives of the rising middle classes
who were superseding the fast-decaying feudalism and wanted
to abolish this outdated social structure altogether. Confucius
was full of praise for the first Protector, Hwang of Tsi, who
called a congress and whom Confucius credited with saving
China from a return to total barbarism through a universal
war—but this was before the post-Confucian wars, which were
far more devastating. The Lords Protectors really worked for
the future in helping to curb and then destroy feudalism,
in preparing, although unwittingly, the birth of the strong,

centralized monarchies, just as Richelieu and Mazarin smashed the French nobility to make way for the absolutism of Louis XIV.

The political impotence of the Chou ruler and his enduring prestige as a religious symbol had a decisive influence on the formation of China's state religion and the crystallization of its philosophic interpretation of man's destiny. The Chinese conceived Heaven and Earth as being complementary halves of the Absolute Totality, perfect duplicates that were mirrored in each other. Man is surrounded by incorporeal spirits and forces, and a complicated system of regulations is necessary to obtain satisfactory relations with these mysterious forces: rituals have to be performed with compunction and admirable precision if the equilibrium between Yin and Yang is not to be disrupted. Failure to perform the prescribed rites and sacrifices on Earth brings down an automatic, immediate and devastating reaction from Heaven, under the form of floods, famines and natural disasters of appalling magnitude.

The Book of Changes itself claimed, upheld by Confucius, that every occurrence in the tangible and visible world was only a symbol, an *image* of an abstract *idea* located in the invisible world. Every event that took place on Earth, in the material world, was a symbolic duplication of a thought originating in the spiritual world beyond man's sense perception, in Heaven. This, in turn, was linked with their conception of Time and History. The Book of Changes, through its welding of matter and spirit, of events and their symbolic meaning, was able to uncover the seeds of events to come and to foretell prophetically; it implied a triumph over Time, a yearning for duration to which the Indians or the Classical Greeks were totally indifferent.

But it implied also a rejection of *causality* in the Western sense of the word. Instead of cause and effect, the Chinese chose to study the coincidental relations between phenomena. Instead of the logical chain of mechanical *causation*, we have *association* between the apparently most incongruous elements; this association is based on their synchronization. In this type of "associative thinking," concepts are not logically deduced from one another but are placed side by side in a *pattern* and are *organically* related to one another.[10] Already strongly pragmatic, the Chinese assumed that synchronism, implying parallelism rather than causal succession, must be meaningful: the *objective* phenomenon is somehow related to the *subjective* state of the observer at the time, and the whole of it is a symbolic reflection of an idea produced in Heaven. From this will follow the peculiar structure of the Chinese mental process in philosophic thought.

This peculiarly Chinese world-picture is essentially based on *magic* (which constrains the higher powers) rather than *religion* (which conciliates). All the great Chinese rituals which have played such an important part throughout history are based on a sophisticated form of *sympathetic magic,* that is on the fundamental *mimetic* principle that "like attracts like." It is not primitive in the true sense of the word, although causality has no place in it. It is based on a subtle conception of the universe as being a vast aggregate of organic entities precisely fitted into one another, a spontaneous and harmonious super-organism in which laws, causes and supreme deities are unnecessary. This type of *weltanschauung* makes religion superfluous since there is no supreme spiritual entity to be prayed to or implored, but it makes a refined form of magic imperative because man has to be in control of his earthly habitat.

Every effort of the conscious Chinese is directed toward following the rhythm of nature, toward following his *Tao.* This Tao is the path which every Chinese must follow in life if he is to be successful—that is, harmoniously adapted to nature's inner rhythm. Anything done by man's will power against or outside the rhythm and periodicity of nature is *Li,* tension or reason, represented by the double trigram, heaven–low ground. Li is the human molding of the Chinese landscape, the historical development of China, its political and social institutions, the physical expansion consciously regulated by the Chinese people. To a highly-strung people such as the Chinese, the cautious following of the Tao was essential to their own nervous equilibrium and Li was only the surplus energy to be used whenever there was no danger of disturbing the harmonious stability of nature.

The greatest psychological characteristic of the Chinese is their close relationship with the earth and the molding of their energy on the normal pattern of nature. The Son of Han never goes straight to his goal as the Pharaonic Egyptian or Western man. He will follow instead a devious path, will feel his way—without, however, failing to reach his goal in his own good time, in a roundabout way. His over-all conceptions, in art or in history, are completely two-dimensional, and to him depth or perspective does not exist. History is an eternal recurrence, not a continuous development of life toward higher forms of life and expression. It has no depth but is projected on a flat, two-dimensional screen, as is his perspective-less painting. In his temples and palaces, especially in his gardens, which represent some of the most illuminating expressions of his artistic feelings, there is an imitation of fanciful, unpredictable nature but no deep, almost infinite perspective such as Western man created in Europe.

All these psychological traits developed gradually during the springtime of Culture and became part of the Chinese inheritance, of the collective subconscious feeling which suffuses the Chinese people and permeates Chinese thinking, in art or in politics. A slow and subtle switch from profound metaphysical inquiries and mystical introspection such as prevailed in India to a humanistic, ethical, sociological and historical world-sentiment had been taking place since Shang times. The remaining priests of early Chou days disappeared progressively now that religious awe before the mysterious forces of nature gave way to a philosophy of history.

A new class of men arose to take the place of the departed priests: the scholars. No other country has produced such a compact and homogeneous class of learned men shrouded with such general reverence. Their task was to memorize the fantastic number of ideograms contained in the Chinese script and to become the depositaries of China's cultural inheritance. They preserved, and in those days often augmented, the traditional moral code, the sacrifices and the festivals. They found in the ruling princes of their days what German scholars found at the courts of the petty princes of the Holy Roman Empire. A new age dawned upon China with the appearance of these men, and its symbol was a man, obscure then but of world-wide repute later on—Confucius. With him the great culture of China begins to crystallize and enters into its autumn; China's "medieval" age was closed.

2

THE SPRING
AND AUTUMN

The transfer of the Chou capital to Loyang in 771 B.C. inaugurated the era known as Ch'un-ch'iu, the Spring and Autumn period. China was entering her "modern" age. Considerable changes took place in the way of life and the ideals of Chinese society. It was an era of considerable development: remarkable expansion, growing political centralization and gradual disappearance of feudalism, growth of state power and growing tension among the various sovereign states, great technological progress and economic development.

The gradual formation of a scholar class was carried out within the framework of an essentially aristocratic social structure. Codes of manners and ceremonies were elaborated; a strict set of rituals designed to harmonize man's behavior with the laws of nature came into being, replacing the religious ceremonies and sacrifices of Shang times. Codes of *law* were being drawn up everywhere (in Cheng in 535, in Chin in 512) to replace the vanishing *traditions* of feudal times.

The prodigious vitality of this period of cultural growth expressed itself in a magnificent development of arts, music and philosophy. Every ruling court played host to poets, artists and philosophers whose works have disappeared for the most part during subsequent "epurations." Nevertheless, imposing if fragmentary remains have filtered down to us. The *Shi-Ching* or "Book of Odes" provides samples of Shang and Chou poetry, some of which are of exquisite beauty.

But philosophers were already beginning to react against old customs, against the accepted metaphysics of the time, against the social order and the growing weight of the rituals, against the validity of the official code of ethics. In this dawn of China's "Age of Enlightenment," the famous philosopher and audacious rebel, Teng Shih, taught the absolute relativity of morality and immorality, of right and wrong, and fought with utmost energy against the ethical dogmatism of his time until he came to be considered a dangerous revolutionary. This unlucky Chinese Voltaire was finally put to death by the Duke of Cheng.

The great cultural movement which had started in earnest under the Chou dynasty culminated between 550 and 400 B.C. But as this cultural growth reached its zenith, political and social conditions began to deteriorate. Doubt and confusion crept into the minds of thinkers and philosophers, as always happens, in every Culture, when the "medieval" Age of Faith gives way to rationalism and skepticism. Increasing political strife was the unavoidable result, and a number of constructive minds began to ponder over the causes of the dramatic changes that were taking place at the dawn of China's modern age; they followed the instinctive bent of all Chinese for historical thinking by poring over the lessons of the past and drawing the pattern of the "ideal state" of a Golden Age which had never existed.

Religion and metaphysics were now fully replaced by history as a source of inspiration and as an ethical guide. The Chinese intellect had fully matured and the best thinkers of the time were mulling over the causes of the political and social breakdown of their times. It was in such an atmosphere of moral confusion and intellectual doubt that two great men arose in China, who symbolized two directly opposite but also complementary aspects of the Chinese mind and suggested two basically different attitudes toward the problem of a disintegrating world: Confucius and Lao Tzu.

One of them summed up the constructive thinking of the past, elaborated definite codes and rituals for the guidance of political and social life, favored meeting the challenge of a decaying society by setting up against it a massive framework of ethical laws and rigid social traditions. This man was a mild scholar by the name of K'ung Fu-tzu, better known in the West as Confucius. Here was a bitterly disappointed sage who traveled from one feudal court to another in search of a wise ruler who would appreciate his talents, unable to keep an administrative or political appointment for more than a few years at a time, until he abandoned all efforts and settled down in his home state of Lu, where he taught his disciples until his death in 479 B.C.

Confucius was a profound, naïve and practical genius with an encyclopedic knowledge and universal interests, a typically Chinese blend of epicurean and stoic whose real greatness sprang from his being the most "true to life" symbol of the wise and incorruptible scholar. Although most of his works were written solely for the benefit of the ruling nobility of his time, his ideals and standards were eventually adopted, to a greater or lesser degree, by the entire population of China for thousands of years. Little known in his lifetime and even after his death, his everlasting fame is due to his historic position as the man who summed up the grand creations of the past, who crystallized the cosmic and ethical concepts elaborated during the Chou period and set the example of the governance of Heaven as a pattern for human conduct on

Earth, who completed the transformation of the early tran-
scendentalism of metaphysics into a cold, rational and precise
doctrine.

The time was now approaching when the organic development of Chinese Culture would come to an end, preparing for
the coming sclerosis of Chinese thought. Inspiration was beginning to wane, the great visions of the past were becoming
blurred, creative power was weakening. Confucius himself
knew that he was not innovating but merely reviewing and
commenting on the wisdom of the past. The *Analects* report
his own candid words: "I have transmitted and do not create
anew. I am faithful to the men of old and love them."

After him, there was nothing more to be done. The rest
would be mere elaboration or amplification—or the useless
hair-splitting of the Warring States era, in the twilight of
Culture. No substantial addition could accrue to Chinese cultural growth unless one followed the opposite doctrine of Lao
Tzu. To make sure that his own doctrine was consistent and
that there would remain no loose ends after his death, Confucius proceeded to make an encyclopedic review of all the
cultural achievements of his time, ruthlessly discarding those
elements which did not fit into his pattern, altering and distorting past history to make it conform to his views. He then
proceeded to write out himself the famous *Ch'un Ch'iu*, his
"Annals of Spring and Autumn," a record of his home state of
Lu—one of the great classics of Chinese literature.

The essence of Confucianist philosophy is that Heaven as
well as Earth—the two components of cosmic totality—submits
to the universal law, to the rhythm of nature, to the Tao. But
under the brush of the Confucianists, the Tao is not so much
a metaphysical expression or the goal of mystical rapture as a
right way of government and the source of morality. Just as
the astrologers observe definite laws in the movements of
celestial bodies, the Son of Heaven, as high priest of the
world, should be able to contemplate his subjects perform-
ing their duties according to the same timeless laws as plan-
ets revolving around an imperial sun. The ruler should **not**

participate actively in politics but merely set an example, just as the sun, the moon or the stars do at all times, (and everything and everyone would automatically fall in place. He should scrupulously observe all rites and ceremonies and exercise the greatest self-restraint in order to follow the most exacting sacrificial rites, in which case his subjects would follow suit and observe all their family rites for their greatest happiness.[1])

Ancestor worship had developed amazingly under the Chou dynasty as a substitute for vanished religious values, and Confucius consolidated this tradition into the most enduring and binding force within the family. To repeat, *ancestor worship* is the religious expression of a concern for Time and is the exact psychological opposite of the *cult* of local deities dwelling in pure Space.

(The family itself is the indestructible cell of society, the organic unit without which life would come to a standstill and to the interests of which the individual must sacrifice himself in all circumstances.) The eldest male is, according to Confucianist dictates, a patriarchal autocrat whose authority should be unquestioned unless he transgresses the well-established, universal rules of morality. Reverent disobedience is permissible in such a case: "When the command is wrong, a son should resist his father and a minister should resist his August Master." (The state itself, being a political extension of the family, has to be regulated in similar fashion, and the ruler, being the patriarchal father of his subjects, can no more transgress the moral law than can any head of family. Political disobedience can therefore become an unavoidable necessity, a theory which Mencius, later on, transformed into a sacred duty whenever circumstances warranted it.

Confucius had no interest in metaphysics. In his collected statements and pronouncements of the *Ta Hsüeh*—the "Great Learning"—it is easy to follow the care with which he avoided any commitments on metaphysical subjects.) His agnosticism was often expressed through terse replies to the inquiries of his student: "You do not yet know about the living—how can you

know about the dead?" and "You are unable to serve men—
how can you serve spirits?" Defining wisdom, he finally declared that "to give oneself earnestly to securing righteousness
and justice among the people and, while respecting gods and
demons, to keep aloof from them—that may be called wisdom." [2] Confucius closed the door to metaphysics and therefore to profound religious thought. He did for Chinese Culture
what Socrates did for the Greek when he turned his back on
the metaphysical inquiries of the Ionian philosophers: he
taught man to turn around and look into himself, probe his
own conscience, get to know himself and cultivate his own
Being.

In a sense, no civilization has been so consistently irreligious
as the Chinese, but nowhere else in the world has such subtle
and delicate enjoyment of nature been indulged in by masters
of polite refinement. Art became a partial substitute for religion; but that was not enough. Some philosophical explanation had to be found, some answer had to be given to the
riddle of man's destiny. Struck by the ethical and social collapse of his time, Confucius never tired of moralizing. Realizing that a great deal of the contemporary chaos was produced
by loss of faith in waning religious values, he refused to
advocate a return to religious beliefs and set up in their stead
a moral code based on an ethical philosophy of history.

The enduring influence of this Time perspective can be
gauged by many instances of historical consciousness which
have no equivalent in any other save our own Western culture. After reading the works of Confucius, a thousand years
after the sage had joined his ancestors, Emperor T'ai Tsung
said: "By using a mirror of brass, you may see to adjust your
cap; by using antiquity as a mirror you may learn to foresee
the rise and fall of empires." Szuma Ch'ien, the greatest historian produced by China, wrote an illuminating preface to
his works when presenting them to the Son of Heaven. Sum-
marizing the entire goal of the Chinese historian, he hoped
that ". . . Your Majesty may pardon this vain attempt for
the sake of his loyal intention, and in moments of leisure will

deign to cast a sacred glance over this work so as to learn from the rise and fall of former dynasties the secret of the successes and failures of the present hour." [3] Countless generations of Chinese were thus indebted to Confucius for a historical perspective which, however distorted it might have been by their ethical and unscientific treatment of the past, gave to their civilization a durability unknown anywhere else in the world and transformed China into a "historian's paradise," into a land where countless official historiographers recorded every minute event of their times in their endless chronologies. In striking contrast, India did not produce one single historian until the advent of Islam. [4]

Historical perspective, in order to be of any practical use, entails a certain belief in determinism; on this score Confucius was most explicit. According to his *Analects*, "Tzu Chang asked whether the state of affairs could be known ten generations ahead. The Master said, 'to what extent the Yin House added to and subtracted from the Hsia ritual, it is possible to know; also to what extent the Chou House added to and subtracted from the Yin. Thus it is possible to know about the successors to the Chou House, even though a hundred generations elapse.' " [5]

Against this attempt to see into the future, against this concern with Time and History, the Taoists raised the vigorous protests of Time-denying mystics. The *Tao Te Ching* claimed that "foreknowledge of events to come is but a pretentious display of the Tao, and is thus the door to benightedness." [6]

In the collected fragments of his discourses known as *Lün Yü*, or *Analects*, Confucius insists at great length on the virtues of music as the most powerful agent working for social and political harmony. This foremost instrument of peace and understanding—the only form of art which he repeatedly mentions in his works—should be taught to all, regardless of social status or intellectual endowment, as the most potent medium of transformation of evil into good.

Why did the wise sage attribute such importance to music?

Perhaps because it is, in Beethoven's words, "the one incorporeal entrance into a higher world," the most ethereal of all arts, unsubstantial in the extreme and yet the most profound of all human forms of expression. Contrary to philosophy, literature, poetry or plastic arts, which "represent" indirectly, music is pure "reality" itself. Being immaterial, it can reach a perfection unknown to plastic arts and, being immensely profound, music can reveal to man's intuition the depths of a particular Culture which gave rise to it as no other medium could.

In his early life, about which he was fond of reminiscing, Confucius would starve rather than forego listening to music. He would undertake lengthy journeys in search of musical material, and it is recorded that he traveled as far as Shantung to collect the ancient songs of Tai-kung. Utilitarian and practical, however, there is already in Confucius a clear decadence which marks the end of art for art's sake, of powerful inspiration and grand creation in favor of the purely utilitarian aspect of social ethics: "When one has mastered music completely and regulated his heart and mind accordingly, the natural, correct, gentle and sincere heart is easily developed and joy attends its development." And he added that "the best way to improve manners and customs is to pay attention to the composition of the music played in the country"; music was not so much a wonderful form of expression for the creative individual as a sort of social therapy.

It followed naturally from Master K'ung's philosophy that Chinese music would strive to express the Chinese feeling for moderate optimism and cheerfulness, for the harmonious balance of an essentially earthy people. Apart from the old classics—the Book of Rites and the post-Confucian *Tso-chuan* —the most extensive musical treatises were written by Ching Fang during the first century B.C. and by Ho Ch'eng-t'ien in the fifth century A.D., considerably revised a thousand years later under the Mings by Chu Tsai-yu, who invented a well-adjusted scale. But these were modifications of detail which in no way affected the substance of the musical theory.

The essence of Chinese music, like all Asiatic, non-Western music, is the absence of harmony and the complete predominance of melody. But the striking feature which China has passed on to Japan and which puts Far Eastern music in complete opposition to the rest of Asiatic music is the pentatonic scale, which eliminated all but five whole tones—roughly equivalent to our A,C,D,F and G—which the Chinese entitled Emperor, Chancellor, Subject People, State Affairs and Picture of the Universe. This exceedingly simple music, whether it is pure melody from the north or more rhythmic in the south, is essentially optimistic and soothing—neither sublime nor soaring, like Western music, nor subtle and vague, like Indo-Persian tunes. It is essentially Tao-like, a brooding over the earth, joyful and contented, in which there is neither longing for spiritual understanding as is the case with Hindu tunes nor the pathetic yearning toward the three-dimensional infinite of Western man. It is essentially well balanced, although northern tunes are inclined to be more sentimental and somewhat vaguely despondent. But the utilitarian function of music has always been emphasized, a view which had already been summarized by Han Yu's comment that the sages "taught man music in order to dissipate the melancholy of his soul."

The endless insistence on good manners and politeness seems to have sprung from an overdose of nervousness among the Chinese, whose excitability had to be controlled by stringent rules and rituals. Confucius taught that external constraint ends by molding our inner personality so that we actually become what we aim at being, and he insisted that "the usages of propriety serve as dikes for the people against evil excesses." [7] Nowhere else on earth has such a people endowed with such immense vitality—the greatest physical vitality of all human beings, according to some Western psychologists [8]—been under the spell of such collective self-restraint. The profound social culture which was fostered for thousands of years by Confucianism perfused the Chinese people with such perpetual equanimity and serenity in the midst of their antlike activity, that they appeared inhumanly self-controlled to many foreign travelers. Yet this apparent calm can be torn away by devastating outbreaks of uncontrollable rage, which the Chinese believe to be due to an accumulation of poisonous *Ch'i,* the substance of anger; "many disturbances in the Chinese organism, some that end fatally, are believed to be due to repressed rage." [9]

The climax of Confucius' teaching is reached when he broaches the subject of the personality of the higher man— a semi-Nietzschean superman endowed with integrity, intelligence and character, a sage-scholar-gentleman all rolled into one, who was largely inspired by the potentialities of the contemporary nobility but who should be recruited democratically through intellectual examination. The *mandarins* of the future were to materialize and embody this Confucian ideal.

But we should not be deceived by this Confucian superman; he is by no means the hero who strives relentlessly to surpass himself and reach unknown heights, by no means a profoundly original and creative individual. He is essentially a *social,* altruistic man rather than an *individualist,* a man who follows in the tracks of the ancients rather than a bold trail blazer such as the men of the Shang and early Chou eras. The Confucian sage seeks "integration" into society, seeks to follow the norm; he is essentially a conformist for whom the Confucian *jen* or human-heartedness is a social quality rather than one which promotes the creative originality of the isolated individual.[10] In other words, the Confucian ideal is essentially that of the Civilization man as opposed to the Culture man of former times; in Confucius, one can already detect the approaching twilight of Culture.

In this grand way, Confucius put together all the innumerable fragments of Chou tradition and welded them into a united, cohesive system which included Heaven, the state and the family. The strict observance of rites made for smooth, musical functioning of the entire social machine. Nothing contributed more to the frictionless contacts of a vast

population perennially crowded into a small space and, for all
the exquisite politeness and delightful manners of Chinese
intellectuals, nothing was more responsible for molding Chinese society into an antlike community in which every member appears to be one tiny cell in a gigantic super-organism. In
spite of his greatness and the obvious inspiration which dic-
tated his works, the sage was essentially true to the practical
and utilitarian genius of the Chinese people. Here was no
excruciating search for transcendental truth or spiritual realization as in India, but a perfect adaptation to the concrete
reality of human psychology, a modeling of social life on the
rhythm of nature, a complete subordination of the part to
the whole which eventually warped creative instincts. Under
Confucianist influence, artistic creation became bound to
social ethics. To a large extent it was "industrialized" and
mass-produced when China's Civilization became petrified,
and from it true emotion and creative imagination were
gradually squeezed out. Were it not for the powerful influence of individualistic Taoism and Mahāyāna Buddhism,
Confucianism would have destroyed all artistic and poetic life
in China.

Wise as he was, Confucius could not entirely exclude pathos
from his life. Largely frustrated in his search for the intelligent
ruler who would appreciate him, the Master wept shortly
before his death and said bitterly: "No intelligent ruler rises
to take me as his master and my time has come to die." This
was the end of a man whose writings were to exert an enormous
influence over hundreds of Chinese generations. Many historical events came to pass before his victory was complete,
however, and although he symbolized one of the most enduring aspects of the Chinese soul he was in no way representative of its totality. From the positive, social, practical and
humanistic pole of Confucius, the Chinese have often been
wont to travel to the intuitive, individualistic, mystical pole
of another great master, Lao Tzu.

Confucianist China was centered on the Yellow River, in

close contact with the vigorous barbarians in the north, compelled to devise sound social structures and strong political institutions in order to stand up against their relentless pressure. But a new Chinese world was being created farther south, along the banks of the Yangtze and beyond. Far away from the flat plains of the north, proud races wandered freely through dense forests and mysterious swamps, at first owing allegiance to no Chinese prince but gradually and more or less peacefully being absorbed by the Chou Culture. Less vigorous and warlike than the nomadic Hsiung Nu barbarians in the north, they merged easily with the growing culture of the expanding Chinese society but molded and altered it to suit their psychology. This new cultural development was suffused with a fervent love of nature, of a nature much more beautiful, with its different skies, its thundering waterfalls and its oddly shaped mountains, than the flat, colorless and monotonous landscape of the north through which the murky waters of the Yellow River rolled slowly toward the sea.

While so much effort was being expended by the great northern scholars to define a workable state of affairs in politics and sociology, to devise codes of ethics and prescribe appropriate rites to conciliate the favor of Heaven, an entirely different trend was started by Lao Tzu. No one knows with precision when or where he was born or where he lived; his influence began to grow centuries after he is presumed to have passed away. His elusive teachings are contained in a small, poetic and concise book, the *Tao Te Ching*, the "Book of the Tao and its Power." Like Jean-Jacques Rousseau, his historical counterpart in Europe, Lao Tzu represents the end-of-Culture sentiment, the growing revulsion against the increasing artificiality of social life in expanding cities, the increasing dimness of the Culture's twilight and the passionate desire to seek refuge in nature, away from the growing complexities of "modern" life. He did not write for the rural intellectual to whom nature came as a matter of course but for the urban scholar who was tired of the town and yearning for the unspoiled, unsophisticated atmosphere of virgin nature.

Some passages of the famous Taoist work *Huai Nan Tzu* sound just like Rousseau's *Social Contract*. Looking back at the distant past, when technical progress and social distinctions put an end to the Golden Age, it claims that "the mountains and streams were divided (*fen*) with boundaries and enclosures, censuses of the populations were made, cities were built and dikes dug, barriers were erected and weapons forged for defense. Officials with special badges were ordained, who differentiated the people into classes of 'nobles' and 'mean' (*i kuei chien*), and organized rewards and punishments. Then there arose soldiers and weapons, giving rise to wars and strifes. There was the arbitrary murder of the guiltless and the punishment and death of the innocent . . ." [11] And it goes on to extol the happy primitive collectivism of the Golden Age before metallurgy was invented and cities were built.

Lao Tzu, like Confucius, preached the way of the Tao and attempted to bring man's life into harmony with the universal rhythm of nature. But instead of Confucius' moralistic rationalism, which sought to harmonize the historical development of the social world with the Tao, Lao Tzu used intuition and emotion for the sole benefit of the individual. Confucius wrote for social and political man who is history-conscious and devotes his life to action. His opponent wrote for the world-weary individualist who seeks refuge in solitude and yearns to obliterate history. His Taoist followers retired from city life to spend their years in the depths of a wild countryside, in a deep forest or on the banks of a quiet river, adhering strictly to the Tao and living according to his great doctrine of W*u-wei*, "passive achievement" or "non-assertion."

The Tao itself, the central core of his teaching, is a perfect molding of man upon nature, a profound and intuitive understanding that the road to human perfection lies in a complete harmony between man and Heaven, upon his adaptation to nature's essential beat, rhythm and periodicity. Lao Tzu's Tao is no longer a definite set of moral laws which man apprehends rationally in Confucian fashion but a more elusive rhythm which follows no rational laws and which has to be grasped intuitively. Lao Tzu advocates non-assertion, action-less activity, and he advises: "Be subtracted and yet again subtracted, till you have reached non-activity. Then through this non-activity there will be nothing unaccomplished." [12] This is the very essence of *Wu-wei*. Once this is achieved, a perfect understanding of the Tao is possible; the Tao now becomes the essence of all things, devoid of morality (which is only a man-made set of rules for social living), devoid of volition and yet immanent in all things. "We do not know its name," says Lao Tzu, "so we term it Tao." [13]

Lao Tzu could not remain content with a doctrine which appealed only to world-weary men. His ambitions or those of his followers were too vast to be confined within such limitations and he tried to extend his doctrine to the world of politics, ending unavoidably by advocating a mild anarchy: "If I work through non-action, the people will transform themselves." Whereas Confucius believed in ritual compulsion from outside to alter man's inner nature, Lao Tzu believed exclusively in change from within through mystical introspection. Taoists never ceased to campaign for pure individualism against Confucius' social semicollectivism, ridiculing Confucianist doctrines and regulations, tirelessly expounding Lao Tzu's thesis that "the secret of the art of living is neither antagonism nor criticism but the clever insinuation through the apertures which exist everywhere."

The sage's concepts, perfectly adapted to the artist and mystic who retires from the world, were totally impractical in social and political life. By an ironic but predictable twist of fate, his doctrine eventually gave rise to the anti-Confucianist movement of the "Legalists," who no longer bothered about altering man's inner nature, either externally or internally. They were content to bind him politically with a ruthless rigidity never dreamed of by Confucius. Thus it was that, like Rousseau and just as unwittingly, Lao Tzu fostered a school of practical, iron-willed fanatics in the world of politics and ended by destroying the *ancien régime* of his days. His uncompromising anarchism, by annihilating the traditional structure of society, managed to leave the individual alone and helpless, the perfect tool in the hands of the Caesarian dictatorship called forth by the Legalists. Thus it is that gentle but impractical idealists such as Rousseau and Lao Tzu foster the implacable dictators, the Robespierres of France and the Legalists of China.

But Lao Tzu's undying contribution to Chinese culture overshadows his destructive influence in politics. In many ways, he represents the counterpoise to Confucianism which was necessary if Chinese culture was not to petrify forever and disintegrate like the Classical culture of the Greco-Roman world in the first centuries of the Christian era. The true Taoist despised official honors and obligations, withdrew from all family entanglements. The spirit of his doctrine was such that the same man could easily be a Confucianist in active, mature life and a Taoist in his old age. His mysticism did not take on a religious coloring because Chinese psychology does not favor such an attitude, but his intuitive doctrine came very close to producing a deeply religious experience and ended by doing so, centuries later, in conjunction with Buddhism. Confucius and Lao Tzu represent the two poles of Chinese tension, the contrast between intellect and emotion, between reason and intuition, between social requirements and individual self-realization. They are therefore two facets of one identical, indivisible China. But the intuitive master's real contribution lay in the world of art and poetry, a world immensely far removed from Confucianist rituals and politics. Most of his nonpolitical followers became painters, architects or poets, and the shining figure of them all was his admirer Chuang Tzu, a poet-philosopher who is one of China's greatest literary figures.

Chinese painting at the time had already reached a high technical level, mostly due to the very nature of Chinese ideograms and to the many years of calligraphic study required of all scholars. But under the influence of Taoism, the Chinese painter used his art as a medium of expression for mystical and emotional materializations of rare power and beauty, adding great profundity to what had been until that time merely naïve craftsmanship. To the basically irreligious Chinese, art became religion itself, the highest expression of his mysticism. He may be entirely indifferent to metaphysical speculation, completely skeptical as to heavens, gods and the survival of the soul. Yet he will feel with the utmost intensity the timeless reality of artistic emotion which obliterates his ego just as effectively as many years of religious meditation. He then becomes immersed in a vast aesthetic "continuum" without beginning or end, an infinite universe of pure beauty and sheer goodness which is beyond time and space, in which everything is undifferentiated, in which object and subject are totally merged. Taoism teaches him how to lose himself in this incorporeal continuum, how to become one with this unending ocean of bliss and give up all subjective feelings, all individuality. There he rejoins the Hindu mystic who traveled on the road of spiritual introspection and meditation; but he is taught to return to the world of form and differentiation, to paint on silk or describe in poetic rhymes the everlasting impressions of his self-realization.

This is why Chinese painting gives such an impression of revealing the very soul of nature as if the painter, after several days of motionless contemplation and absorption, was able to paint the landscape from the "inside." If any religious terminology could be applied to the Chinese artist, he could be called a pantheist, or rather an *immanentist* (since he rejects all notion of a supreme Godhead), not a *transcendentalist* like Western man; for him, the spiritual essence of the universe pervades the whole of nature just as much as man himself. This remarkable faculty for penetrating into the very soul of nature and contemplating it from the inside has often prompted the Chinese painter to criticize Western art by saying that we paint it from "outside."

Since the Renaissance, Western oil painting has been three-dimensional, with geometrical depth and perspective, the only such painting the world has ever known. Chinese painting, like all other painting in the world with the exception of ours, is two-dimensional. Where the Asian in general and the Chinese in particular will take in the totality of the intuitively experienced beauty in a landscape, the Westerner seeks to depict it theoretically and will apply geometrical laws to his work of art. Where the Chinese desire is to merge harmoniously with nature, Western man *dominates* it. This domination Western man can exert only by standing *apart* and by refusing to grasp its essence—which would amount to a merger which he does not want. This psychological disposition of Western man has its deepest roots in his metaphysical outlook: man is the sole incarnation of the divine spark on earth, the king of creation who has a God-ordained right to dominate a soulless nature. The Chinese artist reverses the process. He invests nature in its various manifestations—winds, storms, waterfalls—with humanlike thinking and feeling.

Chinese painting was defined and its canons were explicitly stated by the famous poet-painter Ku Kai-chi; his central theme was "concentration of the dominant characteristic." A century later, Kuo-chi evolved the six canons of painting: first depict the life of the spirit through the rhythm of nature, then consider that the spirit forms the organic structure of painting, *i.e.*, the lines of the drawing; color constitutes the emotional casing. It was only much later that light and shadows came into Chinese and Japanese painting. The great cult of the "line" in China was the result of calligraphy and it finally gave to Chinese linear drawing an unsurpassable, if sober, beauty. The Taoist love for mystical contemplation of nature, of its woods, its rustling rivers, its wild birds fluttering in the reeds, gave rise to a powerful symbolism—its greatest expression being the dragon, the personalization of threatening clouds which change ceaselessly, the symbol of endless "Becoming." In a sense, art became almost a philosophical language.

Painting and poetry in China were two complementary facets of the same artistic inspiration. Both of them were impressionistic, merely suggesting, teasing the imagination and leaving the spectator or reader to fill in the immense gaps

by himself. Sounds, smells and tastes were admirably conveyed by mere suggestiveness and to a degree which never
seems to have been reached in any other culture. As in all
historical times of great artistic creativity, versatility was the
hallmark of Chinese artists; many painters were poets of the
first rank and vice versa, the most famous of all being
Wang-wei.

What is a great asset in many respects can easily become
a handicap in others. For psychological reasons, Chinese painting was sublime in its landscapes but it failed miserably in
the portrayal of human forms—a failure which extended to
sculpture as well. Forms demand light and shade, demand
perspective, a scientific knowledge of the inner structure of
the body and, in fact, a fascination for human psychology
and for individual idiosyncrasy which the Chinese have always
lacked. This triumph of Western art remained unknown in
China. The women portrayed by Ku Kai-chi and Ch'iu Shih-
chou suggest willows bending under a powerful wind, or
clouds being chased across the sky, rather than human personalities. Their faces suggest landscapes rather than striking
expressions of human emotion. The sensual West, having
inherited its passion for the body from Classical Greece, deems
Chinese forms to be unsatisfactory in the extreme; to Western
man, more individualized, permeated with the Christian outlook and stronger-willed than the Chinese, the human being
is the most worthy object of his artistic attention and reproduction.

On the other hand, the Chinese have proved to be far more
earth-bound than the Indian and in that respect closer to the
Westerner. The transcendental, undifferentiated ocean of
bliss beyond sense perception which is the object of the
Hindu's mystical quest is sought for its own sake in India.
The Hindu wants to immerse himself in it and destroy forever the fetters which bind him to the illusory world of *Maya*,
to this very Earth which the Chinese revere and which is as
real to them as Heaven. The Chinese artist pursues the same
quest but always seeks to come back to the contingent world

of everyday life, to translate into form and interpret through his art the profound insight which the mystical Hindu keeps to himself. Spirit has to become flesh in China and express itself through matter, whereas in India it evaporates. There is therefore a greater synthesis of essence and appearance in China than in India, in the Far East in general than in the rest of Asia.[14]

The essence of the Chinese soul is just as profoundly expressed in architecture and gardening as in painting and poetry. Chinese architecture seeks the same harmony with nature as does painting, the same elegant merger with the Tao of the land. Chinese immanentism has imposed this fervent and deep feeling of respect for every form of life, however humble it may be. The main lines of Chinese architecture, strangely enough, are derived from the art of calligraphy. The structural lines are not concealed but are revealed with great care, and many buildings—palaces, temples, pavilions or pagodas—are structurally built like ideograms. A straight axis or a square is always present in the center. But thereafter all the lines are delicately curved, like the strokes of a master's brush. Pillars are straight vertical lines but the sagging roofs are always curved, reminiscent of the sweeping curves of the calligraphist. The Chinese have always been deadly insistent on breaking straight lines, on sundering straight perspective by placing one temple or one pavilion behind another in their great monasteries and palaces, by laying tiers of sagging roofs one on top of the other to interrupt the soaring towers before their dynamic lines take them right up to the sky. Chinese architecture is *rhythmic* whereas the Western is *dynamic* and full of tension. The contrast between them cannot be better expressed than it was by Lin Yutang, who claims that the spirit of Chinese architecture does not, "like the Gothic spires, aspire to heaven but broods over the earth and is contented with its lot. While Gothic cathedrals suggest the spirit of sublimity, Chinese temples and palaces suggest the spirit of serenity." [15] Windows and doors, courtyards, patios and passageways are all built with an eye to fanciful irregularity so that no straight line will run away toward the unknown and infinite, taking with it the reluctant Chinese, who have no transcendental aspirations nor sacrilegious will to dominate nature.

The same spirit can be found in the Chinese approach to gardening, an art which has reached its greatest perfection in the Far East. Nowhere else in the world has such harmony been established between man and his landscape, nowhere has the interpenetration between the spirit of the soil and the works of the human being become so complete. This total integration of the landscape includes architecture as well; no building is ever erected which is not in complete agreement with its immediate surroundings. But it is a rare occasion when one can reach the temple of the country house directly, without having to wander along twisting and spiraling paths, through thickets and dense bamboo groves, over a balustraded arched bridge which spans an unexpected pond or a quiet river. One is in the arms of friendly nature herself and therefore compelled to follow the Tao.

Here harmony with nature's essential beat is complete, and the contrast between the great gardens of China's palaces and the French gardens of Versailles is just as startling as the contrast between a Chinese temple and a Gothic cathedral. The Chinese and the French are both gardeners, deep down in their souls. They are both rooted in the soil, but the Frenchman will not aim at harmony within nature with the tender love of the Chinese. He will attempt to *impose* a human harmony *upon* nature, to dominate the landscape instead of espousing it, to impose an external God's will on a soulless nature instead of discovering God in nature. He will shape the trees and shrubs into cones or spheres, cut the hedges evenly, multiply the straight perspectives running away toward the horizon so as to give the French garden a triumphant feeling of depth, of a third dimension which is at last mastered. This repels the Chinese. Many generations of Chinese and Japanese have found solace in their exquisite communion with nature, in their humble and serene acceptance of a Tao which left no room for domineering instincts.

3

THE TWILIGHT
OF CULTURE

Culture lays the emphasis on *aesthetics*, on Beauty; Civilization promotes *ethics*, moral Goodness. One is intensely creative and fosters individualism, the other seeks to preserve and organize the creations of the parent Culture; to this end, it emphasizes the social side of man and this inevitably entails promoting ethics above everything else. So that while Confucius laid the basis of an orthodox morality which would eventually give an indestructible stiffening to China's social structure for thousands of years, Lao Tzu carefully put aside a fragment of man's individualism and showed him the road to individual self-realization through aesthetic contemplation.

But the distinction between these two outlooks was not as sharp in China as it was to become in our Western Culture. At all times they blended more or less harmoniously. Lao Tzu was not indifferent to ethics and social concerns, and Confucius was extremely sensitive to beauty. Both were aware that Beauty and Goodness, aesthetics and ethics, are reflections of the same basic Truth and that they are actually merged on the highest level. For both of them, and therefore for all Chinese, Beauty and Goodness were far more real and "true" than any objective scientific evidence which conflicted with them. They were both humanists and related everything to man and to his subjective requirements.

In history, for instance, exact and accurate chronology of past events is not as real to man as an intensely wishful account of events as they should have occurred. Whatever the past may have been in reality, its only participation in today's life now occurs through the imagination and memory of living contemporaries. Confucius could become positively lyrical when referring to purely mythical accounts of a distant past about which he could hardly know anything—"What sublime majesty was that of Shun and Yü! The Great Society was theirs but they were not trammeled by it. How great was Yao as a sovereign! The sublime majesty of him! Only Heaven is great; only Yao copied it . . . Sublime majesty, with its sublime achievements of civilization, all glorious to view!" [1] and so on, endless rhapsodies about a past which had never really existed at all.

Confucius felt that he had an absolute right to alter past history and transmute it into a Golden Age because it conformed to the aesthetic and ethical requirements of the present. What matters is not the past as it really was, not the perspective of real events as they occurred or as they really impressed the ancestors who were involved in them, but the result which such knowledge of the past may have on the contemporaries, on the living. Any lie or falsification which will contribute to greater aesthetic enjoyment and more ethical living is permissible, indeed obligatory. The celebrated "face" of the Chinese is nothing more than this preference for aesthetic reality over the theoretical, scientifically intellectualized and coldly impersonal reality prized by the West.

As Chinese cultural processes were being gradually worked out and epitomized by Confucius and Lao Tzu, the systematic and speculative "pre-Socratic" philosophy of China began to die out. As vast, original and all-embracing in its own way as the pre-Socratic philosophy of Classical Greece, the systematic and speculative thinking was then followed—as it was in

Greece and India—by an intensely practical, social and utilitarian philosophy which gradually prepared the transition from Culture to Civilization, from intense inward growth to forceful outward expansion.

In the twilight of Culture, when irremediable petrifaction threatens and enlightened men feel this approaching crystallization in the marrow of their bones, there is always a flare-up, a desperate attempt to break out of the choking citadel raised by the giants of the past. It is the pathetic attempt which the Indians made between Buddha and Asoka. The emotional urge to create gave way to dry, pedantic ratiocination and criticism aiming at the destruction of past achievements, to philosophic schools such as the materialistic *Lokāyatatikas*, the rationalist *Tarkikas*, the sophistic *Paribbajaka*, all of whom attempted to turn their backs on the profound Vedas. India had her cynics like Virocana, her nihilists like Brihaspati, her agnostics like Sangaya—just as Classical Greece produced their counterparts between Socrates and Aristotle, just as the West has been producing them in the past two hundred years. And so was it in China.

The great styles of the past, developing slowly and organically out of one another, were followed by innumerable schools and fast-changing fashions. Philosophers now flocked to the Chi-Hsia Academy in the capital of the state of Ch'i as their Greek contemporaries flocked to faraway Athens and its Platonic Academy, to indulge in endless controversies and confrontations, in fruitless intellectual disputations; this was the age of the famous "Hundred Schools" of philosophy. The utilitarian Mo Ti fought against restricted family ethics and ancestor worship, attempted to extend the *jen* (humanheartedness) which presided at these clannish celebrations to the entire community of Chinese nations, thus removing all friction between rulers and subjects, between clans and families. His religious utilitarianism—whose Western counterpart appeared in Europe's eighteenth-century Age of Enlightenment [2]—forced him to discard the great concepts which had ministered to the birth of Chinese Culture.

Mo Ti condemned warfare as economically unproductive—
but condemned music on the same grounds. Everything was
made dependent on its "economic usefulness"; Confucianism,
with its more generous, comprehensive and all-embracing ethics, now appeared quite outmoded alongside this more "modern" view of life's purpose.[3] The logic of profit drove Mo Ti to
base his entire philosophy on the canon of material prosperity,
but, very much unlike some of his Western counterparts, he
was not hypocritical enough to pay lip service to artistic activities, which he condemned, unashamedly, as being totally
useless and wasteful. It is significant that Mo Ti's intellectual
talents ran to mechanical inventions and military tactics and
that nine chapters of the *Mo Tzu Book* dealt with defensive
warfare. His successors, the Mohists, organized a rigidly disciplined army of supporters and groups of technical experts
which they offered to various rulers during the terrible age of
the Warring States. Furiously opposed by the Confucianists,
the Mohists did not survive this war-torn period and disappeared when the Caesarian Empire was established.

The positivist Mencius extracted from Confucius the useful
and the practical, leaving behind the vast encyclopedic vision
of an inspired sage, and attempted to draw workable conclusions from the rather vague generalities of the Annals of
Spring and Autumn. He decided that the "voice of the people" should select the suitable ruler and that, by the same
token, it would be entitled to remove him if he proved unsatisfactory. Thus justification was given in advance for the
frequent revolutions and changes of dynasty which occurred
throughout history in the name of Mencius' "sacred right of
rebellion." The good ruler would give up warfare and concentrate all his energy on internal problems: abolition of
poverty, regulation of economic processes, institution of compulsory education for all.

The late Chou era was essentially an Age of Enlightenment,
very much "under the impression, as the English Victorian
age was, that there was great virtue in the development of
material civilization,"[4] claims a British scholar. The typical

atomization of philosophic thought which affected the post-Socratic Greeks affected the Chinese, and the Middle Kingdom produced epicureans and pessimists such as Yang Chu, embittered mystics such as Chuang Tzu, and cynical realists such as Hsün-tzu who fought Mencius with ironic delight and insisted that man's fundamental nature was bad. Dialecticians and sophists also cropped up: Kung-sun Lung and Hui Tzu, who developed Chinese logic and rhetoric—such as they were, for the Chinese never discovered the syllogism.[5]

All these conflicting philosophies and doctrines presented the usual facets of the moral and intellectual chaos which always prefaces and accompanies a cultural collapse, bringing with it the agonizing period of world wars that closes the great Culture and prefaces the coming of Civilization. The Mohists were well aware that there could be no social and political order if men's thoughts were not put in order beforehand. But it was entirely beyond their mental capacity to give this philosophical order to the Chinese world. And so world-weariness and romantic archaism seized a Chuang-tzu who yearned for the peace and silence of the rustic countryside, for a scrapping of all technical improvements and the complications which they had introduced into man's life, for a complete rejection of machinery, property and currency, and for an unequivocal return to a paradisical Golden Age when men had no needs and no desires, therefore no cause for strife or conflict. But alongside the archaic yearning there existed dynamic and forceful doctrines which, had they triumphed, would have led China onto the paths which the West trod two thousand years later. Rejecting even the Tao, the agnostic and rationalist Hsün-tzu wanted to develop man's technical power and his control over nature. He remarked sarcastically:

> "You glorify nature and meditate on her;
> why not domesticate her and regulate her?
> you obey nature and sing her praise,
> why not control her course and use it?" [6]

But China did not heed Hsün-tzu's recommendations and the Tao triumphed.

Meanwhile, early in the fifth century B.C., the Chinese world was about to go through the greatest social and political upheaval in its history. The disappearance of the old, small feudal fiefs was almost complete by now, giving way to large national states, stronger and more centralized—as large as those of modern Europe—whose rulers began to arrogate to themselves that title of *Wang* (King) which had hitherto been reserved to the Chou ruler, the Son of Heaven.[7] The medieval unity of Shang and early Chou days—spiritual and cultural rather than political—collapsed. This political metamorphosis was in every respect equivalent to the rise of nationalism in modern Europe. And as in Europe, nationalism soon extended to the cultural field; the language and the script itself soon began to feel the impact of absurd patriotisms. Almost-new languages arose in Wu, Ch'u and Yüeh, as Europe's national tongues arose during and after the Gothic period, promoted by the administrators, ruling classes and scholars of the various nations. Their differences were purposely emphasized, cultivated and jealously nursed along, adding their substantial contributions to the dissensions which began to sear the entire Chinese world on every possible level.[8]

Yet, as in modern Europe, this evolution coincided with a remarkable development in economic activity and communications due to technological revolutions.[9] Canals were dug and roads built, linking all the major cities; and the cities themselves grew steadily, hastening the decline of feudal power and the rise of a genuine middle class.[10] Increased trade and growing prosperity created a money economy whose complexity would probably have baffled those who could still remember the feudal period. New social classes based on wealth began to supersede the old aristocracies based on blood kinship and ancestry. The great increase in the means of production and distribution was accelerated by the utilization of iron in agriculture—and also in the weapons of war. The introduction of the ox-drawn plow and of fertilizers augmented agricultural yield, and the labor thus saved found full employment in the various armies. Increased state-power made possible the construction of important waterworks for irrigation and flood control. And in turn, these economic changes stimulated the proliferation of middle-class merchants and artisans. The development of industries was so considerable in the states of Ch'i and Ch'u that a new bureaucracy of *Kung-cheng* had to be created to supervise them.[11]

The increasing power of the various states over their populations, their assumption of complete and unquestioned sovereignty, the disintegration of feudal nobility and the rise of urban middle classes, technological improvements which made war more costly but more tantalizing—everything conspired to increase the instability of the Chinese world. In the second half of the Ch'un-ch'iu period, a constellation of Great Powers appeared: Ch'i, Chin, Ch'u, Wu, and the most redoubtable of all, Ch'in. Around and between them were secondary powers which guarded their sovereignty jealously, playing one Great Power against another: Lu, Ts'ao, Sung and Wei—the Switzerlands, Netherlands, Denmarks, and so on, of the Chinese world.[12] And there were tributary states and principalities (*fu-yung*) and colonies (*shu*), most of which were condemned to extinction and absorption within larger political entities.

Great Powers, like Chin and Ch'u, could put more than one hundred thousand soldiers in the field and did so with increasing frequency as time went on. Their effective power depended largely on the degree of centralization and "democratization" of their social and political structures. Conscription into a national militia was inaugurated by Kuan-tzu in the state of Ch'i, and simultaneously the nobility lost much of its power through the establishment of the merit system in its administration.[13] Kuan-tzu himself was probably the first of a new breed: the prime ministers or chancellors of the emerging Great Powers. And, preparing and anticipating the future regime of a unified China, Kuan-tzu imposed complete monopoly on salt and iron, and favored the middle class in order to break the power of the nobility. It should also be kept in mind that states such as Ch'i, Chin and Ch'u were as large as modern France or Germany—not taking into account semibarbarian states such as Ch'in, which dwarfed them all.

Elsewhere, social revolutions were carrying out the same social changes which were wrought by peaceful evolution in more efficient states. Southern China, more recently brought under the spell of Chinese culture, produced such leaders as Hsü Hsing, the "shrike-tongued barbarian of the south" who advocated a thorough social revolution and the dictatorship of the working man. In the midst of this universal breakdown, many naïve thinkers such as Sung K'ang still hoped to convert rulers to pacifism and revolutionary leaders to social peace by proving to them that wars and revolutions were not economically profitable, even for the victors. But many more began to realize that such arguments were both immoral and ineffective—the profit motive is no moral argument and political upheavals are usually too fundamental to be affected by it. New ideals, new political and ethical doctrines had to be formulated.

Shunning the impractical philosophers who remained involved in useless intellectual dissertations when survival of the entire Chinese world was at stake, abandoning Confucius who, in those days, appeared to be hopelessly welded to a dying social order, a new political and social doctrine arose out of the dramatic confusion—Lao Tzu's bizarre outgrowth, the Legalists. This Fa Chia, or Legalist school, was not only the logical if paradoxical outcome of Lao Tzu's teachings—as Robespierre's Terror was the ultimate consequence of Rousseau. It was also the natural sequel to Mo Ti's naïve but impractical utilitarianism. It spread like wildfire among the dispossessed princelings and the ruined noblemen, although not among the scholars. The ruined aristocrats and gentry deserted Confucianism altogether, made their peace with the new democratic social order and advocated a strong centralized state under a Caesarian ruler along with a social democracy. Their advertised constitution was strongly flavored with socialism: Capital should be nationalized and trade monopolized by the state, manipulation of prices and concentration of wealth should be forbidden. The people's duty was no longer to discuss and argue but to work and obey the dictates of the all-powerful state.

Han Fei-tzu, the main theoretician of the Legalists, was fiercely opposed to the Confucian theory of a loose, aristocratic government of idealistically minded gentlemen. The ideology of Confucius had been developed during the full bloom of a great Culture when men were still great individuals endowed with real moral stature. Han Fei-tzu was a cynical realist who aimed like Confucius at the creation of a workable political system but who started from the premise that all rulers are wicked, that morality is nonsense and that nothing short of the strict enforcement of drastic laws can paralyze the dishonesty of both the ruling classes and the masses. Family solidarity, ancestor worship and every form of social tradition dear to Confucius had to be smashed in order to leave the individual "common man" face to face with a mammoth state, alone and powerless.

Such views always preface the coming of Caesarism as it did during the last decades of the Roman Republic when the great ideal of the majestic senator, incorruptible, stern and animated by lofty ideals, broke down under the growing demoralization of the aristocracy and the rise of mass democracy. Han Fei-tzu argued that it is nonsense to expect people to be intrinsically good and that the state should see to it that their evil designs are thwarted by effective laws, as well as by a shrewd exploitation of their paltry desires and their fear of suffering. He was, in fact, merely interpreting the general lassitude of the times at the sight of the ruling classes' complete decay, and he proclaimed that henceforth there should be a law "before which the high and the low, the clever ones and the stupid ones shall stand equal," a mechanistic rule for a democratic world which could dispense with wise and talented rulers because of its very perfection. Social equality was purchased with the loss of freedom. And in the *Shang Chun Shu*, we read: "What I mean by the unification of punishments is that they should recognize no social distinctions. From ministers of state and generals, down to officials and ordinary folk, whosoever . . . violates the interdicts of the state . . . should be guilty of death and should not be pardoned." [14] In order to emphasize their reliance on dictatorial authority, all Legalist writers and thinkers, from Shen Tao and Shang Yang to Han Fei-tzu, substituted their stern imperial concept of *jen chu*, which stands for "Master of men," [15] to the more humane Confucianist *jen chun* or "Men's Sovereign." [16]

These ideas were enthusiastically adopted by the "Roman" state of Ch'in in the northwest—contemporary Shensi and eastern Kansu. This strongly centralized realm had already disposed of its internal feudalism and nobility under the stern supervision of Shang Yang, the great Legalist statesman. Lord Shang was a typical Civilization man who saw clearly that the decline of the traditional nobility and the rise of middle-class democracy entailed both the inevitable growth of the bureaucratic state and the systematic development of law. [17] The customs and traditions of the Culture era were breaking down, despised and forgotten. The Civilization that was to follow could only be based, as it was in all other Civilizations, and especially in Rome, on an all-embracing legal system.

Like America in our Western world, the Ch'in state had early found the secret of *organic* growth through the immigration of settlers from other Chinese states—settlers who were encouraged by its more "democratic" institutions. Ch'in's social democracy was established by the antifeudal reforms of Shang Yang when he decided that, by law, farmers were free to buy and sell land as they pleased. [18] As a result, the rulers of Ch'in had in their hands the most progressive and efficient state in the Far East, the only strong power in a world of disintegrating kingdoms: it was "Rome" to the rest of the Chinese world's "Greece," the Civilization state to the Culture nations who were collapsing as the Greek world was to collapse at the other side of the globe two hundred years later. And so it was that Ch'in gave to the entire Sinic world the name "China," as Rome, the small city on the Tiber, was to give hers to the Classical world.

As a border state in close contact with barbarians, Ch'in could survive only through efficient management and a dynamic policy which gave it an immense superiority over the more effeminate Chinese in the east. At the same time, its possibilities of territorial expansion at the expense of the barbarians—who were gradually brought into the social structure and civilized, much as Spain and Gaul had been absorbed by Rome—enabled Ch'in to dwarf the other nations of the Chinese world by its sheer geographical size. And later on, the great historian Szuma Ch'ien, in a striking description of its geographical superiority, explained: "The country of Ch'in was a state whose position alone predestined its victory. Rendered difficult of access by the girdle formed around it by the Yellow River and the mountains, it was suspended a thousand li above the rest of the empire . . . the position of its territory was so advantageous that when it poured out its soldiers it was like a man emptying a jug of water from the top of a high house." [19]

Meanwhile, the increasing cruelty of wars and revolutions led to the famous disarmament conference of 546 B.C., under the auspices of the state of Sung. None of the other states dared flout the general desire for peace, but they undermined the conference through their intrigues.[20] The development of international law had made great progress in the Chinese world but it was powerless to preserve the balance of power between the great states. The development of fierce nationalisms made wars inevitable.[21] Increasing diplomatic activity and expressions of good will, international conferences, leagues of states and alliances for the preservation of peace, attempts to foster collective security, everything was done to solve that most difficult if not insoluble problem of international politics: how to reconcile the existence of a multitude of sovereign states with world peace.[22]

The various Chinese states behaved with the same blind futility as the Greek states in the Classical world. But in the west, the growing state of Ch'in was watching the slow breakdown of China's "Hellenistic" world without sorrow. Psychologically disciplined, administratively centralized, socially democratic, Ch'in was economically prosperous; it was a great importer of southern metal destined for markets in north China, and it had an almost complete monopoly on salt production. Concentrating on the concrete task of developing its economic and military power, growing organically through the incorporation and absorption of neighboring barbarians, Ch'in soon felt strong enough to take an aggressive part in the affairs of the Chinese world. And the precarious balance of power which had been more or less preserved all through the Spring and Autumn period broke down at the end of the fifth century B.C.

In 403 B.C. the Chinese states entered a new era, an era of "world wars," the era of the Warring States. This *Chan-kuo* period, which lasted until 221 B.C., saw conflicts of unimaginable magnitude devastate the Chinese world. It takes the same place in the historical evolution of the Far East as the Hellenistic period from Alexander to Hannibal in the Classical world—which was only a prelude to the world-wide Roman imperium and the establishment of Roman civilization—or, in our Western world, to the period which stretches from Napoleon to our twentieth-century World Wars. The total collapse of spiritual authority and of reverence for some form of moral restraint was symbolized in a dramatic way when the Chou ruler was degraded to the position of pensioner of the Eastern Duke, one of the great ruling princes. Like the French Revolution and the execution of King Louis XVI (or Louis Capet, as he was styled during the Terror), it marked the dramatic ending of China's *ancien régime* and the beginning of almost two hundred years of atrocious warfare and bloody revolutions.

The growing power of Ch'in was now challenged by its alarmed rivals although they never were able to muster sufficient strength to destroy it. Combinations and alliances of states fought each other with a savagery and a ruthlessness unknown in the old days. The North-South axis (Ho-tsong) fought the East-West League (Lien-heng) of states. Most of the small noble families lost their lands and fortunes, becoming itinerant politicians or soldiers of fortune, new recruits for the growing Legalist movement which was making considerable inroads all over the Chinese world.

As time went on, conscription was introduced in the various states and peasants were uprooted by the hundreds of thousands and sent to die on distant battlefields. From the clumsy armed chariot, the technique of war gradually progressed to a massive infantry drawn from the farmer population, backed by a cavalry recruited among the wild nomads of the north. The state of Ch'in kept an eye on all technical improvements and adopted the heavy armored cavalry soon after the King of Chao had introduced it. Wars became increasingly gory and the Ch'in rulers had to start a program of mass immigration to compensate for their appalling war casualties. Implacable destructions and indescribable atrocities in these "total wars" coincided with vast improvements in siegecraft, with its complex machinery, movable towers and artillery of catapults. While "shields floated on rivers of blood" and mechanical ingenuity made fabulous progress, the Chinese world gradually fell to pieces.

Hard pressed as it was at times, Ch'in was better off than many other states—such as the state of Wu, which was completely annihilated. This total destruction would have been utterly unthinkable in the old days, but with amazing technical improvements in the art of warfare and mass slaughter, with an entirely new and limitless ferocity, war—instead of being a desultory sport for small numbers of professional warriors—became a life-and-death struggle for entire populations, a tragic evolution which has been repeated in Western Europe in the nineteenth and twentieth centuries.

Fundamental social and economic revolutions took place. A great deal of land became unoccupied, and, with the relatively recent invention of currency, estates which had been held by noble families for countless generations came into the market. At the same time, no one dared hoard for fear of bandits who were multiplying as law and order broke down. Land became the only safe investment, and the rising middle class, who in the midst of this turmoil aspired to the standard of living and social consideration attached to landlordism, invested heavily in it and became the ancestors of a new gentry. Thanks to the anarchy and breakdown of the administration in most states, these middle-class landlords were soon in charge of tax collections—the first administrative officials in cities and villages, the nucleus of the future mandarin class—while the aristocracy disintegrated, never to rise again.

As the Chinese World Wars reached the pitch of their bloody ferocity, in the middle of the fourth century B.C. Ch'in began to assert its immense superiority. A transit area in full economic development, Ch'in was largely populated by recently civilized tribes from Tibet and Mongolia. To the rest of China it was a "barbarian" state, unrefined and uncultured, as the Roman West was to the Hellenistic East. But its strength and cohesion came precisely from its youth, its still-savage and virile character, its lack of refined culture, its single-minded pursuit of economic and military power and the disciplined nature of its large body of neophytes without any deep-rooted traditions—which explained the ease with which feudalism had been destroyed and a centralized administration imposed upon a tough population. The rest of China, overburdened with a long past and cramping traditions, and with social structures which only wars and revolutions could destroy, was overrefined and weak, as ripe for subservience to the recently civilized barbarians as Greece was to Rome. While poets, artists and philosophers had been honored and prized in the other states, Ch'in bred mainly men of action, men who were comparable to Sulla, Caesar, Pompey and

Augustus—practical men who were acute realists rather than cultured dreamers.

Fighting ruthlessly and negotiating with great diplomatic skill, Ch'in began to swallow one great state after another, extending its rule farther toward Szechwan and Yunnan. The main rival state, the Chinese Carthage to Ch'in's Rome, was the Kingdom of Ch'u in the Yangtze valley; but with its strong constitution, efficiency, iron will and single-mindedness, the Ch'in ruler gradually reduced his opponent to complete impotence. Last-ditch attempts to promote an international league of nations—the famous alliance of the Six Kingdoms in 333 B.C., for instance—collapsed miserably. By now, everyone across the length and breadth of the Chinese world felt that a universal state was indispensable. The lassitude of the people was such that everyone came to accept the idea that the alternative to a voluntary league of nations was the autocratic supremacy of one state over the entire civilized world. And so it was that disunion and demoralization destroyed all possibility of constructive resistance.

In 256 B.C. the last representative of the Chou dynasty, a mere figurehead by now, abdicated in favor of the prince of Ch'in. This young Caesar, reaping the fruit of his predecessors' work, launched his conquest of China at the age of twenty-five. In 230 he took over the state of Han, in 228 Chao, in 225 Wei, in 223 Ch'u, in 222 Yen and in 221 the last independent state, Ch'i. For the first time in history, if not in myth, China was united under the iron grip of a Caesarian autocrat.

Now that he was the supreme master of the Chinese world, the Ch'in prince decided to discard the meaningless title of *wang*—king—which he had inherited after the abdication of the last Chou ruler. There were no more independent kings, states or nations. Referring back to the mythical past, he assumed the title of the imaginary emperors of the Golden Age: he became *ti*—Augustus. Under his full official name of Shih Huang-ti he arose as the first historical ruler of a united Chinese world and styled himself "First Universal Emperor."

"For the first time he has united the world," claimed the famous inscription at T'ai-shan.[23] Just as Rome's Julius Caesar became Pontifex Maximus and thus became the religious as well as the political leader of the empire, just as the Caesarian Turkish sultans usurped the title of Caliph from the last Arab Commander of the Faithful, the Caesarian emperors of China assumed the religious title of Son of Heaven and kept it for more than two thousand years, until 1911. With them, China closed its great Culture epoch and inaugurated the age of Civilization—the age of Pax Sinica, an oriental Orbis Sinicus similar to the western Orbis Romanus.

4

THE UNIVERSAL
EMPIRE

The Civilization of China emerges from the awful epoch of the Warring States as a bright dawn from a dark night. All the great and basic books have been written, the great political and philosophical ideas have been formulated, the great artistic styles have set. The great effort toward original thinking, the trail-blazing progress of inward cultural growth, is gradually slowed down to be replaced by the crystallization of the great achievements, the extraction of the utilitarian contents and the material extension of the civilization over the entire Far East.

But just as India's Civilization started with the violent and temporary reaction of militant Buddhism against the hardening of India's institutions, against the petrifying caste system and the holy Vedas, Chinese Civilization started with a fierce and short-lived reaction against Confucianism and all that it stood for. Both reactions were carried out under the auspices of Ceasarian emperors, Asoka in India and Shih Huang-ti in China.

When the First Universal Emperor ascended the imperial throne which he himself had created, and when the last independent state had been absorbed by the Ch'in Empire, Shih Huang-ti cast an imperious glance over the gigantic domain which he now controlled. The Chinese people were tired of two hundred years of uninterrupted wars and revolutions, of looting, raping and destruction. Men were tired of conflicting philosophies and ideologies, abstract schemes and utopian plans. They were exhausted and anxious to turn their backs on theories which had led them nowhere, as the Greeks became disgusted with Platonic idealism and other impractical philosophies. Skepticism, once so fashionable, waned; empty intellectualism gradually disappeared before a powerful wave of emotional feeling which surged from the depths of the Chinese soul and eventually led to the establishment of a state religion with all its orthodox trappings. The Chinese people were now like soft clay in the hands of the iron-willed emperor, apparently ready to be molded into any form or shape which might appeal to his whim.

Under the leadership of Li Ssu, the stern Legalist chancellor, the Ch'in government set out to curb and eventually destroy altogether what was left of China's nobility. Shih Huang-ti did not have to obliterate it as Augustus had to obliterate Rome's Senatorial aristocracy, at the battle of Philippi and in the frightful proscriptions in Rome. All he had to do was to deport all the ruling classes, princes and kings of the remaining independent nations to the Ch'in capital city and decapitate all the states at one stroke. The internal administrative structure of Ch'in was then extended to the entire Chinese world, the states suppressed and ab-

sorbed and the Universal Empire divided into tightly controlled provinces and prefectures.

The Chinese Caesar brought to the Far Eastern world the
basic ingredients of Civilization: democratic equality [1]—"he
has regulated and made equal the laws, measures and standards for all men," claims the stele at Lang-ya—world-wide
unity and universal peace—"the Sovereign Emperor has pacified in turn the four ends of the earth," [2] adds the famous
stele. But the complete paralysis of the former ruling classes
and the emperor's undying hatred for intellectuals and scholars made it necessary for him to devise some new instrument
through which he could rule the Chinese world.

An imperial civil service came into being, headed by a
number of "controllers" who had full jurisdiction over the
provinces and were directly responsible to the emperor. Each
controller had both a civil and a military governor under him,
and all three officials were permanently engaged in endless
intrigues against each other—a shrewd device which prevented
any one of them from becoming a semi-independent feudal
lord. This was the essence of the philosophy of Chinese administration, as it was to remain throughout history: Rather
paralyze the entire administration into hopeless inefficiency
than encourage any separatist tendency among the powerful
officials in the provinces. The remains of such a system could
still be observed in the middle of the twentieth century in
Tibet, where every province was ruled by two governors of
equal rank and power.

The next task which the Ch'in ruler took upon his shoulders was the cultural unification of China. The great cultural
growth had occurred more or less simultaneously in many
different states and areas of China. There were great differences between the languages and customs of various provinces, indeed differences between the scripts, and the spirit of
nationalism, now obsolete, had purposely emphasized those
differences. A united world begged for over-all unification and
standardization, as the Classical world had begged and received from Julius Caesar free trade and standardization of

laws, weights and measures. And the Chinese world, basically devoted to the principle of centralized uniformity, received it in far more generous proportions than the Classical world. The First Universal Emperor gave his instructions and the imperial government ordered the progressive unification of the language and especially of the ideograms; an official lexicography was compiled and all officials were ordered to conform to it. Weights and measures were also unified. Another problem had to be solved: The growth of colossal cities and especially of the Ch'in capital had made them dependent on food imported, not only from the immediate neighborhood but also from far-flung provinces. There were no roads and the muddy soil had necessitated the use of deep cart tracks embedded in the caked mud. The axles of the carts were of different lengths according to the provinces and a uniform size for the carts had to be imposed throughout the empire—a technical problem which is encountered in the modern world in the shape of railroad gauges.

The fundamental problem of the imperial ruler was the smooth administration of a huge population. According to the Legalist doctrine, a good population was composed of disciplined, obedient and uneducated peasants and artisans. Scholars and philosophers, being nonproducers of goods, were an economic liability and therefore useless, besides being a public nuisance because they thought too much. The greatest enemy of the state was Confucianism with its distrust of strong monarchies, its preference for the aristocratic form of government which the Ch'in had just destroyed, and its reverence for family unity and solidarity, which stood in the way of political autocracy. In 213 B.C. a state-ordered holocaust of all classical books was ordered in which the writings of Confucius and his disciples were destroyed, save for one copy left in the imperial library. The past had to be blotted out of the memory of China, that history might begin with the First Universal Emperor—a drastic action which could be taken only by people who were essentially Time-conscious, to whom history had a definite meaning and conveyed a quasi-religious message. This epoch-making "Burning of the Books" would have been pointless in India, where people had no historical memory anyway. Just the same, it could be done only by people who hankered after uniformity and authority. Scientific books which dealt with technology useful to the economic prosperity of the state were spared.

Confucianism having been restored later on as the official philosophy of life of the Chinese people, the judgment of orthodox Chinese historians on Shih Huang-ti was bound to be viciously biased. Historical objectivity seems to indicate that he was of average intelligence, strong willed and ruthlessly determined to apply the political theories of the Legalist school with the help of his remarkable chancellor Li Ssu. Interfering as little as possible in the actual administration of the state, the emperor traveled all over his vast dominions, following with great precision the course of the sun and the stars, offering public sacrifices at the appointed ritual dates. His gigantic palace at Hien-yang was built according to plans drawn up by the court astrologers, and the orbit of the main stars determined the various apartments in which he had to live.

A hundred and twenty thousand of the wealthiest and most prominent families were either invited or forcibly compelled to live in the capital city under his watchful eye. Scientific knowledge and applied sciences were as strongly encouraged as philosophy and ideological literature were frowned upon. The resistance of poets, philosophers and thinkers of all ranks to the emperor's Caesarian dictatorship was relentless. They violently opposed his revolutionary policies, which appeared to violate every moral, social and political tradition, refused to sanction his policy of crushing the nobility, urged him unanimously to re-create a landed aristocracy by distributing fiefs to his relatives. Keeping their eyes on history, commissions of scholars proclaimed that "for a person, in any matter, not to model himself on antiquity and yet to achieve duration—that, to our knowledge, has never happened." [3] To which Li Ssu replied that times had changed and that history did not flow in repetitive cycles, that indeed a unique revolution had occurred which could never be undone. However, the Chinese mind was already set fast by then and was slowly returning to past traditions; and it was the scholars who were the trustees of this past. No enduring regime could be established against or even without them. But Shih Huang-ti was a volcanic force of nature who could stand no opposition. Violently irritated at the horrified protests raised against his "Burning of the Books," he arrested thousands of scholars, sent them to forced labor on the Great Wall or had them put to death. Terrified, those who were spared retired and kept quiet.

Now that China had brought about its universal state, it became obvious that serious threats to the external security of the empire could materialize only in the vast deserts of the north in the shape of huge, warlike and nomadic tribes which could never be permanently controlled. The south, populated by small, disorganized, backward tribes still living in the Stone Age represented no threat and was destined to become the main field of Chinese expansion. Trading colonies from northern China gradually extended as far south as Canton, forming administrative centers, the nuclei of future provinces. The permanent immigration of Chinese farmers intermarrying freely with aborigines was creating a new Chinese population, while the more savage tribes were pushed back into swamplands, forests and inhospitable mountains where millions of them remain to this day. But the relentless menace from the north and the desire of the Chinese for permanent protection against attacks of the nomadic Hsiung Nu prompted Shih Huang-ti to undertake the construction of the Great Wall, the most colossal and spectacular public work ever completed by mankind up to that time, extending fifteen hundred miles from the heart of Central Asia to the Pacific Ocean. In the long run, however, the Great Wall was no better shield than its Roman counterpart, the *limes*. If China survived intact, it was due to the immense biological vitality

of the Chinese people and its capacity for ethnical absorption
rather than to any fortified and static frontier.

Civil war broke out shortly after Shih Huang-ti's death in
210 B.C. His rule had been too personal, too many people
were disgruntled by the weight of a political oppression which
was out of the ordinary; the Chinese people were, after all,
far more resilient than might have appeared at the close of the
Warring States era. Confucianist ethics were already deeply
embedded and no amount of political pressure could eradicate
reverence for scholarship or ancestor worship. And it was
proved, for the first but not the last time, that no regime
was likely to last in China without the approval of the scholars. The Ch'in dynasty was engulfed in the upheaval, the
Legalists disappeared shortly afterward from the scene of
history, never to reappear again, and anarchy spread all over
China for a few years. According to a pattern which was to
become a regular feature of Chinese history, a clever adven-
turer named Liu Pang eliminated the legal heir to the throne,
crushed eighteen short-lived states which had cropped up
during the civil war and was crowned emperor in 206 B.C.
Having changed his name to Kao Tsu, he founded China's
first historical imperial dynasty, the Hans, who ruled for four
hundred years.

Kao Tsu rendered a great tribute to his predecessor's immense work by consolidating it with all his might—whereas
no one thought of continuing Asoka's work in India. The
rebellious aristocracy was crushed for the last time and disappeared from the scene of Chinese history. And so did
parochial nationalism and the separatist tendencies of local
states. The entire civilized world was united and the universal state became conterminous with it. In fact, the very
notion of *state* and *nation* gave way to the old classical notion of the *Great Society*, that is, of all civilized mankind
"Under Heaven." The Caesarian rule of a universal emperor
was definitely consecrated by tradition—but always tempered
by the possible revolt of outraged subjects who could then

force a change of dynasty according to Mencius' equally traditional "right of rebellion," when the emperor had lost the Mandate of Heaven. The Chinese people had no right to legislate directly, no power of taxation, no voting right, but they had at all times the right of *rebellion*—the crude equivalent in Chinese Civilization of our modern parliamentary control.

The natural corollary was that no one ever had a *hereditary* right to the throne, whether he was a son or a relative of the ruler; the dynastic, hereditary concept, applicable to an aristocratic monarchy issued from feudalism in a Culture era, becomes outdated and worthless in a Civilization era, being incompatible with the concept of a democratic Caesarian ruler who is the spokesman of the "people" as a whole rather than of an aristocratic ruling class: there was no longer a divine right to the throne by *birth*. In the old days of China's *ancien régime* rulers enjoyed a "divine" right to sovereignty, and dynastic prestige was so great that they could not be dethroned (with the two exceptions of the Tsin and the old dynasty of Ch'i). But their power was drastically limited by powerful aristocracies. Now, the new Caesarian autocrats had limitless powers in an equalitarian, democratic society, but they were at all times insecure on their thrones—as their *ancien régime* counterparts never were.

Chinese politics were at all times directly geared to the cosmic order: When torrential rains drenched the plains and rivers rose out of their beds, when earthquakes shook the valleys and toppled mountains, when mysterious comets streaked the skies, a great revulsion gripped the Chinese people and fear seized the Son of Heaven. Having disturbed the order of nature, the emperor failed to keep the rhythm of public life in tune with the rhythm of celestial bodies and cataclysms ensued inevitably; since man is an integral part of nature, human ethical irregularities and immoral actions produced a kind of shock wave or vibrations that spread throughout the vast cosmic organism that is nature. There was no *causal* relationship between human ethics and cosmic

order but *organic* connection—and as the responsible head
of the human half of this cosmic order, the Son of Heaven
was, first and last, responsible for the *health* of the cosmic
organism.

But below the apparent instability of Chinese politics, a
civilization kept expanding and growing to full maturity
during the four hundred years of Han rule, to achieve the
maximum of its potentialities under the following T'ang and
Sung dynasties. Thereafter, the growth slowed down and
stopped, Civilization became petrified, China went on living
on its carefully transmitted stock forms but created no more.
And yet, until the twentieth century, the Chinese were to
believe obstinately that theirs was the only civilized country,
destined to expand ceaselessly and to establish a universal
"civilizing" domination over the "barbarians." "For the ruler
of the Middle Empire there is no foreign land," stated Kung-
yang.

Although the Hans consolidated Shih Huang-ti's mammoth
work, they tolerated and then favored a rebirth of Confucianism, which was slowly integrated into the new imperial
structure. Social reasons as well as the undying loyalism of
the scholars toward the old Master made such a rebirth inevitable—but under forms and shapes which Confucius had
probably never dreamed of.

A Civilization can establish itself only on an *ethical* basis,
and the cynical realism of the Legalists, useful to bring about
the necessary revolution and unification of the civilized
world by fire and blood, had to be discarded as soon as its
limited purposes had been fulfilled. Thus it was that later on,
under the Han Emperor Hsiao Wu, the great scholar Tung
Chung-shu was put in charge of the Confucianist revival.
The synthetic character of this revival can be gauged by the
numerous elements of Taoism which slipped into what was
now gradually becoming China's state religion [4]—the same
change which, in India, metamorphosed Gautama Buddha's
original philosophic doctrine of pessimistic atheism into the

Mahāyāna's optimistic, emotional religion. This religious and philosophic synthesis welded itself to the far-reaching social changes which had turned China upside down since the good old days of Master K'ung.

With the establishment of Civilization, China's social structure was becoming permanently crystallized. Four main classes formed the substance of this structure: the literate class or scholars (mostly drawn from the gentry), the cultivators of the land, the artisans and manufacturers and, lastly, the traders, merchants and bankers. It was typical of Chinese psychology to raise the social value of the peasant above the two last classes and, more significant still, to depress the mercantile element down to the lowest level of the social scale, a fate which they never suffered in any other civilization, an indication of China's profound and enduring contempt for economic pursuits and especially for the profit motive. Even in the highly religious civilization of India, the merchant Vaisya ranked higher than the Sūdra farmer. The Chinese authorities, whatever the dynasty in power, never ceased to curb ruthlessly the financial appetites of merchants and traders. Distrusting the accumulation of capital, they nationalized trade whenever a new expansion in commercial activity threatened to become a boon for capitalists (the nationalization of tea exports under the T'ang dynasty, for instance).

The great new social elite which replaced the departed nobility, and which was destined to play a major part in Chinese politics until the twentieth century, was the rejuvenated landed gentry. The commercialization of the land and the ruin of the old noble families during the Warring States period had produced a new class of landowners drawn from all social strata. The members of this gentry lived on the rentals of their farms, and while a part of a typical landowner's large family remained in the country to look after the estates the other part moved into town and dominated the political life of China. The emperor, who distrusted both the army and the merchants, recruited his officials among the gentry; these landowning officials first functioned as tax collectors—which gave them an effective financial stranglehold over the empire. This gentry was in no way a closed caste such as the Indian Brāhmins, the notion of caste and racial discrimination being utterly alien to the Chinese. The gentry remained a fluid class throughout the centuries, wealth and financial acumen being the vehicle in and out of it and civil wars, revolutions and foreign invasions providing the instability which prevented social coagulation.

As Kao Tsu's successor, Emperor Wen Ti ruled a flourishing realm in comparative peace. Economic progress was remarkable and taxes were lowered. With the steady growth of the population and consequently of the acreage of land under cultivation, the total wealth of China multiplied at a fast rate. The gentry increased its wealth even faster than the rest of the population and gradually became a completely separate class. Freed from all material preoccupations, the members of this *yamen* class were able to devote all their energies to scholarship and to the preservation of China's cultural heritage. They began to identify themselves mentally with the noble lords depicted by Confucius, imitated their polite manners and acquired their discriminating tastes.

As the gentry provided most of the government officials, Confucianism crept back into the administration and the political world, becoming gradually the sole moral code of China's ruling elite. One by one, Confucianist rituals were revived by the imperial court. Heaven and ancestor worship, sacrifices, etiquette and court ceremonials, every element of Confucianism returned and triumphed over the now forgotten doctrines of its opponents, but strongly altered by the Taoistic influences of the Ch'in period. Just as the Brāhmins eventually made their strong and enduring comeback in India after the Buddhist offensive and the Caesarian rule of the Maurya Emperors, the Confucianists began to reassert themselves after the eclipse of the Ch'in autocratic rule.

The revolutionary establishment of China's universal state could never have been accomplished by reverent Confucianists. Such a task could be undertaken only by the ruthless dictator who despised traditions, who was willing and able to adopt drastic and unethical methods. Having destroyed the traditional nobility, condemned ancestor worship, attempted to dissolve family solidarity and reshaped past history to suit his needs, he had been able to build a strong and centralized empire that would endure two thousand years despite countless upheavals. But Confucianism was too congenial to the basic instincts of the Chinese people to be destroyed forever. In spite of bitter persecutions, it remained the only code of ethics which had any chance of lasting success in the Celestial Empire.

The supremacy of the Confucianist "gentlemen" imbued with wisdom and morality was gradually restored. The undemocratic tenet of Confucius that "courtesy should not be extended to the commoners and punishment should not be served up to the lords" returned in full force. A certain dose of social inequality prevailed again over the stern equality enforced by the first Chinese Caesar. But feudalism had long since disappeared and there was no hereditary aristocracy left in the realm. Confucianism had to be adapted to these new and, in the days of the Master, unforeseen conditions. It had to be fitted within the framework of Shih Huang-ti's enduring institutions; a strong autocratic Caesarism could no longer tolerate the rival power of a hereditary nobility. A new and fairer way of recruiting a ruling class had to be evolved which would satisfy the democratic urge of the Chinese and make full use of the overwhelming prestige bestowed by scholarship.

The most remarkable and enduring institution of China was born during Wen Ti's reign. The return of the triumphant scholar to power, the great Confucianist revival among the gentry and the officials, together with the utilitarian trend always evident in Civilization periods as contrasted with Culture periods, gave rise to a new and unique system for recruiting the ruling administrators of the empire. The complexities of the written script, the many years required to learn thousands of characters, the length of the classics and the profound emotional impact of classical poetry gave to the scholar who was able to master this cultural legacy a prestige which has never been paralleled in any other civilization. War had lost its appeal now that all civilized men were gathered in a universal state, and trade had always been despised by the cultured Chinese (except during the Warring States era),[5] leaving government service as the only prestige-bestowing, face-giving occupation.

With the crystallization of Chinese civilization, this learning was progressively codified by laws and regulations and became indispensable to all those who aspired to government service. The examination system grew out of this typically Chinese yearning and admiration for scholarly knowledge. After many years of studious mastering of classical texts, of memorizing poetry, of becoming not merely intellectually learned but emotionally steeped and soaked in Confucianist orthodoxy and classical culture, of learning not only with the mind but with the heart and the whole being, and after satisfying harsh judges, one became a *mandarin*, one of the elect.

The Imperial Examinations became the most important event in the official life of the empire, and mastery of the six major accomplishments—archery, horsemanship, rites, music, history and mathematics—elevated the candidate to the lowest rank of the official hierarchy. The first man in the Imperial Examinations was mounted on a white horse, decorated by the emperor and paraded through the streets as the cleverest scholar of his generation. Wherever he went, a gong was sounded, proclaiming his newly won social prestige, which the greatest in the land could only envy.

Two characteristics of the mandarin system soon manifested themselves. On the one hand, it was a democratic system, whereby anyone could rise to the highest official functions on his own merit. On the other, entrance was most of the time reserved to the rich gentry because of the many unproductive and costly years devoted to studies and the low pay of the officials which had to be supplemented by a private income. This inevitable weakness of the system was partly remedied by the subsequent reforms of the T'ang dynasty, aimed at helping the poorer students financially and contributing to a periodic regeneration of the ruling administration. Even with this unavoidable handicap, the mandarin system was the most democratic that had ever been known. As Lin Yutang contends, with only slight exaggeration, "learning was the privilege of the talented, yet never the privilege of the rich. No one was known to be seriously handicapped in his academic career by his poverty. In this sense, it may be said that there was equality of opportunity for all." [6] And gifted but poor students were often provided with scholarships by subscriptions from their family and clan, whose reward lay in the prestige bestowed upon it collectively if the promising youngster became a mandarin.

Intellectual examination as a method for recruiting the best elements in a country can become, in fact, a devastating weapon against exceptional minds or outstanding characters who have to proceed through a crushing mill set for the standards of an average intelligence and which grinds all nonconformists to dust. All those who did, finally, rise to the top by scaling the examination ladder lost whatever originality and personality they might have had in their youth. They had become completely molded by the implacable structure of traditional scholarship, victims of a majestic "brainwashing" which destroyed their *individual* idiosyncrasies but developed their *social* instincts to the utmost.

This gradual evolution was intimately welded to the Chinese appreciation for perfect *expression* rather than perfect *being*. The original and exceptional personality could never express himself adequately, and could never fit into the smooth functioning of the immense machinery of state. In this, the mandarins remained faithful to Confucius' warning: "to recognize the unrecognizable, to attain the unattainable; to perform deeds which would draw admiration from the coming centuries: these are things which I would never attempt." [7] The ideal was the man who was willing to fit into the norm of the Tao, the exquisitely cultured individual who is not exceptionally endowed by nature but gives perfect expression to this norm according to tradition. The result, judged by a modern philosopher, was enunciated thus: "among the Chinese, original individualities are rarer than anywhere else, the uncultured man is more blunt and failures are sacrificed. But the average reach a high degree of perfection more frequently than anywhere else in the world." [8]

The Chinese are guided by rationalism and common sense to a greater extent than other Asians. The rational mind of a humanist bent on literary pursuits often makes him a bad psychologist. He is unable to judge other men's characters through sympathetic, intuitive identification and, being afraid to trust his faulty judgment, will resort to the palliative of mechanical and impersonal means. Intellectual examinations provide such means; thus no one person but a mechanical system was held responsible for those mandarins who proved inadequate. The closest parallel to the mandarin system in the West is the examination system set up by Napoleon, whereby modern France recruits all its civil and military officials by means of intellectual competition. In both cases, the psychological roots are identical.

But what is originally the most democratically perfect institution for the recruitment of a ruling administration becomes warped and distorted in time. The mandarin is no longer judged according to his efficiency. He has received no professional training—except as jurist or physician. Literary accomplishments are required to the exclusion of almost everything else. The fact that such accomplishments may have little or nothing in common with the future occupation or responsibility, that there is no direct relationship between memorizing pages of poetry and, for instance, supervising the construction of roads or the digging of wells, has given a curious twist to the psychology of a mandarin. His main duty is to succeed in his examinations, to cram as much theoretical knowledge as possible into his mind in as short a time as possible—and forget it as soon as the examination is passed. The actual performance of his duties is often of secondary importance. The appointment comes as a reward for his intellectual accomplishments and his achievement of a certain mental conformism. He is now entitled to a privilege, even if he proves to be entirely useless and unproductive. This was and is a great system to elevate the average scholar to intellectual heights unattainable in other civilizations. But it was destructive of true creative talent and originality. It is essentially an antlike, mechanical system—a typical Civilization-creation.

If the candidate mandarin was nimble enough, he climbed slowly through the various grades, *Hsiuts'ai* (B.A.), *Chujen* (M.A.), to reach the higher echelons: *Chinshih* and *Hanlin*. Each grade had its distinctive marks, precious stones and feathers with which to adorn their hats, so that each mandarin should receive the due reverence and kowtowing to which he was entitled. Great and brilliant as it was, this most democratic bureaucracy became oppressively slow and inefficient. Certain moral guarantees and real honesty and integrity did not outweigh the disastrous clumsiness of the mandarin system. Yet China lived with it for two thousand years, until 1904. It was the price paid by the Chinese for having no castes, no clergy and no hereditary aristocracy.

The *yamen* class remained fluid, open on both sides of the social scale, and few families could claim a long ancestorship comparable to the duration of any Western aristocracy. But the mandarin system was hopelessly welded to a petrified Civilization which could no longer grow or adapt itself when challenged by superior forces from the outside world. Just like the Indian caste system, it became the mechanical extension of a great organic creation of the cultural period, and with this transformation creative thought came to an end in China. "Late manifestations" in art or philosophy represented synthetic efforts aimed at reinterpretations but not real creation. In spite of their shortcomings, however, the mandarins remained for thousands of years the best officialdom in the world, an iron armature of great moral value which preserved intact for countless generations the most delicate culture the world has ever known—mandarins *preserved* but never *created*.

Before the inexorable flow of history sweeps us on and takes us away, we must pause and study one of the most remarkable characteristics of China's political and social instincts. This characteristic recurs relentlessly throughout the history of the Middle Empire: the inherent, fundamental socialism of the Chinese. The psychological background is obvious: the lack of true individualism in the Western sense, the predominance of family and clannish collectivism even long before Confucius was born, its compulsory transfer to society and the state when Caesarism and Civilization came about, and finally, the true compromise of Civilization between two forms of collectivism—family and society. Nowhere in Chinese psychology was there any place for real individualism in the Western sense.[9]

Thus the great socialistic experiments carried out in China were never at the expense of the individual's freedom but at the expense of the more narrow and limited collectivism of the family. They should be seen as repeated attempts to transfer to the entire "Great Society" the loyalty, devotion and abnegation usually granted by the individual to his clan and relatives.

The first such experiment was begun under Emperor Wu Ti, one of the Han monarchs, who reigned from 140 to 86 B.C. and who was undoubtedly the greatest of the dynasty. A man of considerable ability and energy, he launched the first of many socialistic revolutions in which China was to indulge time and again. He started by establishing state ownership of all natural resources in order to protect the lower classes against the greed of the wealthy. The production of salt and iron and the manufacture of fermented drinks became state monopolies. Transport and financial transactions were either strictly supervised or taken over by the authorities. Goods were stored and bought by the state, and prices were controlled to prevent any violent fluctuations so that "the rich merchants and large shop-keepers would be prevented from making big profits." [10] A 5 per cent income tax was established throughout the empire, public works of colossal dimensions took care of unemployment. For a time the system worked magnificently until it came to the same end as most socialistic experiments. Neither nature nor men could put up with it for long and the entire scheme collapsed rapidly into corruption and inefficiency.

But the Chinese had a new try at it a century later under another remarkable ruler, Wang Mang. His socialistic empire set up famous laws which inaugurated great land reforms, turning over to the state huge private estates and giving away to landless peasants the landlords' holdings. By law, the state became sole proprietor of the soil. State-owned communal farms were created; this in fact reduced the farmer to the status of a state slave and pleased no one. The exploitation of lakes and forests was nationalized, wine, salt, gold, copper and iron became once more state monopolies. "Equalization Offices" were created to stabilize the market, purchasing goods cheaply in times of plenty, reselling them at low prices in times of scarcity. Banks were nationalized, systematic inflation was promoted and a 10 per cent income tax decreed. But, once more, this planned experiment ended disastrously. Corruption flourished and the standard of living of the farmers declined catastrophically.

It was under Wang Mang that another enduring institution of China saw its birth: revolutionary secret societies, many of which are still alive today. Most of them were peasant societies (usually with Taoist affiliations) started by influential farmers, and although in time of peace and political stability they were as harmless as any welfare organization in contemporary Europe and America, they could and did become formidable powers in times of emergency and widespread chaos. Secret societies were the only form of peasant organizations which could influence politics directly, but this they did very effectively in many circumstances. In Wang Mang's reign the "Red Eyebrows" started a revolt and marched on the capital, killing

all the officials on the way. Wang Mang's army, sent against
the rebels, disintegrated swiftly and anarchy spread all over
China until the Han dynasty was re-established in the person
of Liu Hsiu, also known as Emperor Kuang Wu-ti. The
socialist state was scrapped and the new emperor reverted to
the good old ways. But several aspects of this episode had
been striking, especially the facility with which Wang Mang
had been able to extract from Confucius' writings arguments
and justifications for his revolutionary attempt.

China had by no means finished with her socialistic experiments, however. The next important one occurred a thousand
years later. The artisan of this bold plan, perhaps the boldest
enterprise of that kind until the twentieth century Marxists,
was the chancellor Wang An-shih. The entire Chinese world
was given a complete cadastral survey, landowners had to
declare everything they possessed, all commodities were arbitrarily priced by the mandarins. Forced labor was abolished,
huge public works were started, moneylenders were removed.
Landless peasants were given land and government loans,
wages and prices were severely controlled, banking and mort-
gages were taken over by the authorities. Trade and commerce
were nationalized and the government became the sole cus-
tomer, distributing its goods according to the need of the day.
Pensions were set up for the unemployed, the aged and the
sick. Even education was overhauled; the literary influence of
the classics was drastically reduced in favor of history, geography and economics. But once more the experiment floundered under the swelling discontent over crushing taxes,
growing inefficiency and inevitable corruption. The emperor
finally gave way to the clamors of public opinion, removed
Wang An-shih and canceled all his reforms.

This was the last spectacular socialistic experiment, although many more were attempted on a more modest scale as
late as the Ming dynasty. But it was not only in thorough-
going revolutions that this inherent socialism manifested itself;
it remained a permanent trait throughout China's history. In
the T'ang era, the state had remained sole proprietor of the

soil, but in practice a great deal of it was owned collectively by the village. When a young Chinese peasant attained manhood he received an allotment of about ten to fifteen acres, but only "for life"; it reverted to the community at his death. In addition, he received a small "property" of about three acres which he could leave to his descendants. The whole of it was inalienable and was paid for by land taxes, forced labor and conscription in the militia. Only the gentry and the officials were entitled to have and inherit large estates which they rented to tenant farmers.

In many ways, Chinese civilization remained the only one which, until our twentieth century, displayed such persistent instincts for socialism and schematic uniformity—except for the Peruvian Incas.

5

THE CHINESE
MIND

China's civilization was based on one of the most remarkable world-outlooks ever to express itself on our planet—in many ways the most remote from anything the West has ever known or experienced. Chinese psychology shaped and molded its civilization into a vast structure which owed less to other civilizations than any known to history (with the exception of the separate worlds of pre-Columbian America). In order to penetrate into this strange mental universe a great intuitive effort is required on the part of the Westerner, to whom the

peculiar European world-outlook is something that should be
taken for granted as being the basic psychological substratum
of all human beings. But even the greatest intuitive effort can
do no more than show us the weird contours of China's
strange world-outlook; this windowless monad, now as irretrievably destroyed as the Egypt of the Pharaohs, will remain
for all times one of those fascinating dreams which an increasingly Westernized world will be forever unable to conjure up.

The essence of the Chinese mind resides in its synthetic
and concrete, almost feminine apprehension of reality and its
deliberate shunning of any kind of analytical form of reasoning, linked with a distaste for abstraction which surpasses that
of any other Asiatic culture. The Chinese mind is therefore
not attuned to generalities, since generalities are perforce
abstract, but to the "singular": there is no Chinese equivalent
for *oldster*, for instance, but there are a number of concrete
evocations of different types of oldsters: *k'i* will designate
the undernourished old man, *k'ao* the asthmatic, *lao* those
who are over seventy, and so on.[1] This multiplication of
concrete and powerfully evocative symbols enriches one's intuitive understanding but paralyzes logical reasoning and
abstract generalization.

This distaste for inductive and deductive reasoning has
given rise to the distinctive characteristic of all Chinese philosophic doctrines and systems. In order to grasp the meaning
of such doctrines, one should not attempt to seek for the
normal articulations of logical analysis, but for the central
core, for the key formula which ties together the innumerable
strands of an essentially illogical system. All the deductions
radiate from this key formula very much as spokes radiate
from the hub to the rim of a wheel.

The Chinese are essentially utilitarian and are forever seeking magic recipes; and no such recipe is worth considering
unless it possesses both an essential originality and all the
qualities of a universal panacea.[2] It must have specific virtues
which will give it its uniqueness, but also an unlimited efficiency. The essence of any such recipe cannot be grasped by

discursive reasoning but only intuitively, and thus remains largely esoteric, out of reach for non-initiates. A great deal of what sounds unbearably insipid or dull or even fantastically nonsensical springs from this essential fact: that these texts were intended to be meditated upon and not just read intellectually, that their aim was to frame a discipline of life which *transformed* the whole individual instead of merely *informing* his mind. These philosophies were not theoretical postulates but mental and emotional gymnastics which altered the inner self, not for the purpose of developing the individual's self-realization as in India but rather to promote his social and moral instincts—very much like a cog which is shaped and refined and polished in order to fit into a gigantic machinery, the machinery of the Great Society. All such Chinese doctrines were not so much concerned with the welfare of the particular *individual* or with his quest for religious understanding as with a proper disposal of the various elements of man's *social* life, but always by taking their "totalitarian" aspect into account and by carefully scrutinizing all their cosmic implications.

There are innumerable examples of the Chinese type of reasoning which always seeks or springs from the master recipe, the "special" key formula which, once it is meditated upon and understood in all its profound implications, will unveil all secrets and all mysteries of the universe and of the human heart. In the famous Great Learning, for example, we are informed that "the men of old who wished to shine with the illustrious power of personality throughout the Great Society first had to govern their own fiefs (*kuo*) efficiently. Wishing to do this, they first had to make an ordered harmony in their families. Wishing to do this, they first had to cultivate their individual selves (*hsiu sheng*). Wishing to do this, they first had to put their minds right. Wishing to do this, they first had to make their purpose genuine. Wishing to do this, they first had to extend their knowledge to the utmost . . ." And now we reach the key formula: "Such extension of knowledge consists in appreciating the nature of things."

Once this key formula has been meditated upon at great length, has literally seeped into the very marrow of the disciple's bones, all the bounties of nature are his: "For with the appreciation of the nature of things knowledge reaches its heights. With the completion of knowledge purposes become genuine. With purposes genuine the mind becomes right. With the mind right the individual self comes into flower (*hsiu sheng*). With the self in flower, the family becomes an ordered harmony. With the families ordered harmonies, the state (*kuo*) is efficiently governed. With the state efficiently governed the Great Society is at peace." [3]

The consequences of this psychological disposition, of this supreme "utilitarianism," were far-reaching. Concrete-minded, the Chinese deliberately shunned the utilization of abstract "signs" and replaced them by "emblems," by active symbols whose efficiency was well tested and which could actually acquire the magical virtue of accomplishing instead of merely representing. The natural and unavoidable corollary was an almost total split between philosophic and scientific thinking, largely at the expense of the latter. Dogmatic and theoretical thinking became almost impossible, since the Chinese remained rooted in their essentially concrete universe, determined to seek practical recipes of action and distrustful of all abstractions.

The Chinese script and language bore the first brunt of this remarkable psychological disposition and, as codified under the First Universal Emperor, acquired all the characteristics of a tool destined to provoke an emotional shock, imbued as it is with the spirit of concrete action but unable to express abstract ideas with even a modicum of clarity. The Chinese script is a gigantic symbolism which is pointed at effective *action*, not clear *thought*, and each symbol is supposed to suggest to the mind a host of related pictures intuitively felt which create a determined atmosphere and eventually evoke the "Totality" of the Tao.

In the innermost depths of his being, the Son of Han feels that man and nature form one single society, not two separate worlds. In order to grasp the universal order, man should not dream of knowing and dominating nature with the help of scientific knowledge, but should seek to integrate himself harmoniously into nature. Instead of *science*, he adopted *etiquette* and ceremony as the suitable agents for the desired integration. Whatever he did or thought, every item of his life had to be "in tune" with nature, related by a set of complicated rules to the revered Tao. The first thing to do, therefore, was to define the directing ideas, the basic concepts around which the related symbols would group themselves in order of hierarchical precedence—and not according to the structural elaborations of logic. These directing ideas, these fundamental "emblems" have to be essentially synthetic: the interplay of the complementary Yin and Yang which regulate the essential rhythm of life and become Tao through their union. Such vast, all-embracing emblems were never defined and no one ever felt any need to define them. Their efficiency was a byword, and that was all that was needed: they were intuitively grasped. But the Westerner who attempts to peer into the unfathomable abyss of the Chinese mind cannot hope to do so unless he first understands its bedrock: the Chinese conception of Time and Space.

The Chinese had no conception of abstract, homogeneous Time and Space and instead conceived of Time as an accumulation of eras, epochs and seasons, of Space as a group of locations, domains and orientations. Time and Space were therefore conceived as being essentially subjective and "discontinuous" and their respective symbols were the circle and the square.

Time and Space were controlled through their symbolic reproduction in temples and gardens with the help of symbolic rites reproducing the cyclical movements of seasons. The discontinuous nature of Space, its heterogeneity, resulted in positively annihilating it where there was no human life and, on the contrary, of giving it a maximum of density in the sacred precinct of the emperor's palace and temple. Space

became a number of spaces distributed according to a pattern
of hierarchy and Time a number of limited cycles; all of these
revolved around the Son of Heaven and acquired the maximum of their density *in* the capital city of the world, at the
time of the great celebrations and festivities. The emperor
lived in "pure," unpolluted space, the focus of all converging
attributes.

The imperial "etiquette" was shaped by these concepts:
The Son of Heaven had to travel around the empire every
five years and regulate his progress so as to find himself in the
east during the vernal equinox, in the south during the summer solstice, in the west when autumn came and in the north
during the winter. Space acquired all its proper density around
the Son of Heaven and gradually vanished into nought as the
borders of civilization were reached; it emanated from the
"pure" center of civilization and exhausted itself on civilization's periphery.

Time was just as much limited by this odd concept of relativity as Space and was ordered in a number of definite, closed,
discontinuous and unrelated cycles emanating, like Space,
from a center. The same fear of the infinite which is so vivid
in the architecture and gardening of the Chinese seems to
characterize their concept of Time and Space, the same desire
to seek refuge in friendly nature and shun all dangerous disturbances of the order of the universe.

When a cycle comes to an end—an imperial dynasty, for
instance—its separation from the preceding one must be rigor-
ously defined and their respective boundaries set, but the
revolved cycle should not come to a bad end. The scions of a
fallen dynasty were endowed, for instance, with an enclosed
estate in which they were obligated to continue the harmonious, microcosmic revolving of the completed cycle. The
revolved cycle was thus preserved artificially and its ghost was
unable to interfere with the harmonious development of the
contemporary cycle in progress.[4] And while his predecessors
thus kept the ghost of completed cycles chained by this magic
charm, the Son of Heaven went about his business of welding

the various Spaces to the various Times, setting the boundaries of contemporary Space every five years and marking its
emanating center during the next four. Condensing the Spaces
into "pure," integral Space around him, the emperor condensed pure Time with the help of official celebrations. The
small density of Time during the dead summer months of
hard work without social life gradually increased during the
autumn to achieve its maximum during the ritual jubilees,
and it was the Son of Heaven's duty to thus endow, at a
given moment and according to the proper etiquette, Time
and Space with their maximum intensity.

One can appreciate how intensely human, in its utter subjectivity, such a world-outlook could become and, in many
ways, how true to man's inner life this external ordering of
things could be. The intensity of social life endowed Time
and Space with a density which is practically nonexistent
where no civilized life exists—among the barbarians or in un-
populated areas.

Fear or dislike of abstraction has always prevented the
Chinese from basing their philosophical outlook on the distinction between Time and Space and has compelled them,
instead, to use the two concepts of Yin and Yang. It is interesting to note that during the contemporary Western controversy over the exact nature of those two words, modern
Chinese, in an effort to modernize them and assimilate them
to Western concepts, translated them as "forces," in spite of
the vigorous protests of Western Sinologists who insisted on
viewing them as "substances"—an interesting example of the
disintegration of a culture's profound essense and of its members' anxiety to adapt themselves to a new Western culture
which proves to be more efficient. In reality, Yin and Yang
were and are two *emblems*, the richest and most powerful of
all in their suggestive potentialities, master symbols around
which all the other symbols are gathered in hierarchical order.[5]

The interplay of Yin and Yang evokes and symbolizes the
cosmic rhythm, the fundamental beat of nature, the relations
of the male and female sexes. Although the Son of Heaven

is responsible for the harmonization of human society on the cosmic pattern of Yin and Yang, each individual has to devise his own rhythm. Nothing has been more instrumental in preserving the harmonious balance of Chinese life than this individual duplication of the cosmic beat, this forced alternance of phases which, for instance, obliged all town-dwelling Chinese to seek temporary refuge in the countryside.

The interplay of Yin and Yang does not portray two contending, antagonistic forces such as God and Satan, but two complementary facets of the Totality: Instead of *opposition*, there is *co-operation* and alternance. The fundamental dualism of other cultures was unknown in China, and nothing but the synthetic result of the union of Yin and Yang had any basic reality—and the task of the Son of Heaven was to see to it that human society reproduced with ritual exactitude this cosmic interplay and resulting harmony.

The supreme goal of Chinese civilized life was always the individual's integration into the Totality, into the Tao. This is the most distinctive notion of Chinese culture and, like many other Chinese notions, largely indefinable. The closest outline of its meaning was perhaps given by the *Huai Nan Hung Lieh*, written by the disciples of Liu An, the famous syncretist philosopher: "The Tao: it overshadows and supports the earth. It makes the vastness of the four quarters and the eight linked boundaries of the heavens and the earth which are so high and so deep that it is impossible to measure them. It envelops the heavens and the earth, endowing them with formlessness . . . a flowing fountain and bubbling spring, empty and yet overflowingly full, both swirling and smooth, muddy and yet more than limpid . . . it binds all space together and is the container of the Yin and the Yang. It links the Space of the universe with the Time of it . . . By its means the mountains have height and the pools have depth. By its means the animals can run and the birds can fly." [6] It is the Totality.

Today we can understand the profound meaning of the Tao through its etymology. Originally, Tao meant a road, an actual thoroughfare; it slowly became metamorphosed into a "way," a way of life, a mental progression. Thus, the Chinese conception of Absolute Totality is essentially dynamic; it is pure motion, evolution, perpetual change. "Everything flows on and on like this river, without pause, day and night," [7] said Confucius; the Chinese focus is on Time rather than Eternity. This endless *Becoming* was the result of the unceasing interplay of Yin and Yang. In fact, it represented in China what Hegelian dialectics represented in modern Europe: Yin and Yang, the active male and the passive female principles, were to them what thesis and antithesis are to our philosophic mind. The Tao is the synthesis, that which is never quite reached because it always transforms itself into a new thesis which calls for a new antithesis and promotes a further synthesis—and thus on and on, a never ending process of development which is the Tao. The process itself is the Absolute Totality, the only Reality.

Let us now link this with the Chinese conception of History and contrast the Indian with the Chinese *weltanschauung*. An allegory will help us: Let us compare them to two travelers walking on a road. The Indian will be surrounded by dense fog on all sides. To him, the road will be invisible; he will see neither where he comes from nor where he is going. But overhead there is no fog to obstruct the sight of boundless Space, and the immutable, eternal sky is clearly visible; that is what the Indian will be looking at constantly, forgetting all about Time, history, social and political development. On the other hand, the surrounding fog dissipates when the Chinese comes along. His vision of the road, behind and ahead, past and future, is perfectly clear. However, the dissipated fog has become a layer of dense clouds overhead which prevents him from seeing the sky. The Chinese does not care; as far as he is concerned, there is no static Absolute, no transcendental God, no immutable Paradise, no eternal dwelling place for departed souls; the only reality is the road which he sees, his walking on it, historical development, the unfolding process of Time from past to future, the endless interplay of Yin and

Yang: that is the Tao. The ultimate reality to the Indian is absolute Being, to the Chinese absolute Becoming. By way of contrast, the Christian tendency, especially in Western Europe, has always been to attempt a synthesis between Being and Becoming—between Eternity and Time, between the Absolute and the Relative. In this sense, it represents a considerable advance beyond the one-sided views of both the Indians and the Chinese, who emphasized exclusively one or the other.

Thorough knowledge of the elements into which the Tao was decomposed involved the creation of *numerical emblems* which would set the hierarchical order in which these elements were gathered. And here the outsider finds himself face to face with another remarkable trait of Chinese psychology: the complete indifference to the idea of *quantity* and the total disregard for any quantitative measurement in Chinese philosophical thinking (except in the philosophy of the short-lived Legalist school).[8] Each philosophy has its own mathematical concepts, each culture its own way of portraying the outer world of nature with the help of numbers—the most rigorous signs of delimitation and demarcation which human cultures have yet devised. The mathematics of the Classical Greeks was geared to the perception of *magnitudes*, that of the West Europeans to the perception of dynamic motion and *function*.

The Chinese conceived of numbers as *emblems*, the most essential and indispensable of all because of their multiple utilizations and great efficiency. Emblematic numbers are used to *classify* Times and Spaces, and then to *qualify* the very same elements according to strict hierarchy. The same dislike—indeed, deliberate incomprehension—of the Chinese for the infinite made them conceive the universe, the cosmic totality of heaven and earth, as closed, finite. All numbers, serving as convenient labels for the ordering of things within a finite universe, are perforce limited. The imperative obligation of remaining close to concrete thinking, of remaining within a limited Space-Time which is essentially concrete, has destroyed for the Chinese any possibility of taking an abstract and *linear* view of numbers. Instead, these convenient, all-purpose emblems have to be ordered in *cycles*, with an attendant power of geometrical and rhythmic expression.

The end result of this Chinese view of discontinuous Time and Space and of emblematic instead of quantitative numbers was this cyclical understanding of mathematics: The number 1 was not the beginning of a series running away toward the infinite, but the center of the mathematical world. As such it was privileged to represent the Totality and to have, therefore, the highest rating of all numbers. Simple numbers, such as 5 or 6, being close to the center, symbolized modes of distribution in the areas of densest Time and Space. But numbers such as 300 were essentially *peripheral*, secondary and less important, subordinate to the simple numerical emblems.

This over-all exteriorization of the Chinese soul, this mathematical expression of the Chinese world-outlook, was injected into every aspect of their culture: in music, geometry, astronomy, time-reckoning in their calendars and cyclical conception of history. Emblematic numbers satisfied the synthetic urge of the Chinese through numerical identification of musical notes with geographical orientations, seasons, geometrical forms and all elements. They were not intended to express quantitative measurements but to adjust the concrete dimension of man's natural world to the presumed proportions of the universe.[9] The number 1, the Totality, occupied the political position of the Emperor in the mathematical world, and all other numbers—and all their symbolized elements—were distributed around this center in hierarchical order. The Totality includes everything else and therefore predominates, and since each number not only classifies but also qualifies, the largest numbers, situated on the "periphery," serve to qualify the lowest echelons of the hierarchy.

All this brings us to another psychological trait of the Sons of Han: a profound feeling that there never is a *succession* of phenomena in nature, but a mere *alternation* of complementary aspects. This concept of "mutation" largely destroys causality as the West has always conceived it. Instead of an effect springing out of a cause, we now have related elements that are "matched," and instead of a *succession* we have *interdependence*. There is a complete absence of *direction* in either Space or Time, and the most fantastic—to the alien mind—liaisons can be established between seemingly unrelated phenomena whose sole test and justification is *efficiency*. Objective knowledge of those phenomena per se, quantitative measurements, are neglected in favor of the subjective, *practical* aspect of their relations.

Since cyclical views prevail over linear, since direction is twisted and broken in favor of devious routes, the notion of *succession* is totally irrelevant and only that of association and *interdependence* should be considered. Thus all of nature's phenomena are not to be viewed as being determined events with their own signification, but as mere *symbols*, as signals from Heaven pointing out related phenomena, portents of things to come.

We are now in a position to take up the matter of Chinese science, or rather the lack of it. Every particular culture engenders its own type of scientific knowledge, and all physical sciences are historically rooted in religious creeds. They are part and parcel of specific world-outlooks, and they develop or fail to develop according to the very nature of such *weltanschauungs*. This explains that the failure of Chinese culture to produce a body of scientific knowledge comparable to the West's is imputable to the main characteristics of the Chinese mind—to its lack of strong religious feeling, first of all. Almost all philosophical traditions in China, especially the Confucianists and the Legalists, turned their backs on physical sciences in order to devote all their intelligence to the ordering of human society. And it was the very same Hsün Tzu already quoted earlier who sounded the keynote when he claimed: "All those things which have nothing to do with the distinction of right and wrong, truth and falsehood, good government and misrule, or with the ways of mankind, are things the knowledge of which does not benefit men, and ignorance concerning which does no harm to men." [10]

It was only those men who were gripped by strong religious emotions, the Taoists, who could have developed physical sciences in China. And once again the same Hsün Tzu attacked them in the name of humanism, morality, positivism and urbane skepticism:

> You vainly seek into the cause of things;
> Why not appropriate and enjoy what they produce?
> Therefore I say—To neglect man and speculate about
>   Nature
> Is to misunderstand the facts of the universe.[11]

The essentially *practical* outlook of Civilization was overcoming the true religious urge, which is essentially *disinterested*, to understand and know. The mystical contemplation of the Taoists might have led to the development of physical sciences if the Chinese had not been so concrete-minded, so reluctant to theorize in the abstract, so exclusively interested in the harmonious functioning of the social body. Instead, Taoistic contemplation turned to "artistic" comprehension rather than "scientific" understanding of nature. And Chinese civilization remained in the grooves set by men of Hsün Tzu's temper.

But this is not the end of the story. The most striking aspect of the Chinese world-outlook is the similarity that exists between its intuitive vision of the universe and the recent conclusions of modern physics. It is seemingly a paradox that, although unable to develop scientific knowledge as Western culture was to develop it thousands of years later, Chinese culture had intuitively seen the cosmic order as modern science sees it today—not as it saw it in the days of Descartes's rationalism and Newton's mechanical universe. Western science has now come to look upon the cosmos as a non-mechanical *field of force* without direction or mechanical impulse. From the day when Max Planck proclaimed the Quantum

Theory in 1900, the mechanical view of the universe began to fade away. But the intuitive Chinese had perceived thousands of years before what the plodding Westerners, traveling slowly but steadily and more fruitfully along the lines of scientific logic, discovered lately: that on the very frontiers of man's sense perceptions *causality* and *determination* disappear. Gradually, modern physical sciences are beginning to see a cosmic order that resembles China's traditional picture to an amazing extent. Causality is gone and now we have Niels Bohr's concept of "complementarity" which is remarkably similar to the Chinese concept of "interdependence." [12] There is no more absolute Space, independent of the objects that occupy it. Space is now what it was two hundred years ago to Leibnitz (the first European philosopher to be strongly influenced by Chinese philosophy): the *relation* of things among themselves.[13] Space is determined, as it was in the view of the Chinese, by its contents. Without contents, there is no space. Similarly, Newton's gravitation was a *force*; today, now that the universe is no longer viewed as a machine, we have gravitational and magnetic *fields*; this is the way the Chinese understood it. And if there are no more *forces*, material *substances* no longer exist either. As Alfred North Whitehead claims, "the event is the unit of things real."[14] The only Reality today lies in the *process* itself, in the *relation* between things, not in things themselves. And we know that to the Chinese the supreme Reality was the *process*, the Tao.

All in all, the Chinese display the complete lack of logic which makes them shun deductive argumentation. But they definitely display a conventional rationalism which could almost be termed "scholastic." [15] For all their synthetic apprehension of all things, they have displayed an amazingly analytical mentality in their observations of things concrete, a passion for empiricism which has eventually yielded rich dividends: the discovery of printing, gunpowder and many other priceless techniques. They always refused to theorize in the abstract, to separate man from nature or from the social

body. They preferred the concept of *model* to that of rigid
√ *law* and in all respects were the supreme "humanists" of this
earth.

The humanism of the Chinese springs, once again, from
their concept of the cosmos as a vast system of "behaviors"
regulated by a protocolar etiquette which is the model for its
earthly counterpart, the court of the Son of Heaven. There is
no dualism in the universe, no opposition of Matter and
Spirit, since everything is intimately related and since the
former is a symbolic reflection of the latter. There is no
Chinese word for *soul* in its Western, purely spiritual sense.
The two terms *kwei* and *sen*—almost impossible to translate,
although they are respectively welded to the emblematic Yin
and Yang—seem to recognize the existence of souls and spirits
or demons, but only to the extent that they "manifest" themselves somehow or other in the world of nature. No culture
known to history has been so consistently anti-spiritual as the
Chinese, none has been more fundamentally agnostic and yet
superstitious, none has been more bent on ordering human
society into a smooth-functioning super-organism in which
everything is socialistically regulated by the cosmic etiquette.

For all their subtle differences, Taoists and Confucianists
always agreed on the "utilitarian" aspect of man's activities,
and also on endowing them with cosmic implications which
satisfied their synthetic urge. The twin arts of rites and music,
for instance, symbolized this eternal interplay of the two
fundamental principles of dissociation and union—rites sym-
bolizing the necessary distinctions between men, music their
harmonic association.[16] Man's personal rhythm, society's
collective rhythm, should correspond to each other and
harmonize with the universe's own cosmic rhythm—with the
result that the Chinese individual was caught in a fantastic
web of rites and obligations which imprisoned him from the
cradle to the grave and even fettered his mind, an oppression
which was far greater than anything experienced by the
Indians in their own oppressive caste system.

How Rites tie together in an indestructible knot the mul-

tiple strands of Chinese civilization is fully explained by the
devout Confucianist Hsun Ch'ing: "Ritual is the highest
administrative duty, the source of a country's strength, the
Tao of majesty in action . . . There are three sources to Ritual: Heaven and Earth are the source of its existence, our
ancestors the source of its being in a class by itself, sovereigns
and teachers the source of its disciplinary power. Without
Heaven and Earth how could it have come to be? Without
our ancestors how could it have emerged? Without sovereigns
and teachers how could it have disciplined men? If any of
these had been lacking, there would not have been this paci-
fying influence among men. Thus it is that there is Ritual,
the ritual serving of Heaven above, of Earth below, the
reverencing of ancestors and the honoring of sovereigns and
teachers." [17] The respective positions of Rites and Music are
then made clear by the Li Chi, the "Record of Rites": "Music
expresses the harmony of Heaven and Earth, Ritual the hierarchic order in Heaven and Earth." [18]

The desire or even compulsion to be in tune with the cosmic rhythm is one of the most profound and unquenchable
cravings of human nature, but the Chinese were probably
the most persistent seekers of this rhythm. With the twin
helps of Rites and Music—studied by the sages in their most
minute ramifications, in their remotest cosmic implications
as in their most detailed physiological impact [19]—the identification of Heaven and Earth was happily carried out. What
the Brāhmin priests of Vedic times performed through their
religious sacrifices, the Chinese mandarins performed under
their own high priest, the Son of Heaven.

In this sense, the Chinese etiquette was a definite religion
in which God, Satan, the human soul, sin, hell and paradise
were purely and simply ignored, a creed based on a complex
set of *magical* relationships, with "efficiency" as its final goal.
The tenets of this creed were, in many ways, the most perfect
from the viewpoint of a smoothly working human society,
and also the most exacting in their meticulous precision and

in the inhuman self-control required of each individual. Their perfection derived from the very persistence of the Chinese in integrating themselves into the world of nature and from their long, civilized effort to model society on nature.

The Son of Han was shaped and molded from birth, bound, fettered and cramped in his youth by a complicated set of disciplines and obediences. His personality was warped so as to fit into the general mold, and as a mature man he became the most perfect example of the sociable man ever produced by a civilization. But never did he become a machine—the inevitable outcome of such a training when imposed upon overintellectualized Westerners. The Chinese thought and felt with all their being, not merely their intellect, and were able to preserve a remarkable vitality within the narrow confines of this most exacting of all traditions. In every respect the Chinese transcended mere philosophy and reached an uncanny "wisdom," a perfect self-control and an unequaled ability to integrate perfectly every aspect of human life. But the price paid was terrific: an extraordinary lack of individual personality and originality, a devotion to the concrete and singular welded to a repulsion for the abstract and general, a utilitarianism and a thirst for sheer efficiency, all of which finally brought destruction to this grandiose system. The greatest weakness was the lack of religious feeling for the *transcendental*. Magic realism destroyed all true spiritualism and promptly transmuted itself into materialistic positivism or agnosticism—and yet was always accompanied by a feeling of holy *immanence* which verged on mysticism and was responsible for the incomparable beauties of Chinese art.

The Chinese remained, in his own way, a deliberate rationalist, but an adept in a type of rationalism which is in some ways remote from the logically intellectual Westerner. His common-sense attitude springs from a mixture of rationalism and humanism; the real expression would be rather "reasonableness," *ch'ingli*—a compound of *ching*, which stands for human nature, and *li* or timeless reason.[20] He is a rationalist tempered by a strong vein of intuitive feeling for the elusive fundamentals of man's mysterious nature.

6
THE WINTER
OF CIVILIZATION

Chinese Civilization crystallized under the Han dynasty (202 B.C. to 220 A.D.), and remained more or less petrified in its stock forms thereafter—that is, until the twentieth century. Of all the elements which make up the structure of a Civilization, *law* is perhaps the most important. And the legal principles of a particular Civilization are of course intimately welded to that Civilization's world-outlook.

There was a great lesson in the decisive collapse of the Legalists after the first Han ruler ascended the imperial throne. (Alone among all Chinese schools of thought, the Legalists had upheld the idea of *Fa* with all that it implied in the way of rigid and merciless positive law. This is what made them the inevitable leaders in the struggle to establish Civilization and the Universal State on a secure basis.) They had inherited all the legal work done under the Chou dynasty, especially the tremendous code of Li K'uei, the greatest legal mind of China who had been minister of the state of Wei about 400 B.C. And even after the disappearance of the Legalists, Li K'uei's basic code was constantly revised and augmented until by the end of the third century A.D. it consisted of more than seven million characters and 26,272 paragraphs. It was the "Justinian Code" of the Chinese world, but one of colossal dimensions. And from all we know of the practical application of law in China, it is clear that, until the eighteenth century, Chinese justice was far more progressive than any other in the world, including that of Europe and America. And yet, the cardinal fact is that law was viewed very differently in China—in fact, it always played a minor role in the social life of the Sons of Han. They looked upon law as too rigid and contrary to the order of nature, and it was this fundamental hostility to legalism that finally destroyed the Legalist movement.

The Chinese conception of law was in tune with their world-outlook: the Chinese ideal was harmony rather than abstract justice. Law was not an application of some Higher Law established by a transcendant divinity with metaphysical or spiritual sanction, as in the West; it was a direct emanation of nature's own moral character. Therefore, rewards and penalties were only a poor alternative to the moral virtue which should be instilled into all human beings. No civilization has ever been founded on a more noble principle than the Chinese ideal of punishing "only to be able to stop punishing." As a result, Chinese law was mostly penal (for the uneducated who "did not know better"), administrative and ritual—in other words, it was mostly *public* law. There was hardly any *private* law at all: custom and tradition took care of private contracts and business deals; family clans, associations and guilds enforced a rigid honesty through sheer social compulsion. Because of their distaste for abstractions, the Chinese did not really develop any legal doctrine or principle; and the application of the law was never strictly according to the letter but rather according to the particular merits of the case. Furthermore, and this is highly significant, Chinese customary law always emphasized human rights over property rights, individual and collective responsibility for the social consequences of all acts.

Thus, just as the Chinese never really wanted to step out

of the realm of nature and detach man from his surroundings, they never conceived of law as we did in the West, as a rigid code to be enforced mechanically and impersonally. *Law* was only a poor substitute for *ethics*, an inevitable abstraction and crystallization of the morality which should be alive in all human beings. And it was the extraordinary *social-mindedness* of the Chinese, their inbred collectivism, which allowed them to dispense with an enormous legal framework without which the most lawful Western people would run riot. *Li* (good customs) was always preferred to *Fa* (positive law); psychological conformity in China prevented immorality before it even arose.[1]

The empire grew in size, soon comprising a colossal extent of land, and administration had to be gradually modified to suit this change. An indispensable decentralization was devised which persisted until the revolution of 1911. Each province had its own government entitled to take many initiatives usually reserved to sovereign states; many of those provinces were larger and more populated than most European nations of our days. Control from the central government was exercised by way of personal checks and spies, of double appointments and frequent transfers of officials. On the whole, it proved to be a workable and satisfactory system.

Art and literature prospered along the set pattern already laid down before the Ch'in unification of the world. Encyclopedias were compiled, history was studied and recorded with great care, and works such as the *Shih Chi* became models for later historians. Great assemblies of scholars—the Shih Ch'ü Conference of 51 B.C. and the Pai Hu Kuan Conference of 79 A.D.—discussed the meaning and reliability of the great classics.[2] Philosophy had become decadent after the brilliant output of the Culture's autumn. Vague attempts to build up scientific knowledge were made in the *Lun Hêng* ("Critique of Opinions") of Wang Ch'ung, in the first years of the Christian era. Pursuing the earlier studies made by the natural philosophers of the late Chou period, he advocated rational thinking and the study of natural sciences. But, like Lucretius in Classical Rome, Wang Ch'ung was a "late" rationalist, out of step with the times; Chinese Civilization was too far gone in its new direction to turn back, renounce the Tao and take up a systematic study of natural sciences. Confucianism had engendered contentment and smugness, as well as a distaste for bold speculations. Any new science might be a threat to the sacred tradition and any attempt at dominating nature through the development of scientific thought would have conflicted with the basic philosophy of the Tao.

Art instead of natural science, the urge to *understand* rather than *dominate* nature, absorbed every ounce of surplus energy and inspiration in China. The artistic evolution of China had conformed to the recognizable pattern of all Cultures and Civilizations: In the Shang and early Chou periods (China's "Gothic" Age), we have the era of trail-blazing creation of new forms, new styles and new symbols, of prodigious activity and profound inspiration, the age when China's "medieval" art was decisively shaped. Then a period of uncertainty, of heaviness and impoverishment, followed by China's "Baroque" Age, coinciding, as it did in the West, with an Age of Enlightenment: the age of conflicting philosophers, of great creative power, of a revival of decorative art ending in an overelaborate Chinese "rococo" at the beginning of the Warring States era. And then, with the Hans and the dawn of Civilization, a gradual epuration and simplification of forms, a remarkable sobriety which made Chinese bronzes look almost like Greek statuary.

From then onward, the organic development of Chinese art came to an end. The same forms, canons, symbols were used over and over again, preserving an eternal freshness of inspiration but remaining in the deep furrows dug out during China's great cultural period. Even so, art was beginning to show definite signs of exhaustion and might have degenerated as did Classical art in the last centuries of the Roman Empire, had it not been for the momentous events which followed the dramatic breakdown of the Hans.

✳   ✳   ✳

The collapse of the Han dynasty was an event of great magnitude, and the temporary breakdown of China's Universal Empire which followed was greatly responsible for the powerful impact of Buddhism and the inroads made by the consoling Mahāyāna mythology of its "Greater Vehicle." The collapse itself was partly due to the natural decay of an overrefined society which had gradually lost the will to defend itself, but also in large measure to the increasing pressure of the barbarians upon the northern frontiers. Coming from Central Asia, Mongolia or Manchuria, the Turkish Hsiung-nu and T'o-pas, the Tibetans, the Mongolian Hsien Pi and Wu Huan, the Tungus, the Uighurs and others broke through the Great Wall and, helped by local civil wars and anarchy, overran a large part of civilized China.

Rehearsing, as it were, the coming invasions of the Mongolian Genghis Khan and, later on, the Manchus, these warlike nomads, hardy and toughened by an active life led in the cold wilds of the northern steppes, took over northern China, settled down on the land, intermarried with the resilient Chinese farmers and ended up by being absorbed by this huge, unconquerable mass of sedentary human beings. The vast empire remained split up into numerous petty states for more than three centuries. And even though the Chinese did end by proving their fabulous capacity for ethnical absorption at the expense of waves of barbarians, a certain amount of indigestion did persist for generations. But this infusion of new blood into the Chinese mainstream had an invigorating effect on a population which might well have decayed otherwise. The rejuvenation of an already old society brought Chinese civilization, after a temporary setback, to the threshold of a new Golden Age. And with it, the permanent tendency of the Chinese toward unity reasserted itself, as it was to reassert itself implacably after each foreign invasion. The Universal Empire was restored, all "civilized" human beings were brought again under one rule; whereas in India the permanent tendency toward dislocation reasserted itself just as consistently, only the Mauryas and the Guptas being able to establish a certain amount of unity, and that for a short time only. Centripetal forces always prevail in China, whereas centrifugal forces always end by tearing India apart.

It was about this time that Buddhism began to penetrate profoundly into China. As is usual throughout the world and especially in basically irreligious China, new religions make enormous inroads in times of stress and suffering at the favor of bewildering confusion and upheavals. A worldly civilization has to be successful in worldly matters if it is to survive at all, and a breakdown suggests immediately explanations of a transcendental order. The breakdown of the Han society, the wars and destructions which followed and plowed up China for generations prepared a fertile ground for the growth of Buddhism.

The Greater Vehicle, completely metamorphosed by the philosopher Asvaghosa into a new religion from which the exhausted pessimism of Gautama had been eliminated, offered new notions and new ideals to the Chinese which, in the long run, did not counteract or contradict but completed Taoism.[3] It was this Mahāyāna doctrine which, having lost out in India because it was no longer congenial to the Hindu soul, slipped into China and espoused the fundamental optimism and positive earthiness of the Chinese, but added an indispensable strain of mysticism and religiosity to soothe them in their great times of trouble. It also brought to China a profound metaphysical doctrine which the more pragmatic Chinese had not been able to elaborate although they had had a glimpse of it more than a thousand years before in early Taoism.

In this age of utter confusion, Confucianism had partly broken down and Buddhism temporarily displaced the official doctrine of the Middle Empire. Art and literature fell almost completely under its spell. Following the usual, recurring historical pattern, Buddhism penetrated into China by a devious route, seeping in gradually from the outlying portions of the empire, Turkestan and Kansu, where it had

converted the "external proletariat" of Chinese society—as
Islam was to convert it later on. Then it converted the "internal proletariat," made up of millions of impoverished farmers
and ex-landlords ruined by wars and revolutions. Women,
especially, embraced it with great fervor. Confucianism, with
its essentially "masculine" stoicism, could bring no solace
to populations crushed by the magnitude of the disaster.

With Buddhism came a widening of the cultural horizon
of China, which had to acknowledge for the first time the
existence of alien cultures and alien philosophies. The amazing
success of Buddhism was due to its revolutionary character,
to its consoling message of reincarnation and Karma which
promised automatic rewards and punishments after death.
Oppressors and exploiters would pay for their sins under the
iron rule of Karma, and the lower classes of China saw a ray
of hope in the Great Doctrine. Buddhist associations soon
became the best-organized institutions in the Middle Empire. Powerful monasteries were built all over the country
and merchants often used them as safe-deposit banks and
warehouses. The interest paid to the monks served to raise
magnificent temples and increase their already large estates.
Monasteries became the most important and, at the same
time, the most humane landlords of their day. Thanks to the
temporary eclipse of Confucianism at the courts of alien
rulers, the well-educated Buddhists became indispensable and
their influence extended all over China. The holy scriptures
were translated into Chinese, Asvagosha's Buddhism of salvation spread like wildfire among millions of suffering peasants.
The messianism of the Maitreya school which introduced
the idea of historical redemption had a powerful appeal for
many of those Time-conscious Chinese, and more than one
political revolt was inspired by it. Taoism, largely decadent
as an organized religion, was compelled to reorganize itself
completely in order to compete with the new faith.

Yet, with all that, Buddhism had quickly metamorphosed
itself in China. Its real historical function was to rejuvenate
all those elements in Chinese civilization which had become

petrified and hollowed out, to pour the old contents of Taoistic mysticism and artistic inspiration into a new bottle labeled "Buddhism" which had little in common with Gautama's original world-outlook. This new creed did not come to China as Christianity came to Western Europe, and it never played the same part. It did not cater to masses of barbarians like the Germanic hordes, did not undermine what was left of Civilization as Christianity did in the Classical world of pagan Rome. It came to a highly civilized land, became integrated in this civilization, provided a fresh stimulus which reactivated Chinese art and Chinese religiosity at a time when they were threatened with deathlike petrification. It fitted into the inelastic fabric of China's civilization like hand in glove: it became a specifically Chinese creed. The key concept of Nirvāṇa, which to the Indian implied the evaporation of the soul into a voidlike nothingness, was translated into Chinese as implying a return of the human spirit to *nieh*, "slimy black mud," the primordial chaos of Mother Earth.[4]

Although the religious faiths which took hold of China at various times were not mutually exclusive, as they might have been in other civilizations, and although a gradual understanding was worked out between them to the extent that one man might be a Confucianist during his active and mature life, to become a Taoist or a Buddhist toward the end, the fact remained that the Chinese were typically human: petulantly religious in bewildering times of stress and suffering [5] but carelessly irreligious in times of prosperity and contentment—although at all times highly superstitious.

The powerful impact of Buddhism on the art of China was noteworthy, especially in its typically Chinese garb known as Ch'an Buddhism—the ancestor of Japanese Zen. Ch'an soon incorporated the main elements of Taoistic philosophy, proving once again that no foreign influence can make itself felt if it does not appeal to basic, deep-rooted elements of the local psychology. Ch'an Buddhism, indifferent to scriptural authority or iconolatry, shaped Far Eastern art decisively, but by doing so merely revived and continued the

Taoistic strain. Long before Ch'an and Zen Buddhism, hadn't the Taoist sage Chuang Tzu advised man to abolish his rational logic and "vomit his intelligence"? Yet that was the essence of Ch'an Buddhism's teaching.

T'ang and Sung art, however brilliant, was mostly a continuation and a fulfillment of Chou and Han art. It was not long before statuesque Buddhas and Bodhisattvas, impregnated with the grave mystical spirituality of Gandhara, metamorphosed themselves into gently ironic sages who seek the positive Tao of nature rather than the annihilation of an Indian Nirvāna. The fat, hilarious Buddhas of China had little in common with their ascetic counterparts in India. And in the moving poetry of Li Po and Tu Fu, we find more cosmic wonder in the Taoistic strain than Buddhist melancholy at the impermanent illusion of this earth which the Chinese could never bring themselves to share. But the religious adjunct of Ch'an influence certainly contributed to give it a freshness of inspiration which the advanced historical stage of Chinese history did not warrant.

The apex of Buddhist influence in China coincided with the reign of the T'ang dynasty (seventh and eighth centuries), itself the zenith-like "Age of the Antonines" of Chinese civilization. Emerging slowly from the post-Han chaos, the new imperial dynasty guided China through the most brilliant and refined age any civilization had ever known. The great Emperors T'ai Tsung and Ming Huang saw to it that their lengthy reigns had the most massive cultural flowering of all times. Economic prosperity and the use of printing gave them the material means required. Peace and flourishing foreign trade brought fabulous wealth in their train. In the sumptuous atmosphere created by palatial estates and gorgeous gardens, silk-brocaded clothes, exquisite food, carved and painted pleasure boats gliding quietly along canals and across lakes, China engaged in a mass production of cultural elements on a staggering scale. When, a thousand years later, a Manchu emperor ordered the compilation of an anthology of T'ang poems worthy of literary immortality, a severe screening produced thirty books containing more than forty-eight thousand poems written by twenty-three hundred poets; Chinese cultural production had long since outgrown the artisan phase and had reached the assembly-line stage.

Buddhism never faded completely from China. Even after the final petrification of Chinese civilization, Buddhist revivals, often encouraged by the barbarian conquerors, swept China. Furthermore, Buddhism had seeped into the Confucianism of the scholars and mandarins. Introspection had become popular, and in Mahāyāna mysticism many found a useful counterpoise to the desiccation of Confucianist intellectual life.

By now, a final synthesis was needed before Chinese civilization could enter its final slumber. A compromise had to be worked out intellectually and embodied in a firm, workable doctrine—just as Shankara's final formulation of the Vedanta doctrine crystallized Hinduism for all times or al-Ghazali formulated the final synthesis of Islamic thought. The magnificent house erected by their great parent Cultures received from the descendant Civilization their keystone. From now on they are completed: nothing more can be added or subtracted from those formidable structures. They all embody distinctly petrified world-outlooks and can no more merge with entirely alien civilizations than a Gothic cathedral could be combined with Peking's Temple of Heaven. Their sclerotic structures can no longer grow because they are inwardly dead and a slight shove from an alien civilization sends them crashing to the ground.

The artisan of this final synthesis in China was Chu Hsi, and with him Confucianist positivism triumphed decisively although it incorporated many Taoistic features; he summed up and put the final touch to the Neo-Confucianist revival which had started under the T'ang. Entering into the positivistic mood of the great Master, combining it with some elements of Taoistic cosmology and Buddhist metaphysics, Chu Hsi advocated a practical, common-sense investigation of Reality, which he equated with nature. He accepted the fundamental dualism of the Yang and Yin interplay, the active and the passive, expansion and contraction. He also incorporated the dualism of *Li* and *Ch'i*, of rational "Organization" and Matter, or rather, Energy-Matter. Basically, Chu Hsi's *Li* is a sort of structural pattern of the world, a combination of all the "fields of forces" within their respective "levels of organization": it is *cosmos* as opposed to *chaos*. He also fused the Tao of the Taoists with that of the Confucianists into an all-embracing monism that was more catholic and spacious than the original arid Confucianism of the great Master. He had a clear conception of a sort of Darwinian evolution of nature throughout the ages, going from lower to higher levels of organization according to an almost dialectical process. And although he viewed ethics as emerging gradually from nature according to this process of evolution, his morality was a perfect copy of old Master K'ung's.

One essential characteristic of all enduring syntheses of this kind is that they are harmonious structures whose terminologies and symbolisms are valid for *all* members of a particular society, from the lowly uneducated peasant who takes them literally to the most brilliant philosopher who sees in them expressive symbols and apprehends the Reality concealed behind them. For example, Chu Hsi claims that "when wind, rain, thunder and lightning occur, this is the operation of *sen*." To the illiterate farmer, *sen* is a conscious, willful deity; to the Neo-Confucianist scholar it was an impersonal "expansive force." Similarly, *kwei* was a demon to the former, a "contractive force" to the latter.[6] The fact that they all use the same terminology is the essential trademark of a *living* philosophy which satisfies and unites all social strata and all intellectual levels in a given society, rather than a dessicated doctrine for mere scholars. The fact that it inevitably acquires religious undertones merely points to an enduring craving of the human spirit for spiritual understanding.

All in all, Chu Hsi's philosophy was a grandiose synthesis which satisfied the Chinese urge toward all-embracing totalitarian explanations by welding ethics, human destiny and cosmic order into a coherent doctrine. But, basically, it was nothing more than a reorganization and blending of the great thoughts of the past, an impressively encyclopedic reorganization which gave its final shape to Chinese orthodoxy when it petrified.

Against Chu Hsi's Neo-Confucianism, Wang Yang-ming raised a saintly but feeble voice in defense of Buddhist metaphysics and individual subjectivity. Although they both agreed on practical ethics, Wang Yang-ming emphasized subjectivism and introspection. He turned away from the examination of external things, even from the great classics. Solitary contemplation and meditation, not the study of nature, would lead to righteous living: "The mind itself is the embodiment of natural law. Is there anything in the universe that exists independent of the mind? Is there any law apart from the mind?" But Wang Yang-ming's blend of idealistic Buddhism and Neo-Taoism could no longer fight a winning battle for official favor against Chu Hsi's Neo-Confucianism. The final synthesis of Chinese social philosophy was formulated by the rationalists, although the Chinese artist, as an individual, remained always attracted toward the other pole.

But by now, all this mattered little. Real cultural growth was out of the question. Original thought could no longer emerge. These were "late" movements, mere rehash of the grand creations of the past. Basic energy and vitality ebbed, and what was left was increasingly devoted to the things in which the Chinese excelled: plastic arts, poetry and social wisdom. The rest was taken care of by the compilation of vast anthologies, dictionaries and encyclopedias—some of them so vast that they were never equaled in any other civilization.

The coming of the Sung dynasty closed the great period of China's civilization. The innate tendencies of earlier ages crystallized slowly. Socialistic periods alternated with periods of return to more conservative forms of economic government, but the socialistic trend remained in evidence throughout the centuries, cropping up from time to time and as late as the Ming era. The Chinese individual remained, ethically, a collectivist. His individualism was at all times crushed by the colossal weight of family duties and responsibilities, the semi-socialistic organization of the Great Society and the grinding conformism which choked to death any tendency toward creative originality. The natural corollary was a certain passivity which, although it never reached the almost incomprehensible extreme witnessed in the Peruvian Incas, undermined the political energy of the people and made barbarian invasions inevitable. Their biological vitality remained unimpaired, however, and each new barbarian dynasty was eventually wiped out by the swelling anger of a vast population becoming conscious of its shame—after which the Chinese would revert to their traditional calmness and contentment.

During the great periods of strength, unification and imperial expansion as during the periods of civil wars and anarchy, under Chinese dynasties as under barbarian dynasties, the Chinese people preserved this biological vitality. That China should have survived and preserved its substance long after its civilization had petrified, while the Roman Empire strained, cracked and dissolved under the Teutonic invasions, is due to its remarkable power of "physical" resistance and ethnic absorption. Whereas the Roman Empire's motley population decreased and remained in economic stagnation, its countryside emptying itself in favor of large cancerous cities, the prolific Chinese dug their roots deeper into their fertile soil and kept unbroken the tradition that bound them to the great masters of the past. The balance of numbers between the Romans and the Teutonic barbarians constantly increased in the barbarians' favor until the empire toppled. The balance between the Chinese and the Mongol or Turkish nomads of the north constantly increased in China's favor.

The Chinese owe this amazing vitality and power of absorption to the family system. By now, Confucianism—itself the intellectualization of the deepest Chinese instincts—had "democratized" itself and seeped back into the broad masses of Chinese peasants, giving them a code of ethics sanctified by ancestor worship. The extreme stability of the family, its complete, unquestioned devotion and obedience to the chief of clan, its unquenchable yearning to procreate in abundance because of the increased power and prosperity reflecting on the family, the immortality conferred on departed parents and ancestors because of the pious homage still paid to their memory, all this was quite enough to seduce the barbarian thirsting for peace, quiet, stability and durability. Gradually taken into the family system through intermarriage and converted to this very high code of ethics, submerged by the sheer weight of numbers, the barbarian streams soon disappeared in the Chinese ocean. Nor should it be overlooked that the barbarians injected new vigor and dynamism into a race which, despite its great stamina and physical resistance, lost its aggressive energy after every few centuries of peace and security. And so, Chinese history proceeded in a rhythmic, cyclic fashion, with the seemingly unending recurrence of barbarian invasions, their absorption by the Sons of Han and the consequent increment of energy, then a few hundred years of dignified prosperity until the gradual weakening and decay of the whole upper stratum of Chinese society called forth a new wave of northern barbarians—and the same cycle started all over again.

The constant obligation to live in the family community—where one had to submit to the authority of family elders and rub elbows with innumerable relatives—together with the pressure of perennial overpopulation helped to intensify another universal trait of the Chinese: an exquisite and refined politeness which was not merely a matter of form but was actually part of the essence of their being. They developed a consideration for other human beings which smoothed and oiled the relationship between crowds of people and kept them from stepping on each other's toes. Unlimited patience and equanimity went hand in hand with an indispensable courtesy to make life tolerable in circumstances which might otherwise have been unbearable. The smooth functioning of the whole social organism throughout the history of Chinese civilization has always filled the foreigner with unbounded admiration. More than one Western thinker echoed the words of Hermann Keyserling: "China is the only empire which has solved the social question for an extended period; the only one in which the mass of the population was ever happy; and the only one which has ever embodied the absolute social and political ideal in the world of appearance." [7]

The Chinese kept close to the soil, molding it not always too happily; many of the subsequent disastrous floods were due to the complete disappearance of primitive forests in the north. For all their delightful Taoistic absorption in the wonders of nature, especially in the mountainous south, the energetic and patient Chinese had a great formative power which the Indians lacked. They had no desire to upset the laws of Heaven and Earth, but neither did they bow unconditionally to a landscape. Over a period of many generations, they altered it to suit their needs and discover a new, harmonious relationship.

By now, the final form of China's civilization had matured. While the tenacious energy of the peasant shaped the immense garden which is China, the cultured intellectuals and artists no longer created anything new or original. Most of the rulers were dynamic Turks, Mongols or Manchus; the Chinese slowly withdrew from History, which was now made on Chinese soil by alien barbarians. The Chinese world-outlook congealed, no inward development took place and the fixity of death seized the Chinese soul. Successive imperial dynasties worshiped Heaven in the same traditional way and the emperors played their part as main mechanism in a cosmic clock more or less successfully; but revolutionary retribution fell swiftly if the part was so badly played that the whole mechanism was thrown out of gear. The languid mandarins spent their exceedingly refined lives reciting subtle poetry. But there was no more real inspiration.

The sense of Historical Destiny, so powerful under the Ch'in and the Hans, disintegrated. The spans of time changed, and from an intensely *historical* epoch the Chinese relapsed into *zoological* eras in which centuries passed uneventfully like the dream of a second. The great Chinese comet had now become a slow-moving star, revolving around its petrified cultural center, waiting for a new, profound shock to explode the fetters of old age. History was now made elsewhere.

part two

CHINA
AND ASIA

1

THE MOONLIGHT
CIVILIZATIONS

Isolated though it was by the formidable barriers strewn by a provident
nature all around it, the Celestial
Empire was gradually dragged out
of its isolation by the steady progress in transportation, the swelling
currents of trade, the proselytism of
daring missionaries. China had received with more or less good grace
the flood of Buddhist missionaries
but had long since sent out her own
missionaries—priests, not of a transcendental religion of salvation, but
of a secular way of life, of a worldly
and refined civilization. Expansion
in Turkestan and Central Asia took
place simultaneously with expansion
in Southeast Asia. As fast as the
famed Silk Road started winding
itself through thousands of miles of
Eurasian deserts, swamps, jungles
and mountains toward Persia and
the Mediterranean world, increasingly numerous fleets of junks began

to ply the warm waters of the tropical south. Cultural influences spread everywhere, intermingled and soon gave rise to remarkable historical phenomena: the Moonlight Civilizations.

Moonlight Civilizations began to sparkle throughout Asia when the darkness of cultural death had spread all over China, India and the Islamic world. They arose in many different ways, adapting themselves to local conditions and local psychologies, generally continuing the sunlike Civilization they were reflecting—but altering their essence to suit their needs. They reproduced their classical models, but added little or nothing to the real cultural growth of the human race. Their Civilizations were often brilliant but their cultural adaptation was usually skin-deep. When the growing impact of the West shattered Asia's original Civilizations along with their cultural standards, the "Moonlight" people adapted themselves far more readily to the "modern" way of life than those whose roots were still deeply embedded in their cultural past—roots which could not be torn out in the short interval of a few decades.

Each one of the three great Culture-Civilizations of Asia created its own Moonlight satellites: Islam fostered the Ottoman and the Moghul, India the cultures of Southeast Asia, China those of Japan and Korea. In a sense, even south India and south China were "Moonlight" areas themselves, having been settled by Aryans and Chinese relatively late, long after their Culture had passed into Civilization in their northern areas. And they both made substantial contributions to the rejuvenating processes which stirred up new cultural life in civilizations that were already old. In that sense, Chinese Civilization proper petrified in Han times—that is, in its old homestead north of the Yangtze River. But the frequent invasions and ravages which afflicted the north, contrasting with the long peace which reigned for centuries in a south in full development, had momentous consequences. The center of gravity began to shift toward the fertile and increasingly populous valleys of the south, in Han times a mere "colonial" territory.

And while the T'ang era was the last great epoch of the north-west, the subsequent Sung was the first great one of a maturing south. Both, however, were truly "Moonlight" Civilizations, feeding on the crystallized forms of the old Culture. As if to symbolize this new era in Chinese history, the Cantonese speak of T'ang jen, "men of T'ang," when referring to the Chinese people as a whole, whereas in the more northern parts they still use the ancient expression Han jen, men of Han.[1]

But in T'ang days, it was not only south China that was brought into the pale of Chinese civilization. Korea and Japan were also incorporated into this expanding civilization. From then on, we are no longer dealing with an isolated Chinese world, but with a "Far Eastern" world falling under the spell of a great Chinese civilization. Yet in no area of this Far East did the spiritual essence of historical progress manifest itself in great organic creation along the lines of an original Culture. They were all Moonlight Civilizations blooming in a semi-artificial way against the background of a culture that was not truly theirs.

Standing on the shores of the Pacific and blinking toward the rising sun, the Chinese at first could see nothing but an endless ocean fading away into empty space and marking the end of the world. Then during the Han era, some daring sea-men rolled back the boundaries of the known world and dis-covered a strange archipelago lying off the coast of Korea and northern China like a bent bow, which became known to medieval Europe as Zipangu. Japan was at the end of the known world and in contact with one culture and one civiliza-tion only, the Chinese. Japanese Culture was therefore entirely molded by Chinese cultural forms, although the insular char-acter and basic originality of the Japanese people was never seriously challenged. From the early beginnings of their cul-ture in the state of Yamato, the Japanese were hospitable to foreigners. Throughout the centuries, Chinese as well as Sini-fied Koreans came to Japan in droves and settled down in the archipelago, around the Inland Sea, bringing with them all the elements of an already fast petrifying Chinese Civilization. From this civilization the Japanese took their religion and philosophies, their dress, sports, writing, cooking, music, artistic forms and concepts, gardens, architecture and even administrative methods.

For more than a thousand years, every element of Chinese Civilization seeped into Japan, and yet the Japanese character remained unimpaired in its essence. What the Japanese did later on with Western Civilization they did at this early stage with Chinese forms and ideas, and in such a way that no other people known to history have ever been able to adapt themselves so promptly and readily without at the same time destroying their own personality.

The essence of their peculiar character was already well shaped in these early days and it has not changed since. The Japanese were and are neither creators nor imitators but exploiters and adapters. Intensely realistic, they were probably and still are the keenest observers in existence, expert at understanding the empirical significance of all outward expressions, geniuses at extracting the maximum of practical advantages from these observations and from their understanding. The Japanese man can enter into any alien appearance without betraying his inner self. He does not understand profoundly the alien form which imposes itself upon him, but neither does he imitate it externally. Having intuitively, rather than intellectually, grasped the peculiarity and uniqueness of the alien appearance or civilization—although seldom its essence—he enters into organic relations with it through an instinctive but always creative metamorphosis. This was made relatively easy in the case of China's civilization, not only on account of a certain racial kinship, but because of the very Chinese assumption that "form creates content." The Japanese were therefore able to live perfectly at ease within the Chinese mold, fashioning all forms and appearances to conform with Chinese canons, and yet preserve their inner, instinctive self absolutely intact.

From all this it follows that there was no fundamental contradiction between Japan's assumption of this formidable cultural debt toward China and, at the same time, its ethical assumption of complete and absolute superiority over all other countries in the world—a difference not of degree but of kind, which springs from the deepest and most complex psychological sources. The materialization of this belief in the "divine" nature of Japan and the Japanese took the shape of Shinto, the national religion of Japan, the "Way of the Gods" —probably the most difficult religion in the world to understand intellectually, because the intellect never had any part in shaping it. One of its sources was the slow infiltration of Confucianism into Japan, with its ancestor worship and family cults. But in the archipelago, ancestor worship soon developed into a communal cult of all clan ancestors and finally merged into an overpowering state cult of imperial ancestors who then became transmuted into the ancestors of the entire Japanese nation.

This evolution came about gradually, in step with the slow development of Japanese society. The Japanese went through the same social metamorphosis as China, but two thousand years later. During the first centuries A.D. Japanese society was organized on a tribal basis. Around the sixth century a leading clan established its domination over all other clans, and in the seventh and eighth centuries it set out to duplicate the Chinese political structure by creating a centralized empire on the T'ang model. This was the pre-feudal, "Carlovingian" phase of Japanese history, the T'ang empire of China serving as a model just as Byzantium served as a model for Western Europe's Charlemagne. It was essentially a barbaric empire and its subsequent collapse in the ninth century was almost inevitable.

Japanese feudalism then started in earnest, with the typical feudal institutions—*sho*, the ruling manor, and *shiki*, the feudal tenure. A warrior clique of feudal knights gave to the local populations the protection which the collapsing central government could no longer extend to them. The year 1185 is usually deemed to have seen the beginning of feudalism under the strange institution of the *shōgun*, the military generalissimo who superseded but never destroyed the imperial dynasty. The first dynasty of shōguns, the Minamoto, saw the beginning of primogeniture, the aristocratic transmission of wealth and power to elder sons (any one of the sons in the case of Japan) which the Chinese had suppressed after the Warring States era. Japanese feudalism reached its full bloom during the Ashikaga period, approximating the institutions of European feudalism at its height. And its remarkable feature was not only its extraordinary similarity to European feudalism but the fact that it was almost contemporary. Had Japan been less isolated geographically, Japanese feudalism would have collapsed in the sixteenth century, almost simultaneously with European feudalism. But the Tokugawa shōguns closed the country to all foreigners in the seventeenth century and preserved the feudal institutions artificially in order to safeguard their power against the authority of the powerless emperor, who remained as a ghostly reminder of the earlier days of the barbaric but unified empire. In the seventeenth, eighteenth and early nineteenth centuries, Japan was in a state of *arrested* development with a fossilized feudal structure that was bound to collapse when the first foreign breeze blew into the Empire of the Rising Sun.

The preservation of the same imperial dynasty all the way from prehistoric times to our days is a remarkable example of historical continuity and veneration for hallowed traditions. It is also a valuable clue to the Japanese character. From the start, the emperor was surrounded by a cloud of magic and was endowed by his subjects with all the attributes of divinity; the word *matsurigoto*, which implied political government, signified also religious observance. The innate superiority complex which the Japanese have never been able to wrest from their souls created a mythical history in which the origins of both the Emperor and the Japanese people were divine and wholly incomparable with the origins of any other nation in the world. Logic and reason had no part in this fundamental and instinctive belief, and the historian Hirata could write with fervent conviction that "between the Japanese people and the Chinese, Hindus, Russians, Dutch, Siamese, Cambodians and other nations of the world, there is a difference of kind rather than of degree. It was not out of vainglory that the inhabitants of this country called it the land of the gods. The gods who created all countries belonged, without exception, to the Divine Age, and were all born in Japan, so that Japan is their native country, and all the world acknowledges the appropriateness of the title." [2] Patriotism is too weak a word to describe Japan's unshakable belief in its divine nature, its profound feeling against which no intellectual argument could ever prevail.

Intense loyalty toward the emperor, toward the divine Tenno, became the main object of Shinto, and this loyalty itself constituted an act of ancestor worship, worship of the ancestors of the ruler and by the same token of all the Japanese.

To this peculiar Japanese concept of a Confucian ancestor worship blown up to mammoth proportions so as to include the entire Japanese nation, another and just as important psychological element has to be added: the uncompromising veneration of all Japanese for nature. Even in this respect, Shinto started as a fabulous polytheism, as a worship of the multiple forces of nature, so incredibly numerous in a varied and highly differentiated country such as Japan. Everything in Japan's countryside conspired to instill in the Japanese a fanatical feeling of reverence for a country of exquisite beauty, a feeling of belonging soul and body to this particular homeland: the warm climate, the lovely coastline with its small, mysterious bays, its miniature "Mediterranean" seas, its wealth of fish and maritime fertilizers, the mirrorlike rice fields climbing up the neat little hills, the dark forests and mountains which take up so much space in the overcrowded islands—a whole world in miniature, aesthetically self-sufficient, happy in fact to be isolated from the rest of the globe.

From this fervent love for Japanese nature springs many psychological characteristics of the island dwellers—among them their reluctance to emigrate in spite of their having, in our century, the highest density of population in the world, and also their feeling of total communion between man and nature which goes far beyond the traditional immanentism of the Chinese.

But this instinctive polytheism began to evolve slowly, as it did in China, into the creation of historical myths. The early Chinese had transmuted *space* into *time*, nature into history. The Japanese did likewise, but, following their natural bent, nature and space were transmuted into a history and a conception of time which did full justice to their immense superiority complex. Here we are far from the universalism of the Chinese, from their feeling for a superiority which was based on a unique civilization and which could compare with no other in the world. Japanese superiority, being insular, is superior *per se* because, regardless of cultures or civilizations, the gods have so decreed.

With all this, their feeling of religious reverence for the imperial dynasty was never extinguished, even during the historical phase of the shōguns. Because of the religious aura which surrounded the divine emperors, no Japanese could ever dream of actually throwing out the dynasty to replace it with another. Here we are far from Mencius' "sacred right of rebellion" according to which the Chinese Son of Heaven was only a mandatory of the heavenly T'ien. The Japanese Tenno was an actual part of the Divine and no mere man could dare challenge his spiritual attributes. But the explanation does not lie entirely in the psychological difference between Chinese and Japanese; it is also historical. The Chinese emperor was "a democratic" *Caesarian* ruler, removable at the will of the people. The Japanese Tenno was a monarch of "divine right," the keystone of a feudal structure, comparable to the aristocratic kings of China in late Chou times.

Underlying this overpowering feeling of reverence for the imperial dynasty, there is the Japanese sense of historical continuity, his dynamic rejection of the concept of recurring historical cycles dear to the more static Chinese. Also, an intense realism which makes the Japanese grasp the essence of power at the exclusion of its superficial trappings. With a sure, animal-like instinct, the empirical Japanese strikes at the heart of the matter and grasps the reality of power wherever it may be, whether it is the Tenno's power which he will acquire for himself while keeping the empty shell for the benefit of those who are under the imperial spell, or whether it be the industrial power of the West. Such intense realism requires immense strength of character and contrasts strongly with the weaker-willed Chinese, who do not bear misfortune with the same stoicism as the Japanese. All through their history the Chinese have had to look for scapegoats, and their numerous imperial dynasties stream through historical time as more or less innocent victims, sacrificed on the altar of history to atone for their piteous lack of character. The Japanese, going through countless political upheavals and fearful earthquakes, always found enough great and noble-minded men willing to disembowel themselves through *seppuku*—but the emperor always remained untouched, the living symbol of Japan's eternal and unique greatness.

The real starting point of Japanese culture coincided with the introduction of Buddhism into the country in the sixth century. To a people who had felt no Taoistic influence, Buddhism was to be the cradle of their art and by far the most important single influence on their culture. The optimistic Mahāyāna creed of Asvaghosa had already secured a sound foothold in China when it penetrated into Japan under the robes of highly cultured monks. It came to Japan, not as a unified religion but as a medley of sects, and with very few exceptions the Great Doctrine reached Japan through the filter of China, not directly from India. Shinto borrowed from and then gave a great deal in return to Buddhism, absorbing an amount of Mahāyāna metaphysics and influencing Buddhism into modifying its doctines and methods to suit the Japanese temperament.

This temperament itself was not and could never be deeply religious in the Hindu sense. The Japanese lacks imagination and profundity of recognition. Nor can he ever feel deeply and fanatically passionate like the Western Christians. But neither is he a humanist or urbane moralist like his Chinese cousin: "The processes of thought are nothing essential to the Japanese: what is most essential, most profound in him, appears in his sensibility. I say in his sensibility, not in his feeling, his soul, his heart; it is in the manner in which the surface, not the depth of his psyche answers to the impression of the internal and external worlds. The inner life of the Japanese takes place on the whole in the domain of sensibility, just as in the case of children and young women. Here, too, his religiosity is expressed. The faith of a child is not profound faith, and yet it leads directly to God." [3]

The most outstanding, indeed perhaps the most remarkable, outgrowth of Buddhism as a whole was the Japanese sect of Zen (meditation), a form of Buddhism which has had such immense influence over generations of Japanese artists and warriors that it would be impossible to overstress its importance. Zen was the end result of the slow evolution of the Ch'an school of China; it became the most remarkable embodiment of Japanese religiosity and satisfied the most profound aspirations of the Japanese in every walk of life. Their lack of emotional and intellectual depth is too great to allow them to use their rational powers, as the Hindus and even the Chinese have done, along the road to self-realization and up to the point where intellect has to abdicate and give way to direct experience. With the Japanese, there is no question of even traveling part of the way on reason and intellect. Experience has to start right away; the perfect, although complex, rationality of Indian Yoga is too slow. Some other method had to be devised and the result was Zen.

In Zen, the intellect abdicates immediately and unconditionally. The Zen monk is a basic iconoclast who strives toward Supreme Enlightenment, not with the substantial and fanatical faith of the Muslim, but with the help of a powerful method devised over a period of centuries. Rites, scriptures, devotions, everything is thrown out ultimately, although they may play a certain part in the early stages; they are scorned and discarded as soon as enough progress has been made to dispense with their help. Zen is a great technique of meditation, of intense concentration of the mind; it strives to get immediately beyond the intellect, which knows only *about* things and never knows *directly*. Immediate perception, an intuitive and complete assimilation of object and subject, is the goal. Intellectual description or explanation, implying opposition and selectivity, distorts automatically the real "essence" of things described and explained. Zen, therefore, is the bridge which takes the devotee from *thinking* to *knowing* and this bridge is essentially personal, wholly dependent on the character of the individual. The ultimate goal is *Satori*, the total Enlightenment which can be reached only through the destruction of all intellectual fetters and the annihilation of self.

Zen's influence in Japan has been immense. It became eventually the greatest school for the Japanese *samurai*, and its contribution toward the strengthening of his warlike fanaticism is incalculable. A famous fencing master is reputed to have told his most accomplished pupils: "Now that you have completely mastered the knightly techniques, my teaching must give way to Zen." [4] It is probably the only example of a mysticism which has finally been shaped in such a way as to actually increase the militaristic character of the nation's leading elements.

Springing from their fervent superpatriotism, a remarkable affinity for warlike struggle seems to have developed among the Japanese in the earlier days of their history. In this they veered sharply from their cultural mentors, the Chinese, who had looked down on the professional soldier ever since the distant days of the Warring States era. The undaunted, almost inhuman courage of the samurai and the utter contempt of the Japanese for individual life became famous all over the Far East. In the seventeenth century this reputation was so well established that an Englishman wrote of "the Japons not being suffered to land in any port in the Indies with weapons, being accounted a people so desperate and daring that they are feared in all places where they come." [5] To this natural bent of the Japanese, Zen brought the full measure of its remarkable technique, ideally suited to unintellectual people who have definite tendencies toward fanaticism, total disregard for the life of the individual and an equally total devotion to their homeland.

Zen became the main school for a truly Spartan stoicism, a school in which the samurai went through a mental training which gave him no particular concepts or symbols to venerate and no ethical code of action, and which strengthened in him all the instinctive, unintellectual feelings of fanatical devotion to his overlord—whether the latter be the local feudal *daimyō* in the old days, or the emperor in times of national unity. Samurai, and modern officers as well, would make long retreats in Zen monasteries, galvanizing their powers of mental concentration until nothing existed in their minds save their goal—and this goal was no Satori. From the traditional samurai to the modern Kamikaze pilot of World War II there is an unbroken thread. Hojo Tokimune, the Japanese hero who defeated the attempts of Kubilai's armies to invade Japan, would spend many hours in meditation, and a more modern Zen master, Soyen Shaku, impressed a Western philosopher thus: "I have never yet had such an impression of inwardness coupled with equal martial energy; this delicately built monk is thoroughly military in appearance. How he must have inspired the troops whom he accompanied through Manchuria!" [6] In Japan Buddhism had reached the limit of its possible metamorphosis and seemed to be determined to affirm the exact reverse of Gautama's gentle and pessimistic world-outlook in almost every respect.

Zen's influence on Japanese art was just as profound. Shinto had rather discouraged painting and elaborate architecture, favoring simplicity of lines and pure abstraction. Shinto architecture kept strictly to its imposing *toriis*, its large wooden gateways and its spotless but almost empty temples in which the main element often seemed to be a sparkling mirror [7]— the symbol of character-strengthening introspection. Buddhism softened this rather stoic outlook and taught the Japanese to follow their Chinese cousins in their appreciation of the beauties of nature. To the basic concepts which they borrowed from China the Japanese added original elements. Compared to Japan, nature in China displays a certain uniformity on a gigantic scale. But the manifoldness of nature in the miniature islands of the Rising Sun is unsurpassed anywhere else in the world. The very mellowness of the climate has created the most subtle and delicate scale of shades, compelling the inhabitants to regard such subtle distinctions as being of the greatest importance. Color and form can assume far more incarnations in Japan than anywhere else, and they combine to create in the Japanese certain additional senses with which they listen to the inner rhythm of nature as no other human being ever could—even in China.

From their apprenticeship during the Nara period to the full bloom of an emancipated Japanese art in the Fujiwara era to the sternness of the Minamoto epoch, the Japanese evolved slowly toward their cultural zenith under the Ashikaga shōguns. Their martial instincts came to the fore and the Fujiwara effeminacy was brushed aside; warrior-monks came into being. Heads were shaved, monks' frocks were often slipped over the armor of the samurai and these professional warriors transferred to their military commanders the complete obedience and devotion of the Indian sannyasin to his guru. The Ashikaga knight applied the strictest tenet of Zen: to merge oneself with the object of contemplation, to become one with it through the evaporation of all distinction between subject and object. The artists used this technique to become one with nature, but the samurai adapted it to his own profession, no longer using his sword as an external adjunct but literally becoming one with the sword. He became the weapon itself, pure, ironlike and unshakable. The soul had to be tempered into steel. And such monastic brotherhoods as the

Ikko (the Single-Minded) blended the religious and warlike elements in their paramilitary structures until they became undistinguishable.

These were dangerous neighbors to have. But China was so large and powerful, Japan so distant, that the Sons of Han were not concerned. Chinese influence made itself felt again under the Tokugawa shōguns; Neo-Confucianism became the official doctrine of the state, but a reaction set in under the influence of Wang Yang-ming. The Oyomei school which sprang up under his influence brushed aside the rationalism of the Neo-Confucianists and promoted introspection. Joining up with Zen, which was in disfavor under the Tokugawas, the Oyomei movement abandoned the capital and made its headquarters in the distant provinces of Satsuma and Choshiu —whence came all the leading statesmen of the modern "Meiji" era, in the second half of the nineteenth century. The doctrine of this school can be summed up thus: Knowledge is totally useless unless translated into action. Action is the highest form of expression, the constant effort to defeat the resistance of inert matter, to create and shape anew higher forms of existence. The break with the sclerotic passivity of the Chinese mandarins was complete; and it was the essentially dynamic outlook of the Oyomei school which made possible the remarkable metamorphosis of Japan in the nineteenth century.

Thus, the unconcerned Chinese found themselves saddled with vigorous but distant neighbors dwelling far away in the eastern seas, toward the rising sun, neighbors who owed almost everything to Chinese culture and civilization but who never felt part of this schematic Totality which the Chinese thought of as including all civilized mankind. The Japanese remained staunchly insular and retained all those distinctive traits which set them in complete opposition to the Chinese: warlike temperament, strong aristocratic feelings, superb powers of adaptation and a sort of mental collectivism which makes even the relatively unindividualized Chinese look like the most individualistic of all men. Neither the Chinese nor the Japanese ever really felt that they belonged to the same human community, and they kept on looking down on each other from the tremendous heights of their respective vainglories.

Toward the south, things were entirely different. In the vast and varied areas of Southeast Asia arose a great many Moonlight Civilizations, empires and societies which reflected, no longer one major civilization, but, at one time or another, all Asiatic civilizations. Several Southeastern moons revolved around several suns and each one of the three great cultures of Asia found congenial reflections in the warm and humid climate of the tropics. The essentially maritime and tropical character of Southeast Asia is probably the most outstanding feature of those lands and is responsible for the damp, hothouse atmosphere which pervades this most fertile and productive of all oriental lands. It is an atmosphere in which human volition diminishes with alarming rapidity, in which the human being tends to adopt a purely vegetative life devoid of creative desire or ambition. Here we are far from the invigorating climate of China or Japan.

In this area the fabulous vitality of the vegetation has, until this day, defied all the efforts of man to mold nature to suit himself and create a strong, deep-rooted civilization which might possibly stand the test of time. The ruins of man's former greatness are strewn all over the world. But nowhere else, save in the Central American tropics, can the modern traveler contemplate more horrifying examples of former civilizations literally crushed and choked to death by the pitiless vitality of nature's jungles.

Nothing gives a more concrete picture of Southeast Asia's Moonlight Civilizations than these grandiose temples, palaces and cities which were created under the powerful stimulus of spiritual inspiration and have now reverted to nature, which have become so much part of the exuberant jungle that plants have curled themselves around the columns like an army of snakes about to strangle helpless men. Plants take the place of man's mortar and shape anew the former buildings, trees grow through the former roofs and cupolas of throne rooms or audience halls. Life in its boundless richness and multiplicity destroys ceaselessly and breaks through the empty forms of a forgotten past as it would crunch the bones of a skeleton to re-create.

Here creation is unindividualistic, senseless and effortless. The speedy rise of jungle trees is followed by just as prompt a decay, and it is impossible to isolate any one tree from the formidable mass of entangled and intertwined trees and creepers. The very speed with which decay succeeds growth and growth decay suggests immediately the essential transitoriness of all things and the lack of permanence of all material or spiritual forms. The climate is never extreme and dry as it would be in an inland steppe, nor invigorating as it is in temperate latitudes. It is perpetually, relentlessly warm and humid, destructive of the very notion of effort and striving.

It was in such an atmosphere that Asia's three great civilizations combined or succeeded one another to shape, in a very impermanent way, the life and thoughts of Southeastern people. And from the start, their thought processes and mental life could take shape only along botanical lines. The very history of their Moonlight Civilizations could be understood only as a vegetative process combining the sterner teachings from the north with the wild luxuriance of nature's boundless vitality. This tropical climate blunted the impact of China's culture and civilization, whereas it favored the penetration of India's own semitropical influences.

While the Indians gave to Southeast Asia its scripts, vocabulary, calendar and cosmology, literary epics, religious philosophy, artistic canons, legal system and a considerably mellowed caste system which Hinayāna Buddhism could not destroy entirely, Chinese civilization contributed little, save in the Indo-Chinese area populated by the Vietnamese. Certain general standards of morality and political ethics seeped in, but on the whole Hindu influence was preponderant even in the Indo-Chinese peninsula, and the reasons are not far to seek: Hindu and Indian Buddhist penetration was, first of all, peaceful and largely individual—even when organized by the southern Indian kingdoms. The Chinese, on the other hand, proceeded by conquest, assimilation and absorption into the conformist, all-encompassing Chinese civilization—the "only" civilization in the eyes of the Sons of Han.

The Hinduized kingdoms were loosely knit and their political links with India were nonexistent. Cultural admiration replaced the political subservience imposed by the more vigorous Chinese. Tolerant and broad-minded, the Hindus were always respectful of the individual or of the nation's characteristic personality, but the Chinese were always eager to impose their schematic uniformization, to clamp forcibly their institutions, language, script and code of ethics, to absorb, digest and finally destroy the cultural and political autonomy of the conquered populations. As a result, their prestige and popularity in Southeast Asia suffered heavily and the Moonlight Civilizations turned to the easy-going, all-understanding Indians. Having for the most part fled from the relentless Chinese advance on the mainland, the Indo-Chinese people were gratified to be treated by the Indians as political and cultural equals instead of having to behave as barbarian tributaries at the court of China—a distinction between the respective influences of India and China which has bearing in the twentieth century.[8]

From China, however, came by a very devious route the transformation of India's cynical philosophy of politics into a more optimistic and ethical outlook on worldly matters. Southeast Asian kings were endowed with the divine *devarāja* halo which was refused to the Indian rulers, and this metamorphosis could be traced to the religious character of the Chinese Son of Heaven—in spirit, if not in name. So that although art and religion came from India, the methods of government and general political philosophy came from China, to provide a durable and ethical framework for their political institutions which was nonexistent in India. The *cynical* character of the Indian philosophy of politics, as expressed in the

Arthasastra, gave way to the more *ethical* concepts of the Chinese. The Indian myth of the *Cakravartin*, the universal ruler of the world, was retained and merged with the picture of China's real Son of Heaven; several attempts were made to materialize this myth within the compass of huge maritime empires which astounded both the Indians and the Chinese. But the corroding influence of the tropical climate made short shrift of such grandiose political combinations and the civilizations embodied in those empires disappeared with them.

The exquisite refinement of Chinese civilization, its incomparable power of expression in the world of art, its great political sense, its impressive moral code, everything that China had to offer was more or less absorbed by Southeast Asia and welded to the Indian influence. But one of the fundamental weaknesses of Chinese culture was its basic dependence upon its highly complicated system of ideograms which, for all its immense aesthetic superiority, could not possibly compete with the simpler and more efficient phonetic scripts from India. Japan, geographically situated as she was, had no choice. Neither had Korea. But Southeast Asia could pick and choose, and its choice fell on the simple phonetic scripts. Even today, the Burmese or Thai scripts are derived from Sanskrit—as is even Tibet's—and it was only among the Vietnamese, living on the eastern shores of Indo-China, that the Chinese ideograms struck root. Similarly, the whole mandarin bureaucracy was adopted only by the same Vietnamese, whose eventual incorporation into the vast Empire of the Middle could then proceed without too much difficulty. But their anti-Chinese nationalism remained almost as virulent as among all the other yellow-skinned people of the Indo-Chinese peninsula. They never really became part of the Chinese body and insisted on remaining staunchly separate even though the Chinese themselves looked upon them as satellites.

In the frosty and mysterious vastness of the northern lands beyond the Great Wall, matters were again quite different.

Stretching twelve thousand miles from the plains of Poland to the grazing grounds of Mongolia and Manchuria, this waterless ocean remained the home of extremely mobile nomads who represented a permanent threat to the civilized rimland of Asia—and by the same token to its West European extremity. Like a gigantic mass of clouds forming, bursting, raining floods of wild horsemen down into the settled and civilized lands to the east, south and west, reforming again and hovering somberly and permanently over Eurasia, a large number of tough wild tribesmen of Turkish and Mongolian stock populated these wide open spaces, this concrete infinity of steppes and deserts. Shifting their ground ceaselessly and with uncanny speed, the same Mongols were likely to threaten Western Europe, pushing the frightened Germanic tribes into the weakened structure of the Roman Empire and, only a few months later, attempting to storm the Great Wall of China along which the tireless Chinese peasant was doggedly sowing and reaping away their grazing land. Seasonal changes of the weather might make them swing north or south and launch them on gigantic expeditions covering many thousands of miles.

However, a considerable climatic change, noticeable over the centuries, had been taking place in the heartland, gradually replacing the swamps, parklands and forests of Central Asia with steppes and unproductive deserts. The milk-drinking and raw-meat-eating Mongols were slowly compelled to accentuate their geographical swings into greater amplitudes and gradually faced the threat of slow extinction. Traveling with their tents, herds and wagons, these wild, uncultured men of the Eurasian heartland represented nothing but a blind force of nature—soulless beings who cared not a whit for individual life or death, fragments of successive storms of the desert who, if compelled by an unfriendly nature, could easily wipe out empires and wreck civilizations.

Toward the end of the twelfth century, the mammoth mass of clouds hovering over Eurasia looked darker and thicker than it ever had before. Its center of gravity lay in the heart of the

Gobi desert, south of lake Baikal, and there it was that one of the most spectacular military geniuses of all times was born and raised. To this day the name of Genghis Khan signifies the utmost in inhuman savagery and cruelty—but also in superhuman greatness, in breathtaking imagination and incredible accomplishments. His early years were devoted to the casting and training of an extraordinary military machine, to agglomerating and disciplining innumerable Mongol tribes and organizing them into a highly disciplined and fanatically brave army in which the hard core was made of Khirgiz, Uighur and Khitan tribesmen.

When the Central Asian storm finally broke out, the most inhuman forces of nature ever embodied in men took the shape of a gigantic hurricane sweeping nations and empires before it like particles of sand shifted at high velocity across the desert. The first attack of Genghis Khan was directed at China, and although he was never able to conquer the entire Celestial Empire during his lifetime he sowed the seeds for his descendants. He destroyed the northern state of Kin—one of the large states into which post-Sung China had broken up—and absorbed most of it. Turning west, the army of Mongols galloped into Turkestan, overwhelming the local Muslim states, stormed into northern India as far as Lahore, swerved back to Persia and engulfed Armenia, crushing every hostile army on the way. Genghis Khan then led his horsemen to the Caspian Sea and destroyed the Russian army of the Grand Duke of Kiev, who was taken prisoner. Mongol generals swept clear across the Ukraine and down into Bulgaria, conquering the entire area of the Lower Danube. Constantinople, struck with terror at this unexpected disaster, reconstructed its fortifications while panic swept across the Seljuk dominions.

Genghis Khan died in the midst of his triumphant sweep, but the Mongol Empire kept on expanding. Most of what was to prove durable in this purely military empire was due to the genius and integrity of a great Chinese mandarin (of Kitan origin) who had sought service with the Mongols: Yelu Ch'u-ts'ai, who had become prime minister at the barbaric capital of Karakorum. To him China's petrified civilization owed the curbing of the destructive fury and ferocity of the Mongols. Nevertheless, the Mongolian expansion went on relentlessly. Ogotai was elected Genghis Khan's successor and under his leadership the whole of Russia up to Poland was absorbed and Kiev destroyed. The Mongols pushed into Germany and destroyed a European army in Silesia. Overwhelming numbers, fantastic energy and durability, high mobility, the most perfect strategy and tactics as well as steely discipline had made the Mongols invincible. They could strike east, west and south simultaneously, crushing every opposition and instilling a holy terror into the hearts of all civilized men. But the very extension of this colossal empire was fatal to it. Ogotai's death was the first signal of a breakup, though the Mongols still had much unspent energy. While Kublai Khan conquered the whole of China and Upper Burma, Hulagu Khan took over Persia, invaded Mesopotamia and destroyed the entire irrigation system which had lasted uninterruptedly for eight thousand years, looted and set fire to Baghdad and ended his startling career by subjugating the Seljuk Empire and Palestine, only to fail in his attempted invasion of Africa.

This staggering campaign had at last come to an end. Perhaps the most remarkable feature of the entire Mongol adventure was the complete indifference of these amazing men to any form of religion save their primitive Shamanism. Now that the Eurasian World Empire had almost become an accomplished fact, Karakorum became the focus of missionary efforts from all the surrounding religions and cultures anxious to weld the invincible dynamism of the Mongols to their respective civilizations. The imperial court of the Great Khan became the center of the known world. Emissaries from medieval Paris mingled with highly civilized traders from Peking, Italians met Indians from the Punjab. It was as if, the storm having cleared away, the atmosphere had become purer than it was before and vision had become amazingly clarified. Transcontinental trade and travel reached their zenith, law and order prevailed throughout eastern Europe, Russia and Asia, and yet the Mongol adventure was nothing more than a phenomenon of nature. Culturally, it meant nothing more than a gigantic tidal wave or a volcanic eruption. A few centuries later, nothing was left except a few scattered, miserable Mongolian tribes at the epicenter of the great Mongolian earthquake, slowly converted and pacified by Buddhist Lamaism beyond all recognition.

While the Eurasian heartland emptied itself once more, the dislocated fragments of Mongolian domination crystallized along the fringes of the vast land mass, setting themselves up among the populations belonging to the petrified civilizations —China, Persian and Central Asian Islam, and later on India or occupying for a time the area of a fast-increasing population in its premedieval stage: Russia under the Khans of the Golden Horde. The fate of the Mongols varied with the nature of their conquests, but in China Kublai Khan's successors were absorbed and digested by their civilized subjects until their very Mongolian homeland was drawn into the Chinese world and partly flooded by Chinese immigrants.

This was the end of the great Mongolian menace. The biological vitality of the Chinese, the impermeability of their civilization and their comparative isolation from the rest of the world always made them immune to nomadic "barbarians" in the long run. Others came a few centuries later—the Manchus, from the northeast—and, in no time, they too were Sinified beyond recall in spite of the social barriers raised by their rulers. Truly, China seemed invulnerable.

However, in the sixteenth century, a new, slow, methodical wave of different "barbarians" came across the vast lands of the north, across what was to China almost another continent: Russian emigration began to pour into the void of Northern and Central Asia, into the empty spaces of Siberia and the Mongolian borderlands. This immigration of strong, simple, naïve people who are ethnically the youngest people in the world and who mix well with Asians of all descriptions was beginning to alter the entire geopolitical situation of China. This gigantic filling up of waterless oceans meant that instead of having at her back unexplored immensities from which hurricanes of wild nomads came pouring down every so often, China now had a huge new continent which was being settled by a very different breed of men. When other foreigners came to China, along the Silk Road or from the south seas, the Sons of Han could always hope that they would return to their native lands beyond the oceans and the deserts. The landbound expansion of the Russians bore no resemblance to the coming colonial expansion of West Europeans because they filled up the continental fringes of China with emigrants. The empty vastness of Siberia's five million square miles, a continent in itself, was theirs because it had never really been part of Asia. The momentous significance of this new phenomenon was that never again would China be threatened with nomadic invasions. Drowned by the simultaneous pressure of Russian and Chinese settlers, the nomadic threat disappeared for all times in the nineteenth century.

Meanwhile, early in the sixteenth century, a new type of barbarian sailed in from the southern ocean and was washed ashore in Kwangtung province. The arrogant mandarins thought that these West Europeans were hardly worth bothering about. With an indulgent smile, the viceroy of Canton allowed them to settle down on the fringe of the "civilized" world and offer their pitiful wares to the local Chinese merchants.

Fifteen hundred years after the birth of Christ, the whole of Asia fell asleep. The organic growth of the great Cultures was now far behind, and, in the semidarkness of the clear tropical night which set historically over the vast continent, the forms and moonlit shadows of petrified Civilizations were outlined quite clearly. Organic growth of inspired Cultures was replaced by the mechanical expansion of refined Civilizations. The trail-blazing men of Vedic or early Chou times had given way to countless generations of disciplined successors who remained obediently in the grooves laid down by their great ancestors. But even their mechanical expansion had come to an end, their energy exhausted.

Their destiny was now fulfilled and their civilizations had reached the extreme limits of their possibilities. Small wars and invasions were still carried out, innumerable political plots and revolutions took place in India, China or the Islamic world. But all this took place in the jungle-like world of nature in which biological impulses had replaced spiritual inspiration. No event had any historical significance.

The fiery energy and inspiration and selflessness of youth had vanished with the disappearance of will-to-power, and the final world-sentiment of China could be expressed as it was by one of the most articulate Chinese writers of our times: "There comes a time in our lives when the innocence of spring is a memory and the exuberance of summer a song whose echoes remain faintly in the air, when, as we look out on life, the problem is not how to grow but how to live truly, not how to strive and labor but how to enjoy the precious moments we have, not to squander our energy but how to conserve it in preparation for the coming winter . . . I like spring but it is too young. I like summer but it is too proud. So I like best of all autumn, because its leaves are a little yellow, its tone mellower, its colors richer and it is tinged a little with sorrow and a premonition of death." [9]

part three

CHINA
AND EUROPE

8

THE SPIRITUAL IMPACT
OF THE WEST

Completely unnoticed in China, a new world had emerged from the collapse of the great Roman Empire. At the extremity of the Eurasian land mass's occidental peninsula, while the refined Sungs ruled China in full splendor, Western Europe was in the barbarian throes of a cultural birth. Ten centuries after Christ, after having been repeatedly devasted by ruthless invaders until hardly anything remained of the great Civilization of Rome, a new Culture was born. The transition from Romanesque to Gothic, the birth of a new breed of men—offsprings of the rape of old civilized people by Germanic and Scandinavian tribes—set Western Europe on a historical course which China herself had trodden more than two thousand years before. And when the barbarian Carlovingian dynasty gave way to the clever Capetian,

Europe began to discover its soul as China had when the
Shang dynasty was replaced by the vigorous Chou.

The birth and rise of Western Christendom after the completion of the Germanic and Norman invasions was immediately followed by an organized and consciously directed
missionary effort. The new faith of Western Europe, a radical
departure from the original Christianity, was already stamped
with the expansive, dynamic spirit of Western man. Organized by the Roman pope, the historical heir of the Caesars
and emperors of the past, Christian missions assumed immediately a political character which has, since then, never
been totally absent from their undertakings. Rome's ambition
was to reclaim the Eastern Roman Empire, which had been
almost entirely snatched away by the tidal wave of Islam; and
a large part of its early missionary effort in Central Asia and
the Far East was directed toward securing powerful allies who
could strike Islam in the back. This was a preview of the unparalleled boldness and vision of Western man, of his feeling
for geographical perspective and his daring belief in strategic
action-at-a-distance, a notion which was completely alien to
the aggressive but two-dimensional Muslim who expanded the
area of Dar-ul-Islam by plodding along, sword in hand, and
continuously annexing contiguous, neighboring countries.

Catholic missionaries became explorers, traveled into the
depths of an Asia which was far more unknown and mysterious to them than to the Nestorian Christians who were close
neighbors and who were in fact Asians themselves. But as far
as they were concerned, conversion to Western Christianity
was no longer a matter of recognizing the true faith and the
gentle, humble message of Jesus. It became the unconditional
acceptance of papal authority, an authority which was as much
political as it was religious in Gothic Europe.

The first significant contact took place in Karakorum, the
splendid capital of Genghis Khan; the second occurred in Peking at the court of Emperor Kublai Khan. Tirelessly the
popes sent one missionary after the other, and the time soon
came when the Mongols began to swerve slowly toward Chris-

tianity as a result of their confirmed hostility toward Islam. As responsible head of Western Christendom, the Pope viewed a Mongol alliance with pleasurable anticipation, hoping to derive from the crushing military superiority of the Great Khans a decisive advantage against Islam. At the same time the Mongol rulers were in search of a faith, and under Kublai's instructions a great conference of Muslims, Christians, Hindus and Buddhists was convened in Peking. Taking the initiative, Kublai sent an embassy to the Pope in 1269 requesting the dispatch of a hundred learned Christians to attend the conference—a request which his mortified Chinese subjects deemed typical of a barbarian and ignorant Mongol who could not appreciate the overwhelming superiority of Chinese culture.

Unfortunately, the Westerners had no conception of the real nature of Asiatic civilizations, of the depth and astuteness of the Oriental mind. They carried over with them the whole epic atmosphere of Rome's evangelization of the savage Celtic and Germanic tribes and still thought that they were dealing with uneducated barbarians. Their vigorous narrowmindedness was hopelessly inadequate. When confronted with Buddhists, Taoists or Confucian scholars they usually had the worst of the arguments, and the dynamism of their faith could not compensate their immense inferiority in the world of subtle dialectics. Their Western mind was still immature and undeveloped, unable to compete with the sophistication of highly civilized Asians.

On the other hand, gradually enlightened as to the psychology of the West and the political implications of its missionary effort, the Mongols slowly lost interest in Christianity. The great Khan Mangu summed up with crystal clarity their position in his reply to William Rubruck, a Franciscan envoy of the French king St. Louis: "We Mongols believe that there is only one God . . . but just as God has given different fingers to the hand, so He has given different ways to men. To you He has given Scriptures, but you Christians do not observe them. To us He has given diviners and we do what they tell us and live in peace." Being acute observers, the Mongols had quickly perceived the difference between the dynamic aggressiveness of Western Christianity and the actual teachings of Christ, a difference and even a contradiction which thoughtful Asians have been prompt to point out ever since. Nestorian priests, who were in fact apostles of a different religion of Syriac origin, untouched by such accusations and untrammeled by political aims, went on living at the Mongol court, enjoying a rare degree of influence.

Many more Western missionaries went to China, some of them exceedingly brilliant: the Franciscan John de Monte Corvino, for example, who worked for thirty years in the Celestial Empire and died in Peking. He was typical of the Gothic missionaries who made no religious impact but thoroughly impressed the Asians by their towering strength of character, fixity of purpose and noble-mindedness. For a time, Western missionaries were allowed to build churches and establish congregations, but most of their converts were Chinese-born foreigners who had been rejected by the Nestorians. With the downfall of the Mongol dynasty in 1368, every shred of their work was destroyed by the violent antiforeign reaction which swept through the entire Chinese Empire, and Christianity retreated to a Europe which was slowly emerging from its medieval age. In contrast with the amazing vigor and persistence of the Muslim faith—which was beginning to make great inroads in western China, unhampered by the prevailing xenophobia—the first phase of Western proselytism had ended in a complete collapse.

For a while, Western Christianity had to remain within its West European boundaries. Rome had failed utterly in its attempt to evangelize the populations of Asia and, with the growing danger of schisms and heresies, with the Reformation and the Renaissance, with the disquieting rise of scientific inquiry and religious skepticism at home, the popes had no time to think about converting the Orient.

Yet, two hundred years later, a new and stupendous effort

was made by Roman Catholicism to free itself from growing
political entanglements and spread the Faith on its own
merits without material backing from the growing power of
the West. Its greatest tool in this bold undertaking was the
new "Company of Jesus" founded in the sixteenth century
by a Basque mystic and fiery man of action named Ignatius
Loyola. The spirit of the Jesuits was like no other in the Western world, a strange combination of fanatical devotion to the
Church and the pope, iron discipline under the unlimited
powers of the general of the order and at the same time a
broad-mindedness and depth of psychological understanding
which baffled all other Christians, Roman Catholics as well
as Protestants. It was the most perfect tool for proselytism
ever invented by man.

The most remarkable disciple of Loyola was his personal
friend and Basque compatriot, Francis Xavier, one of the
most adventurous if naïve missionaries of all times. Having
reached India and having promptly realized the hopelessness
of missionary endeavors in the land of the Brāhmins, a chance
meeting with a Japanese traveler sent him off to the mysterious islands of Zipangu in 1549. Xavier started out, determined
to apply the new strategy of the Jesuits—the only one, in fact,
which might have set Christianity firmly on the map of Asia.
It was not enough to preach to the poor and ignorant masses;
the leaders, political and intellectual, were the real target. The
cultures, psychologies and philosophies of the heathen should
be studied with great care if the road to successful proselytiza-
tion was to be uncovered. Xavier's temporary success was due
to this shrewd but arduous policy of meeting the real opponent on his own ground, of striking directly at the head rather
than attempting to undermine the heathen structure from
beneath.

In devising their policy, the Jesuits had clearly in mind the
overwhelming success of the Christian conversion of the
Roman Empire; and they hoped to see in the various Asian
monarchs so many new Constantines ready to embrace the
true faith. But they forgot that if Christianity had converted

Rome, it had also become completely impregnated with
Roman traditions and in fact had served as substitute for the
empire during the Dark Ages, when the clergy took over many
of the duties of Rome's bureaucracy. The Roman Church had
inherited Classical Rome's concept of authority and legalism;
its theology and dogmas were the spiritual counterparts of
Rome's laws and political structure. To a large extent, what
the Church attempted to export to the Orient was a residue
of Roman civilization rather than a mere religious creed. Under these circumstances, Christian proselytism in China could
have nothing in common with the natural expansion of Buddhism or Islam. The only way it might have succeeded was if,
under the direction of the Jesuits, Catholicism in China had
in fact become completely Sinified.

Xavier failed in the land of the Rising Sun, but long before
the final eclipse of Christianity in Japan he had understood,
and so he had argued with Rome, that to achieve a substantial
and lasting success in Japan an effort should be made to convert China, the Mother Civilization whose brilliant sun Japan
was still reflecting, although with diminishing ardor. And so
it was that the Company of Jesus launched its boldest, truly
colossal enterprise toward the end of the sixteenth century.

In 1601, the Jesuit Matteo Ricci reached Peking and was
introduced to the imperial court by a eunuch. Following the
shrewd policy of the order, he had promptly discarded his
Western clothes on his arrival and robed himself in the usual
garb of Buddhist monks. But he had miscalculated his step.
Noticing the contempt with which the ruling Chinese scholars looked upon a now decadent religion, he promptly discarded the clerical *tsia-cha* and clothed himself in the glittering
dress of the revered mandarins. He applied in China the policy
which had now become the official tactical method of the
order: the policy of striking at the head of the empire instead
of attempting the mass conversion of millions of illiterate
peasants and artisans. It was far better and more effective to
convert the ruling circles of Peking, the intellectuals and the

mandarins. If the higher social strata went over to Christianity, the Jesuits believed, the rest of the empire would follow suit.

The success of Ricci and of his successors was immense, but such success as they achieved was mostly due to their scientific knowledge and not to their religious work. That the Church should have benefited from scientific discoveries against which it had struggled at home for centuries would have been one of the great ironies of history—but history has a stern, cold logic of its own and no such thing could possibly happen.[1] When, later on, relations between Peking and the Vatican began to cool off, Emperor K'ang Hsi stated the practical Chinese viewpoint without any ambiguity: "As to the Western doctrine which exalts the Lord of Heaven, it is opposed to our traditional teaching. It is solely because its apostles have a thorough knowledge of mathematical sciences that they are employed by the state. Be careful to keep this in mind." [2] But hopeful that the religious obduracy of the Chinese would be overcome in the end, the Jesuits pursued their remarkable work. They built and staffed hospitals, made guns for the Chinese army and made possible the military expansion of the Manchus. Matteo Ricci was clever enough in his geographical work to draw a map of the two hemispheres which was centered around the Middle Kingdom and not around Western Europe—a rare example of full understanding of relativity in those early days and a symbol of the nimble-mindedness of the Jesuits.

They had become cunningly Sinified, adopting in its entirety the mandarins' way of life: they cultivated a distinguished Chinese-style beard under the chin, wore round silk hats adorned with peacock feathers and the ritual, distinctive jewel, ate Chinese food and spoke Chinese like mandarins. Being gifted psychologists as well as profound philosophers, they had soon noticed that Confucianism and ancestor worship did not constitute a religion so much as a moral code and that, under certain conditions, they could be amalgamated with Christianity. Ricci, who had mastered many intricacies and subtleties of the Chinese language and ideograms, wrote several works of Christian apologetics for his Chinese public. The greatest, the "Teaching of the Lord of Heaven"—*T'ien-chu Shih-i*—quotes profusely from Chinese classics, demonstrating great friendliness toward Confucianism but attacking Buddhism and Taoism with severity. In this, he was astute enough to realize that Confucian ethics were the foundation of the entire structure of Chinese civilization and that they were therefore sacred. Buddhism was no longer in favor and he could afford to attack the Great Doctrine without fear. He intermingled his religious exhortations with practical advice on scientific matters which made him indispensable at court. Observing the paramount importance of the calendar and of astrology in the regulation of Chinese life and agriculture, he persuaded the Vatican to dispatch an outstanding astronomer to Peking. Father de Ursis arrived in 1606 and within a year had reformed the Chinese calendar, altered the whole outlook of Chinese astronomy and caused the downfall and ruin of the Muslim mathematicians, who had made crass errors in their celestial calculations and therefore were endangering the throne itself.

The Jesuits soon felt sure enough of their ground to attempt a grandiose syncretism which would have fused Confucianist ethics with Roman Catholicism. They drew up a bold plan advocating the establishment of an autonomous Chinese Church with its own Chinese Rites and dispatched it to the Vatican. The first ruling of Pope Innocent X in 1645 was unfavorable to the Jesuits and the last one in 1742 ruled against them with deadly precision. The century that elapsed between the two rulings was filled with confusing and bitter controversies which only too often had nothing to do with theology and in which the Dominicans took part with unusual acidity against the Jesuits. The Chinese Rites controversy remained famous in the history of the Church and was carried on relentlessly by Ricci's dedicated successors, Fathers Schall and Verbiest. The Chinese themselves became involved in the controversy, and Emperor K'ang Hsi took part in the theological arguments on the Jesuit side, with considerable intelligence and with a certain amount of humor at first, then with growing impatience and finally exasperation. The mere fact that he took sides with the Jesuits did them untold harm in Rome, and their enemies, outraged that a "heathen" monarch should be consulted on theological matters which concerned only the Church, finally obtained the devastating "Ex Illa Die" Bull in 1742. The entire structure so carefully built by the Jesuits in China was wrecked beyond repair. Two centuries later, on December 8, 1939, the Vatican reversed its decision and stated officially that ancestor worship and Confucianist rites were not incompatible with the Catholic faith —too late by two hundred years.

Few episodes in history have been as enlightening as the Jesuit effort in China. This long and enduring contact between petrified China and the dynamic West on the highest cultural level had sparked many brilliant flashes which throw a valuable light on their respective psychological dispositions. The Chinese often remarked on the illogical attitude of the Europeans. When a Chinese minister chanced to witness the opening of St. Francis Xavier's tomb in Goa toward the close of the eighteenth century, he exclaimed: "You Europeans are odd: you refuse to let us keep the memory of our ancestors alive because it smacks of superstition. Yet you do not hesitate to worship a human body as if it still retained and could communicate its sainthood through mere physical contact." [3] Often irritated by the Vatican's amazing intolerance and lack of comprehension, the Chinese Emperor wondered whether Chinese missionaries would be half as well treated in Europe as the Westerners had been in China.[4]

But in spite of the psychological bafflement and the occasional irritation, cultural contacts could be extremely enlightening, especially in the realm of art. One Jesuit missionary commented on the Chinese reaction to Western architecture and mentioned that "their eyes, accustomed to their own architecture do not favor our way of building . . . these large houses, those tall pavilions frighten them. They view our streets as being deep tracks carved through ugly mountains and our houses as rocks pierced with holes . . . Our floors, especially, piled on top of one another, are insufferable." [5] The great artistic activity of the Jesuits was at one time almost as valuable as their scientific work. They opened schools and academies, one of which was located in the emperor's Summer Palace and was attended by many young mandarins. One of them explained the Chinese outlook on Western painting and pointed out that "the Westerners take advantage of theoretical rules in their pictures which gives them a vivid representation of depth and distance. They always add shadows to human beings, houses or objects painted on the canvas . . . shadows which end in a triangular point. Their frescoes depicting buildings are so real that one is tempted to walk right in. Our students could use with benefit a small part of these techniques, which are, however, totally devoid of personality . . . such works cannot be termed real painting." [6]

In spite of all the obstacles thrown in their path, the Jesuits had labored on doggedly in China, but with conspicuous lack of timing. The last Ming pretender to the imperial throne was converted, but shortly afterward the Mings were overthrown by the Manchus. The new dynasty was, at first, just as favorably disposed toward the Jesuits as its predecessor. They showed more interest in the scientific part of their work but remained even more antagonistic to religious influence.

A double misfortune finally wrecked the influence of Roman Catholicism: the appearance of Western pirate ships on the southern coast of China and the disorderly conduct of Western traders who, describing themselves as "Christians," impressed Peking very unfavorably. The Jesuits were hard put to convince the Chinese authorities that they were in no way responsible for those doubtful representatives of the West. But the second and final blow fell when the Jesuit monopoly was broken and Franciscans and Dominicans settled in Fukien and Chekiang. Bitter quarrels soon started between the various orders and the Chinese began to lose patience. Emperor K'ang Hsi had remarked sarcastically to the missionaries that "you go to a great deal of trouble, coming from afar to preach contradictory opinions about which you seem anxious to slit each other's throats." [7] The Catholic missions were now slowly collapsing under their own dogmatic weight, torn by inner strife and dissension, dangerously compromised by the piratical behavior of Western traders and seamen, and gradually involved against their wishes in the political expansion of the West in Southeast Asia. It was not long before Emperor Shih Tsung banned Christianity, now suspect of being a secret political organization, and all missionaries were expelled from China. Thus ended, in the middle of the eighteenth century, the most spectacular phase of Western Christianity's missionary effort in Asia.

The Jesuits had attempted evangelism on a cyclopean scale and had set themselves against all the other Catholic missions, against the Franciscans, Capuchins and Dominicans, who all believed in the "tabula rasa" policy, in the total absence of compromise with alien cultures and modes of thought. According to this opposite doctrine, the Christian missionaries should attempt to convert the masses and destroy the heathen civilizations from the bottom up. The Jesuits, on the other hand, believed in an "elitist" policy of converting the intelligentsia—the only policy which, historically, might have had any chance of success in Asia and which was definitely abandoned after the condemnation of the Jesuits in Rome. But the dramatic struggle underlining this whole Jesuit epic was the attempt of Western missionaries to impose, not Christianity as such, but the Westernized version of Christ's teachings with all its symbolism and psychological twists suited to the West only and to no other civilization in the world. The Jesuits were the only Europeans who saw the problem in its true perspective, who felt that this was a fundamental clash between alien civilizations, and their immense work went down in ruins before the narrow-minded and the bigoted.

The cardinal change in the policies of Christian missions took place in the early part of the nineteenth century. From now on, Western missions were to keep out of local political involvements, refuse to seek the protection of the local rulers, turn their back on all compromise with local customs and traditions, and concentrate on mass conversions. Attempts to win over the ruling class and native intelligentsia by entering into high-level confrontation of doctrines were discontinued. A great deal of this basic alteration in missionary policy was motivated by an important consideration which was more sensed intuitively than understood clearly by the religious authorities in the West: the beginning of the breakdown of Asian civilizations, the collapse of their cultural values and the approaching downfall of their ruling classes.

In China, the authority of Peking was gradually weakening and anti-Christian persecutions in the provinces could often coincide with favor at the imperial court, or vice versa. It became, therefore, useless to seek the favor of a disintegrating power. It would be a waste of time to strike at the head when the head itself was already wobbling. Yet the fatal error of the Christian missions was to give up entirely the "elitist" policy of the Jesuits instead of adjusting it to altering conditions. In times of collapse and upheaval as well as in times of stability, Asian countries were ruled by small groups of more or less capable men—the main difference being that in times of quick changes the turnover was far greater. To court only the masses in times of revolution when the West Christian message was obviously unpalatable and misunderstood was heading automatically toward defeat. It would have been far better to retool the Jesuit technique of seeking assiduously and capturing the ablest and most intelligent men of the younger generations, of attempting to shape the coming leaders of the inevitable revolution. But that involved reshaping the fast-crystallizing doctrines of the various Christian churches—an obvious impossibility.

At the same time, the modern missions would never be as totally on their own as the Jesuits were in China—in those days as geographically remote as a distant planet. Christian missions would become increasingly involved in politics and would often be backed by imperialistic power, big guns and

Western diplomacy. The growing expansion of the West in Asia was bound to drag the missionary effort in its wake, to make use of it for its own political purposes.

Napoleon had sounded the keynote early in the nineteenth century when he declared that "the religious missions may be very useful to me in Asia, Africa and America, as I shall make them reconnoiter all the lands they visit. The sanctity of their dress will not only protect them but serve to conceal their political and commercial investigations." [8] This became, often unconsciously, the policy of all Western powers.

Looked at from the viewpoint of their contemporaries, there was nothing immoral in the establishment and protection of the missionaries in foreign lands. But from the viewpoint of history, which is just as concerned with subconscious motivations as it is with conscious political goals and decisions, the policy was just as Machiavellian as Napoleon had expressed it. As early as 1789, the French missionary Bishop Pigneau de Behaine asked for a French military expedition into southern Indo-China and personally raised an army to fight for his candidate to the throne of Annam.[9] How such a bellicose attitude on the part of a priest could be justified by the Gospels was never clearly explained.

The most brazen link between power politics and Christian missions was the Opium War between Great Britain and China, which ended in the capitulation of the Celestial Empire in 1842. According to the terms of the Nanking treaty, China had to allow free importation of Indian opium—following which Christian missionaries, who had been banned for a century, returned in droves. The fact that Britain waged war to foster her economic interests and that prestige-conscious France followed up right after with increasing demands in favor of Catholic missionaries was not analyzed in great detail by the Chinese. To them, both offensives were part and parcel of the same Western expansion. Each treaty and each gain by the West was followed by a sanguinary reaction of Far Eastern xenophobia. Emperor Tu Duc of Annam wiped out all the Christian bishops and priests—only to provoke a devastating retaliation. China herself was not yet convinced of the power of the West, and a second conflagration broke out twenty years later while the Celestial Empire was in the throes of the T'ai P'ing Rebellion. Peking was occupied, the magnificent Summer Palace was recklessly burned by Lord Elgin and new treaties were signed with the Western powers, the French text embodying as usual a virtual protectorate over Catholic missions in China. The poison of opium, extraterritoriality and Christianity became inextricably mixed with Western imperialism in Chinese minds.

From then onward, West Christianity was viewed in China —and in most of the rest of the Orient—as a Trojan horse; Christian missions were seen as merely softening up the Chinese for their eventual subjugation by the West. Everything pointed that way: the extraterritorial rights enjoyed by the missionaries, their frequent involvements in local politics, their backing by the armed gunboats and military garrisons of the Western powers. Never had the contrast with the peaceful missions of the Buddhists of old been so blatant. Unconcerned, Western missionaries began to flock into China; but in spite of their efforts they remained divorced from the great masses. Most of the clergy remained European or American until well into the twentieth century. Even the alien pseudo-Gothic style of the churches built in the Celestial Empire reminded the Chinese that this new faith was just as much Western as it was Christian, and it worked automatically against Christian propagation; they called such churches Yang-tang, "European temples." Wherever missionaries struck enduring roots, it was mostly on account of their scientific or technical work, on account of their "Western" rather than specifically Christian contribution. Medical and educational help were at all times appreciated. But the basic flaws were too deep to be removed and the fundamental contradiction between the actual message of the Gospels and Western behavior remained unexplainable to the Chinese.

The greatest weakness of Western Christianity was its inability to convey its implied metaphysical truth in a simple,

direct and understandable language, in a shape that might
have the almost universal appeal of Mahāyāna Buddhism, for
instance. The complexities of Western psychology were partly
due to a multiplicity of contradictions which modern Western
man had at times resolved intuitively, but not intellectually.
His creed, in its allegories, symbols and dogmas, was essentially a "historical" growth suited to a peculiar breed of people in Western Europe rather than a coherent doctrine. It
was an illogical, irrational, hieroglyphic compilation and amal-
gam of unrelated or discordant elements from Judea, Greece,
Rome and the barbarian Teutons and Scandinavians, which
had accumulated over a long period—but which never became
an explicit doctrine with a universal appeal.

If, instead of the Gospels, Western missionaries had come
forth with a Western Koran or a Nietzschean proclamation in
which the spiritual sources of the West's immense power were
clearly revealed, if instead of the kind and loving message of
Christ they had preached the dynamic virtues of audacity and
courage, of man's Promethean duty to dominate nature and
to evolve higher forms of life regardless of the suffering entailed—all those psychological characteristics which had made
the West powerful—China would have willingly lent an ear.
Most of the resentment against the "hypocritical" West would
have disappeared. But the message of the West was never
really conveyed to China for the simple reason that the West
itself did not understand its own message—it lay deep in its
subconscious, but no one had formulated it in terms understandable to the whole of mankind. China could not help
being either baffled or infuriated by the split personality of the
West—a split personality from which the West itself was
beginning to suffer inwardly.

The irony was that in spite of all their errors and lack of
understanding, the missions did have a profound impact on
the disintegrating civilization of China. But blinded by their
own aggressive dynamism, strangely oblivious to the real message which they were in the process of conveying, Western
missionaries misunderstood the powerful and revolutionary

impact of their Christian teaching and refused to recognize
their spiritual children.

The most spectacular of such spiritual children was the
fantastic T'ai P'ing rebellion. The words and teachings of the
Gospels had spread far and wide in China and Christ's
message had reached one Hung Hsiu-ch'uan, an exacerbated
visionary' with a great gift for leadership. Blending the new
teaching with the idealism of old China, he proclaimed his
God-given mission to establish Christianity in China and
establish the Kingdom of God on earth. Claiming that the
Christians were followers of the true God, the anthropomorphic Shang-ti of China's antiquity who had been discarded in
favor of "false gods," he styled himself "Christ's younger
brother" and called his coming kingdom *T'ai P'ing*, "Supreme
Peace." He started in the usual Chinese fashion with an agrarian revolt, redistribution of land and the expulsion of all
Manchu officials. Progress was amazingly swift and the movement spread all along the Yangtze valley with a growing nationalist, anti-Manchu momentum. Hankow was captured in
1852, Nanking in 1853, and the following year Peking and
Tientsin were threatened. The movement was considerably
helped by the numerous anti-Manchu secret societies such as
the Triade, the White Lotus and the Celestial Reason, by
numerous anti-Chinese aborigines such as the Miaos and
Lolos. The T'ai P'ing rebels never ceased proclaiming their
Christian faith, and they treated missionaries extremely well.
They ruled their socialistic empire with an iron hand in the
area of the Yangtze but lost their dynamism in the broad, flat
plains of North China. Their inability to organize themselves
without Western help led to internal conflicts and eventual
self-destruction.

Of course, in the process they antagonized the Confucian
scholars and mandarins—and only a rudimentary knowledge
of Chinese history would have been needed to predict the
eventual collapse of any movement which did not enjoy the
backing of the scholars. The full backing of an idealistic West
would have been needed to counteract this grave weakness.

But, frightened by the revolutionary aspect of the T'ai P'ing rebellion and repelled by the unwelcome prospect of a strong China replacing the weak and pliable Manchu regime, the Western Powers refused to cooperate with a movement which their spiritual message had indirectly fostered. When it came to a choice between political interests and spiritual advancement, the West unfailingly chose to sacrifice the latter.

Furthermore, dissensions within the body of West Christianity itself would have wrecked any chance if there had been no political or economic consideration. The T'ai P'ing movement was inspired by the Protestants; this, alone, was enough to set the Roman Catholics against it. The Protestants themselves were puzzled by the bizarre shape of this Chinese Christianity, the ecstatic visions of its fanatical prophet and the exasperated violence of the movement. Worse still, they had no direct part in shaping it, since Hung had drawn his inspiration straight out of the Bible. This sort of new offshoot from the original stem would have given birth to a distinctive *Chinese* Christianity which would have discarded a great deal of the purely *Western* accretions. But the missionaries, unconsciously, were really trying to sell them a *Western* creed rather than universal Christianity itself.[10] In many ways, this was a prefiguration of the coming struggles within the Marxist world when Mao Tse-tung and his followers found their inspiration directly in Marx, bypassing Moscow and the Russian high priests. Moscow and Stalin lost out, but they had the realistic good grace to see the writing on the wall and to understand that any powerful movement in China would have to be, first and last, specifically Chinese.

So it was that the "Supreme Peace" movement degenerated into an appalling civil war which lasted many more years and is alleged to have cost twenty million lives, to peter out finally, crushed by the Manchus and deserted by the West. The T'ai P'ing rebellion was the one and only example of a mass movement in China—or anywhere else in Asia, for that matter—directly initiated by the spiritual influence of Christianity; and the West turned its back upon it.

Christian missions were to attempt to convert China for another century after this *débâcle*. But it was a hopeless struggle. Torn between their various Protestant denominations and the Roman Catholics, they presented no united front. Catholics and Protestants could not even agree on the accurate translation of the word God. While the Roman Catholics usually contented themselves with the word *T'ien-chu*, "Lord of Heaven," the Protestants resurrected the archaic, anthropomorphic concept of Shang-ti, which the Chinese had discarded three thousand years before. And all this was not mere squabble over semantics; the very substance of the Christian message was mortally seared through and through by such superficial, conflicting translations. If the missionaries were listened to at all, it was largely because they had the financial means which enabled them to be in China in the first place—and because they were, somehow, mysteriously connected with the awesome power of Western technology.

But, worse still, when the leading Chinese went to Europe and America, they saw that many Westerners had nothing but scorn for this same Christian faith which was being exported to them; they listened to all the philosophic and scientific arguments against the Bible and against Catholic dogmas generously provided by the Westerners themselves. Was it any wonder that the missionary effort ended in complete failure? And that by the middle of the twentieth century, barely one per cent of the total Chinese population was converted, most of it made up of "rice Christians" anyway?

The failure was tragically evident. West Christian proselytism failed to reach the vital centers of Chinese thought and emotion, never really touched the nervous system of China at all.

9

THE INTELLECTUAL IMPACT
OF THE WEST

While the West Christian missions were fighting a losing battle for the Chinese soul, the startling progression of the military, economic and technical power of the West went on at an accelerated pace in the nineteenth century.

Western man had extracted from the depths of his soul an inexorable drive toward a third dimension of infinite extension which was utterly incomprehensible to the children of other civilizations. He had raised his flamboyant Gothic spires toward heaven, he had thrown depth into his painting, injected a three-dimensional harmony into a hitherto flat and depthless music. He had listened in to the rhythm of nature with rapt passion, had applied his acute logic to the elaboration of mathematical laws, prodded on toward the discovery and mastery of the physical world by a Promethean urge. From the mere use of the forces of nature he drifted on to creating the Machine, an independent cosmos which was the materialization of his mathematical dream, an animated universe in miniature made, by man's genius, out of inorganic matter. With this new world in constant creation under his command, his power fabulously increased, Western man hurled the Machine at Asia, smashing the delicate and refined civilizations which had taken thousands of years to build.

During the second part of the nineteenth century, the growing domination of the West began to seem unchallengeable. Backed by an amazing increase in its technical power— itself derived from a constant stream of new scientific inventions and discoveries—and by an energy and a dynamism which appeared inexhaustible, the West extended its power into the innermost corners of the world. Harnessing unsuspected powers of nature, creating steam and electricity apparently out of nothing, the West was gradually abolishing time and space, presenting itself with uncanny ubiquity in all corners of the globe at once.

Domination over the forces of nature went hand in hand with political domination over the world. With irrepressible energy Europe threw a metallic web of railroads and steamship lines all over the East, and with levers and screws Western man fastened his grip on the Orient. Western floating cities of iron and steel appeared simultaneously in every port, disgorging battalions of disciplined, energetic, far-seeing and highly skilled men before whom mighty emperors, kings and sultans trembled, imposing colonial administrations, starting the economic exploitation of the new lands by regimenting millions of Asians on a Pharaonic scale, boring holes through mountains, digging subterranean labyrinths to extract a new form of natural wealth which was completely baffling to Easterners. Colossal cities were built out of swamps, as Shanghai was, or on barren rock, as was Hong Kong. Giant bridges spanned China's great rivers, giant machines extracted her wealth, and millions of Chinese coolies worked and slaved—not just as they had in the past, but for a new god, more inhuman, mysterious and esoteric than all the other gods: economic prosperity, the economic prosperity of the West.

In the process of revolutionizing China and the world, the West brought down in ruins the vast rural industry of China and the rest of Asia. Craftsmanship was shattered by the importation of cheap manufactured goods from the West. Disaster struck in all directions at once. The synchronization of Western man's technical mastery over the forces of nature and his political assault on the Far East overwhelmed all but the most backward form of resistance to his domination. He had a fabulous secret, the secret of the Machine.

Dragging herself wearily through the dark night of baffling impotence, China saw lights flickering in the distance, lights which, furthermore, were carried by Westerners in search of an accurate historical past which the Chinese themselves had long ago garbled. The first great step was taken when armies of European historians, philologists, ethnologists, anthropologists, archeologists and paleontologists started searching into the mysterious past of the vast continent—searching in *time* as other Western explorers had searched before them for mountains, rivers and cities, in *space*. The third dimension of the West was now brought to China with a staggering increase in perspective both in space and in time, in geography and in history.

Digging, reassembling, collecting, cataloguing the innumerable elements of forgotten worlds and of civilizations which had been blotted out of men's memory by pitiless sands and jungles, cleaning away the cobwebs of myths and legends which had become inextricably mixed with factual data, Western scientists began to extract fragments of a forgotten past which slowly added an entirely new dimension to Chinese consciousness. Although sketchy and patchy, the past of China was slowly emerging under the cold glare of scientific research, in good chronological, historical, geographical and ethnical order, a new gleaming monument of frozen history. China's *subjective*, two-dimensional appreciation of a mythical past which was to be nothing more than an ethical model for those who were living in the everlasting present gradually collapsed before a three-dimensional view based on incontrovertible scientific data and a coolly *objective* understanding.

Historical perspective, which was deemed to throw light on a past that had no intrinsic reality because it lived only in the memory of the living, now began to detach itself from the human observer and stand outside of him, encased in the objective rigidity of scientific research. As historical perspective was brought to China by Western research, as the real past finally came to light, a new yearning toward an unsuspected future began to grip the thinking Chinese; they began to search for a complete reassessment of all those baffling elements.

It became clear from the start of this momentous revolution that China was not interested in the fundamentals of Western culture. The basis of Western religious thought, Western art or Western literature was of no apparent interest to the Chinese. The Gothic world, the Renaissance and the early beginnings of scientific thought were thrust aside by the Sons of Han who were being slowly strangled to death by the Machine. If a few enlightened Chinese had in former centuries pored over the fascinating history of Western thought and if they had sought to achieve genuine comprehension of the Western soul, it was due to the remoteness of the West, to its apparent harmlessness and quaint originality. Chinese leaders had always been glad to compare and exchange views with Western theologians and philosophers, to import Western scientists and artists, but always on terms of equal and free exchange, never on terms of subordination. Throughout the sixteenth, seventeenth and early eighteenth centuries these scant intellectual contacts had not been too unhappy, and if they often reached an unfortunate ending it was mostly due to what they considered to be the inexplicable intolerance and narrow-mindedness of the Europeans. With their conception of time flowing in repetitious cycles, their two-dimensional world-picture, the Chinese had been in no particular hurry to understand the secret of the West, felt no great urge to reform a world which had become apparently stabilized through the petrifaction of their great civilization and no desire to comprehend a culture which was soon to overwhelm them.

In a famous letter to Lord Macartney, a British ambassador who had attempted vainly to establish diplomatic relations with Peking in the latter part of the eighteenth century, Emperor Ch'ien Lung, the "ruler of all that is under Heaven," explained his world-outlook with great clarity: "Swaying the wide world, I have but one aim in view, namely to maintain a perfect governance and to fulfill the duties of the state. . . . As to your entreaty to send one of your nationals to be accredited to my Celestial Court and to be in control of your country's trade with China, this request is contrary to all usage of my dynasty and cannot possibly be entertained . . . our ceremonies and code of laws differ so completely from your own that, even if your envoy were able to acquire the rudiments of our civilization, you could not possibly transplant our manners and customs to your alien soil." [1] Thus did China quash the audacity of a remote state which attempted to treat the Son of Heaven as the equal of its "barbarian" king—and then, only a few decades later, Western guns crashed the Chinese gates wide open.

The terrific impact of the West, the deep contradictions within the Western message itself, the humiliation and intolerable loss of traditional values, switched the Chinese intelligentsia around. It no longer sought to probe quietly the oddities of the Western mind, with the genuine desire to comprehend and appreciate which is the privilege of men who are free to take it or leave it, in Emperor Ch'ien Lung's fashion. Now that the scientific materialization of Western culture was upon them in their own homes, devastating and implacable, they searched with savage bitterness for the secret of that terrifying power and, unconsciously, for the grave weakness which might be hidden within the structure of the West.

The trouble was that this great weakness existed: the West was, unknowingly, on the threshold of cultural decline, was beginning to wallow in its own "Warring States" era of World Wars and revolutions. The West was reaching the stage through which the Chinese had proceeded more than two thousand years before, suffering from the same intellectual disorder, the same cultural cleavage, the same rise of destructive nationalism which were eventually to leave its European homeland in shambles. Dwarfed by its own scientific discoveries, the West was turning its back with scorn on the great synthesis that had held together the fabric of its culture during the full splendor of its organic growth.

The Western mind was becoming skeptical, suffering from this atomism which the Chinese and all other great civilizations, each one in turn, had rejected with horror. Drunk with power and economic prosperity, the victorious West saw no need for an all-embracing philosophy that would attempt to integrate all the conflicting creeds, dogmas, philosophies, doctrines; it neglected to put an end to the searing contradictions which had divorced ethics from religion, economics from ethics, which had set conflicting religions against scientific theories. What could the Chinese, with their long tradition of synthetic integration behind them, understand in this incredible jumble? Where was the connecting thread, the all-embracing formula, the keystone of this new and perplexing world? Where was this Western orthodoxy which would substitute for the disintegrating Confucian orthodoxy?

However, there was such an all-embracing formula, a vast philosophic synthesis of Western thought; but it originated in Germany and did not find much favor with those Western powers who were physically present in the Far East—France, Britain and America (Germany's political activity in the Far East was slight and short-lived). And it was from this grandiose synthesis worked out by German philosophic thought that, by a very devious route, the Chinese mind was to extract the new connecting thread, the new orthodoxy that would one day replace the bankrupt Confucianism of a Civilization in ruins.

Throughout the nineteenth century the Germans "thought out" philosophically the whole historical process of Western growth and expansion, while the British were in the process of actualizing it. The practical Anglo-Saxons shaped decisively the history of the century, quite content to let the Germans "rule the clouds" while they "ruled the waves." But with their metaphysical bent, their passionate subjectivism and their inward conviction that Teutonic blood was the main contributor to the creation of Western culture, the Germans extended the three-dimensional vista of Western culture to a field of human consciousness which had been out of bounds to Western thought for centuries and created a new intellectual discipline: the study of the development of historical institutions and, through its agency, the recovery of the lost synthesis of Western culture's Gothic springtime.

Out of this new branch of philosophy, the great secular "religions" of the following century were to arise. And to a slumbering China that had become historyless, that had lost all consciousness of a moving past projecting itself into a dynamic present, this notion of historical perspective was to become the great revelation, the new factor behind the rise of an anti-Western nationalism and the new shield which would protect her wounded pride. Through an often biased and subjective utilization of historical perspective, China eventually challenged the insufferable superiority complex of the West, explained and justified her present plight and prepared the future.

The remote origins of the Western conception of history are clear. Christian Revelation itself, the notion that the Son of God dwelling in Eternity had to manifest Himself in Time, at a particular stage of history, was the cardinal fact in this development of a new world-outlook. The Chinese had been able to substitute a philosophy of history geared to the process of Time for a religion geared to the Timeless. The creeds of the Middle East—Judaism, Christianity and Islam—joined both and fused a religion of Eternity with a philosophy of Time: the notion of the "prophet" who sees the will of the Almighty manifesting itself not only in spatial Nature but also in the development of History, the messianic idea, the apocalyptic expectations, everything pointed to a new psychological outlook.

To this notion of Time, Western Europe was going to add its own specific contribution: the three-dimensional vision which contrasted with the two-dimensional views of Eastern Christians and Muslims, a world-outlook with depth which compared with that of other civilizations as the three-dimensional sight of a man with two eyes compares with the two-dimensional, depthless sight of a one-eyed man.

The Catholic Church embodied in its constitution this

chronological view with its precise ordering in time of numbered popes, with its concept that Divine Revelation had to be reinterpreted every so often in order to remain adapted to altered historical conditions. Ecumenical councils, dogmatic pronouncements, and a precise reckoning of the steady progress of the Church in *time* were part and parcel of the same Western spirit which thirsted for the third dimension and had introduced perspective into its oil painting. This ecclesiastical feeling for time-reckoning soon overflowed into the political world until it became, in the Protestant countries which had stepped out of the orbit of the Roman Church, purely dynastic and political. Theological fluidity and consequently progress had finally come to a halt in the Roman Church after the Council of Trent. All such theological speculations were soon discouraged in the Protestant Churches. Philosophically, on the other hand, Descartes broke with the long historical traditions of the Roman Church by expelling historical perspective from philosophy in the first part of his *Discours de la Méthode.* Western philosophy after him disregarded history in favor of natural sciences and, viewing with suspicion all efforts at organizing historical knowledge and endowing historical evolution with metaphysical significance, drew most of its philosophic concepts from mathematics and physics.

But as Western thinking lost sight of this intellectual notion, German thinking began to fasten onto it and finally emerged with an entirely new philosophy of history which filled a growing intellectual need. This new intellectual outlook allowed the Germans to complete Luther's Reformation, to compensate his subjectivism with a new sense of time-conscious objectivism which was wholly based on a feeling for historical relativity. With the exception of a few unimportant precursors, Kant was the first to raise, in his *Idea for a Universal History,* the possibility of elaborating such a discipline, indeed to insist that the logical ordering and understanding of *history* on a rational basis was as essential as the scientific understanding of *nature.* History had to make "sense" somehow, and the philosopher's new frontier lay on this objective view of mankind's memory. "What use is it to glorify and commend to view the splendour and wisdom of creation shown in the irrational kingdom of nature if, on the great stage where the supreme wisdom manifests itself, that part which constitutes the final end of the whole natural process, namely human history, is to offer a standing objection to our adopting such an attitude?" [2] Kant went on to demonstrate that, if history makes sense and can be ordered rationally, the existence of Divine Providence can no longer be questioned. Moral life is intimately tied to the process of mankind's evolution on the historical plane, and proceeds according to an intelligible plan. Therefore, a philosophy of history becomes morally indispensable. Confucius himself could not have put it better.

This revolutionary awareness of the need for a philosophy of history was based on the Germanic yearning for a synthetic explanation of all the startling developments of the post-Renaissance period, of an urge to reunite the disconnected fragments of man's fast-increasing knowledge. While French thought remained in the grooves set by Descartes and British thought in those set by Hume and Bentham, Kant merged the main ideas of the Cartesian knowledge derived from mathematical thought and those of the British empiricists and sensualists. This was a first step toward the philosophic reunification which the other Westerners had neglected.

In addition, Kant was able to justify, discreetly and unobtrusively, an important psychological trait of the Germans: their lack of individualism, which contrasts strongly with the marked individualism of the Latins and the British.

Let us take a closer look at the incidence of geography on national psychology. While the Latins in Europe were able to form their nations behind natural boundaries (France, Spain and Italy are, each of them, well-defined geographical units, protected by massive mountain ranges), the Anglo-Saxons (in Britain, America and Australasia) formed themselves even more naturally into *insular* nations, well protected from neighbors by even more formidable seas and oceans. Both the Latins and Anglo-Saxons could afford to base their philosophic outlook on an individualism which sought freedom *from* their respective states. But the situation in Germany was diametrically opposite. The first and basic concept of the Germans is that of frontier, of "March," of a border in perpetual motion, shifting back and forth in the vast plains of northern Europe where no natural borders exist. Except for the Persians, the Germans were the only neighboring people who were not absorbed by the Roman Empire, and their extensive migrations took them all over the Western world, often depriving them of their national identity.

From the Elbe and the Vistula to the Yellow River in northern China, there are no natural barriers—nothing but immense plains stretching for thousands of miles through Poland, Russia, Siberia, Mongolia and northern China, halfway across the world. Any philosophy elaborated around the Elbe and the Vistula is bound to be influenced by this geographic situation. German nationalism could not be rooted in natural geographic circumstances; instead, it became an *idea*. German power and unity waned during the Middle Ages, the Renaissance and the Age of Enlightenment; its political structure weakened and was reduced to dust for centuries. Political fragmentation meant political impotence and denial of liberty. Real, true freedom could only mean the growth of a German state-power which would free the Germans from this impotence; subordination of the individual to the state was the first step toward freedom. A great deal of German philosophy was shaped by this geopolitical situation, and it is no wonder that Kant could conceive of the state as a Categorical Imperative, of the citizen as morally bound to unquestioning obedience.

So it was that Kant was driven to lay the foundation stone of this obliteration of the individual by stating his metaphysical subordination, the final outcome of which was the obliteration of political freedom of the individual as conceived in the

West.[3] Kant himself drew no such conclusions but left it to his successors to complete his work. Like Jean-Jacques Rousseau, whom he so much admired and from whom he borrowed the notion of a distinction between the general will of the people (which has to be interpreted almost metaphysically) and the will of all (which is the statistical result of the deliberation of the people and is deemed to be inadequate), Kant was finally driven to lay the foundations of a totalitarian and anti-democratic philosophy. Extreme subjectivism is compelled to choose between political anarchism and dictatorial autocracy. Twenty-five hundred years before, Rousseau's Chinese counterpart, Lao Tzu, having advocated a mild political anarchism, had unwittingly given birth to the stern autocracy of the Legalists. The same phenomenon was now manifesting itself in the West through the medium of Rousseau's disciple, Kant.

But Kant's awe-inspiring philosophy remained dualistic to the end, unable to synthesize his twin unrelated philosophies of scientific knowledge and metaphysical morality. This dualism became insupportable to his successors, and the German passion for synthesis could not leave such a gap wide open. The whole process of German thought from Kant to Hegel was one of overcoming this static dualism which Kant had clearly stated and of reaching Hegel's profound dialectical, dynamic monism.

Hegel's philosophy was the exteriorization of a deep mystical urge, the intellectualization of a powerful awareness of a metaphysical "Reality." It had all the characteristics of Teutonic psychology: intuitive, pantheistic, dynamic and synthetic. The divorce from Western philosophy was now complete, and German thought rocketed past its predecessor and, leaving it far behind, soared into a stratospheric world of ideas hitherto unknown to philosophic thought. But dominating Hegel's mind was a powerful awareness of the basic unity of all things, of an urge toward a monism which could not possibly countenance Kant's dualism. It was the task of Hegel to transcend it, as once Aristotle had transcended Plato's, and to project beyond the apparently irreconcilable dualism of thesis and antithesis, the unifying synthesis.

Hegel stated that the Absolute Reality is spiritual. Being Absolute Reality, it is also Absolute Thought; and thought is logical and rational. But he stressed immediately the limitations of logic: a predicate, if applied to the whole of Reality, becomes a self-contradiction. However, the synthetic urge which all men feel prods us onward and toward an increasingly accurate conception of this Absolute Reality. The vehicle for this historical journey is to be provided by Hegel's famous "Dialectic Logic," a threefold development of logical thought: From the Thesis which is the predicate applied to the Absolute, man goes to the Antithesis which demonstrates its insufficiency, following which the Synthesis reconciles both viewpoints by taking the whole problem onto a higher plane. But the Synthesis itself is incomplete and automatically brings forth a new Antithesis—and so on. The mere force of logic will take us from any predicate to Absolute Logic. Therefore, rational dialectic directs systematically and imperiously the evolution of the universe. Hegel does not merely classify phenomena but deducts them necessarily from one another. Pure spirit materializes itself in nature and returns to its source through the manifestations of conscious intelligence.

All the triads which are responsible for dialectic evolution and change in every aspect of life culminate in the great Triad which presides over man's Historical Destiny: the thesis is Spirit, the antithesis is nature, the material, physical, concrete world which challenges man's abstract ideas, and the final synthesis is the Absolute Idea going back to its original, spiritual home. The Idea is ever requiring its materialization in nature, which man can bring about only through pain and effort and as a result of which it finally returns to its original home, the Absolute Spirit. This endless Becoming, in Hegel's view, equated logic with metaphysics and was the law of thought. But Hegelian dialectics are, in fact, *translogical* and, instead of expressing the mere law of thought, express in fact the law of natural, *organic* evolution. Synthesis is never willingly deduced by logical process, but is always imposed by life itself; and all the great philosophies of the world, after having elaborated their rationalist structures, have finally come to terms with nature and reality through the compromise of a more or less rudimentary dialectic synthesis. Hegel himself referred to his Indian predecessors. And, in line with the profound trend of Chinese philosophic thinking, Neo-Confucianism's "organistic" philosophy was essentially a dialectical materialism.[4]

Everything—religions, philosophies, sciences, arts—is a contingent materialization of Pure Spirit and sinks back into a relativity of time and space, as being the endless manifestations of the Absolute, traveling in historical time from the less to the more perfect. Freedom then becomes the freedom of the Will, not the individual but the collective Will of which the individual is only a reflection. The embodiment of the "collective Will" or of what Kant termed the "transcendental ego" is the highest human society of the time in the form of the state, the real agent of historical evolution. Therefore, the highest achievement of freedom will lie in complete subservience of the individual will to the will of the state. In Hegel's own words, "The state is the Divine Idea as it exists on earth . . . the embodiment of rational freedom, realizing and recognizing itself in objective form." [5]

The new dynamic philosophy was born which would engender the great secular creeds of the twentieth century. That Hegel's idealistic thinking was a projection of the innermost feelings of the German soul is obvious, but it was also the most powerful and profound synthesis of modern thought, the only synthesis which explained and justified all modern activities, theories and concepts.

When viewed from the standpoint of Asian thought, however, Hegel's thinking was not as revolutionary as it was from the traditional standpoint of the West. German subjectivism was a break with Greek and early Western thought, which was always objective, but Eastern philosophies—philosophies of attitude and "transformation" rather than of "information," *psychological* philosophies rather than *theologies*—had always been more subjective than objective. Hegel had gone beyond the confines of Greek logic but by so doing he came closer to the traditional thinking of the Orient, and this he owed to the deep mysticism which pervaded German thought from the earliest days of the Gothic Age. And, what is more, he had justified philosophically the obliteration of the individual's autonomy, a development which was intensely distasteful to the West but brought him even closer to Asian thought in general and Chinese thinking in particular. Hegelianism was bound to deal a shattering blow to Western individualism.

The most extraordinary aspect of this East-West relationship on the intellectual level is not so much the record of the influence of Europe on China as that of the influence of China on Europe. Let us go back from Hegel and Schelling to Herder and to their common ancestor Leibnitz, the founder (in Western Culture) of what could be termed the "organic" trend in Western philosophic thinking that was at variance with all Cartesian philosophies inspired by Newton's "mechanical" universe. Now, of course, we know that the post-Newtonian views in physics as well as Darwin's evolutionary theories have destroyed this *mechanical* vision of the universe and, with it, the philosophy that had been inspired by it. But this mechanical outlook was still triumphant in the eighteenth century. When German idealism took over the philosophic leadership of Western culture, its direct ancestor was Leibnitz. And where, essentially, did Leibnitz find inspiration for his theory of "monads," those autonomous, indissoluble organisms participating as cells in a hierarchy of organisms and culminating in an *organistic* universe? In Chu Hsi's Neo-Confucianism.[6] It is well known that Leibnitz was for many years in close touch with the Jesuits in China, corresponded with them regularly and read thoroughly most of their translations of Chinese works. Leibnitz's original contribution to Western philosophy, his organic naturalism, can be traced, in part, directly to Chinese sources. And from

Leibnitz to Hegel's dialectical pantheism there is a clear, unbroken thread. In a sense, it is not too far-fetched to state that Hegelian dialectics have one of their remote sources in Chinese philosophy itself.

Hegel's ardent interest in oriental philosophy was due to an unconscious feeling of kinship, to this common pantheistic yearning toward a cosmic totality of which man is but a small detached part and to which he must eventually return. The main features of Hegel's philosophy—pantheism, historicism, the dialectical and organic rather than logical and mechanical outlook—were also the main characteristics of China's traditional philosophic outlook.

This Hegelian concept of human destiny was fated to stimulate an entirely new school of thought. A bold and revolutionary transmutation of Hegel's dialectical idealism into Feuerbach's dialectical materialism launched this new philosophy on its dramatic career. This metamorphosis adapted the materialism prevalent in Europe as a result of the Industrial Revolution to Hegel's dynamic dialectic. But whereas Hegel stated that thought creates the object, Feuerbach claimed that the object creates thought. From this simple premise, the successors of Feuerbach derived a "materialistic" philosophy which had, in fact, all the earmarks of an unconscious idealism.

The founder and main apostle of this new creed was Karl Marx, the last of the great "Semitic prophets" whose philosophy of history became the "Koran" of our century's great revolutions. The hard core of his philosophy was succinctly explained by his famous collaborator, Friedrich Engels: "Marx discovered the simple fact (heretofore hidden beneath ideological overgrowths) that human beings must have food, drink, clothing and shelter first of all, before they can interest themselves in politics, science, art, religion and the like. This implies that the production of the immediately requisite material means of subsistence, and therewith the existing phase of development of a nation or an epoch, constitute the foundation upon which the state institutions, the legal outlooks, the artistic and even the religious ideas are built up. It implies that these latter must be explained out of the former, whereas the former have usually been explained as issuing from the latter." [7]

It is obvious that, although he rejected Hegel's idealism and metaphysics, he retained all the other important features of Hegelian thought: the unindividualistic viewpoint, the historical approach and the monistic outlook. Retention of the first feature was essential to the intellectual integrity of the whole system. The dialectical development of the individual self-consciousness is merely a reflection of the dialectical development of historical societies; being mere reflection, it is inevitably subordinate.

Retention of the second feature gave to Marxism its dynamic quality. His was a philosophy of history, geared to the process of Time. His "historical" materialism is a radical departure from Greek or European materialistic doctrines, all of which had ignored history and had adopted a totally dehumanized matter, the matter of the old atomists. Into their static outlook Marx injected Hegel's dynamism. The dialectical development of the universe, in his opinion, is not due to a motivating spirit but to motivating matter—and he criticized the earlier materialistic theories for considering sensation as passive, whereas sensation is really engendered by interaction between subject and object. Knowledge is acquired in the handling of matter itself and the driving force of the dialectical evolution of history is therefore man's relation to matter—or rather his mode of production.

But his retention of the third feature of Hegel's philosophic outlook—monism—is really what transformed Marxism into a prophetic religion. We can detect it in the very tone of Lenin's subsequent comments: "The teaching of Marx is all-powerful because it is true. It is complete and symmetrical, offering an integrated view of the world . . ." [8] This is the tone in which the caliphs used to comment about Muhammad's teachings. This integrated vision of cosmic totality was also explained by Lenin: "His teachings arose as a direct and immediate continuation of the teachings of the greatest representatives of philosophy, political economy and socialism . . . It is the legitimate inheritor of the best that humanity created in the nineteenth century in the form of German philosophy, English political economy, French socialism." [9]

His was essentially a philosophy of action—"philosophers have only 'interpreted' the world in various ways, but the real task is to 'alter' it." [10] Determinism, in Marx's system, becomes inhumanly implacable and he goes on to prophesy the inevitable rush of the capitalistic society toward an unavoidable and apocalyptic breakdown under the weight of its own industrial creations and iniquities.

Powerfully struck by the growing industrialization of his day and by the appalling misery entailed by the increasing mechanization of the Western world, Marx drew one set of logical conclusions out of the evolution of German philosophy but forgot the rest. His materialism was as vague and groundless as all other materialisms, and although he professed to be an atheist he "retained a cosmic optimism which only theism could justify," in the words of Bertrand Russell. [11] The new vehicles of history's dialectical movement are no longer states and *nations*, as conceived by Hegel, but *social classes*. The destruction of the capitalists and the eventual rise to power of the proletariat are viewed with all the tensely dramatic expectancy of the Christian waiting for the Second Coming, but there is no more individualism left in this turgid fresco.

Time and again, Western socialism would strike out at Marx, point out that his entire doctrine is unscientific, that it is essentially dogmatic belief, that he has remained on the threshold of the pre-socialist, pre-scientific phase of socialism. Marxism became a religion against which no intellectual argument could possibly prevail. Hegel had attempted to formulate a philosophy of Time and Eternity, and to him History was the "autobiography of God"; [12] but to Marx, the historical process itself was God: Marxism is a religion of Time, exclusively. Its philosophy became transmuted into a potent faith which was destined to have the same power of expansion in the twentieth century as Islam in the seventh.

The intrinsic truth or falsehood of a doctrine such as Marxism is purely a matter of academic dissertation. What matters to the historian and to the man of action is its effectiveness, and when any such doctrine finally rises to historic power it is on the strength of its representative character. Marxism is, like any other historical phenomenon, a symbol. It is a symbol of a civilization which is in danger of being destroyed by those very forces of nature which it has tamed physically, because it is no longer able to relate its scientific activities to some higher spiritual purpose.

Marxism, as an economic doctrine, could scarcely be differentiated from any form of Western "bourgeois" socialism. But as a new faith, it acquired global significance because of its conquest of the Russian Empire in 1917.

As an all-encompassing philosophy, Marxism sought to integrate an economic doctrine with the most abstruse metaphysical conclusions of Hegelian thought, as reviewed by Feuerbach's materialism. As such, it ended by being the most potent result of a frequently overlooked phenomenon of our age: the psychological impact of the Machine Age upon man's mind. Western Europe and America took the appearance of an industrial civilization, which they had themselves fostered, with a greater amount of casualness than Eastern Europe, Russia or Asia. The material benefits of industrialization were taken for granted, the incredible hardships entailed by the technical revolution taken in stride, and for many Westerners the millennium appeared to be just around the corner. The major form of protest which arose in the West took the shape of socialism. In its non-Marxist incarnation, it was essentially an economic and social doctrine dealing with the concrete problems created by the Industrial Revolution, not an all-inclusive philosophy claiming all the privileges of a revealed religion. Socialism, in its essence, was a "Western" doctrine, a reaction against industrial capitalism and against the virtual enslavement of the working classes in the nineteenth century.

Marxism was a radical departure from this ordinary, commonplace socialism. It was an integrated philosophy, a new way of life which was bound to involve not only man's intellect but his whole personality, his feelings and emotions, his artistic and scientific activities. Socialism, in Marx's doctrine, became almost a secondary matter, being completely overshadowed in importance by his Hegelian conception of the dialectical unfolding of history. But under Marx's impulse, Hegelian philosophy acquired a much broader significance and its appeal became global as Marx substituted the industrial proletariat for the Western nations—and especially the Germanic nations—as the chosen instruments of destiny, as the predestined agents of historical evolution.

Marxism, as such, was nothing more than a doctrine. It became a living reality and a powerful historical movement under Lenin's direction, and as it materialized into a revolutionary manifestation of great magnitude it acquired an entirely different outlook. Marx and Marxism after him remained essentially a Western phenomenon. Marxist and non-Marxist socialists alike viewed the Western world as being the only portion of the globe where the Industrial Revolution had made socialism possible; and as far as Marx was concerned, the West was the only geographical setting for "dialectical materialism." Asia, unindustrialized and completely historyless, was of no consequence. The Orient would automatically follow in the wake of the great Western revolution to come. Russia was a backward giant to be feared and tamed by the West. But between Marx and Lenin many historical events had occurred which justified an entirely new outlook on Eastern affairs: Anti-Western nationalism was beginning to make itself felt all over Asia, Japan's victory over Tzarist Russia had stirred the hearts of many Orientals, and the rapid industrialization of various parts of the East had become a powerful factor to reckon with. At the same time, Western imperialism seemed to be at the height of its glory and aggressiveness, ruthlessly and carelessly destroying the pride and self-respect of Asia.

At this juncture, Lenin and his group of Bolsheviks began to look toward the Orient for new historical clues. For all the rigid dogmas which already encompassed Marxism, it was always assumed that historical evolution altered conditions ceaselessly and that, everything being in a state of permanent flux, all dogmas had to be reinterpreted under the new light of existing conditions. So it was that Lenin began to discern a powerful force which would rank with class warfare as the major instrument of world revolution: anti-imperialism, the revolt of non-Western people against their Western overlords, in fact the political awakening of Asia and its consequent rejection of European domination. Lenin's new position was defined by his successor Stalin, as he himself had once defined Marx's historical role: "Leninism is the Marxism of the era of imperialism and of the proletarian revolution." [13] Although the proletariat, as a social class, remained the chosen instrument of historical destiny, a new factor was becoming just as important: the existence of "proletarian nations" struggling against "capitalist nations," the East attempting to overthrow Western domination. Class warfare now became transcended into a global struggle in which all colonial people and especially Asian nations had their appointed battle stations. This apparently slight adaptation of Marxism to a fast-changing world implied, in fact, a return to a purer form of Hegelian philosophy of history; but now the "chosen" nation is no longer Prussia or Germany or the most civilized state of the time but the "proletarian" states—that is, the non-Western states. It was really Lenin who created this new doctrine which was to promote the anti-Western upsurge of Asian nationalism in our century.

With all its instinctive adaptation to altering world conditions, Marxism-Leninism remained essentially a philosophy of history with religious undertones, the final, all-embracing explanation of all human phenomena, integrating science, art, ethics, economics, politics, linking human destiny with the structure of the universe—and all this, thanks to a dynamic synthesis which was geared to the process of Time.

Against those who refused to realize the transcendental importance of history, Stalin pronounced that "it is clear that without such a 'Historical' approach to social phenomena, the existence and development of the science of history is impossible, for only such an approach saves the science of history from becoming a jumble of accidents and an agglomeration of most absurd mistakes." [14] Stalin harps endlessly on this historical theme: ". . . Social life, the history of society, ceases to be an agglomeration of 'accidents' and becomes the history of the development of society according to regular laws and the study of history of society becomes a science." He adds further on that the "science of history of society, despite all the complexity of the phenomena of social life, can become as precise a science as, let us say, biology and capable of making use of laws of development of society for practical purposes."

He then proceeds: "If there are no isolated phenomena in the world, if all phenomena are interconnected and interdependent, then it is clear that every social system and every social movement in history must be evaluated not from the standpoint of 'eternal justice' or some other preconceived idea, as it is not infrequently done by historians, but from the standpoint of the conditions which gave rise to that system or that social movement and with which they are connected. The slave system would be senseless, stupid and unnatural under modern conditions. But under the conditions of a disintegrating primitive communal system, the slave system is a quite understandable and natural phenomenon since it represents an advance on the primitive communal system." [15]

This view of mankind's history introduces the notion of "historical relativity" which German philosophy had set up against the frozen "absolutes" of Western Christianity. Time and place condition every idea and notion and there are therefore no more fixed, permanent and transcendent, but only relative, values and standards. This world-outlook gives to

Marxism an amazing fluidity, which prevents its dogmas from becoming petrified into deathlike rigidity, and even a certain objective realism in its understanding of contemporary politics in the world at large.

And although the Marxist jargon insists on introducing its fixed, permanent stock of beliefs in the absolute possibilities of rational, scientific knowledge, in a materialism which could be transmuted into idealism with only very slight modifications, the basic feeling remains that everything should be scrutinized under the light of historical relativity. This basic feeling found its practical application in the world of contemporary politics when Stalin extended it to a geographical relativity which made him accept Mao Tse-tung's new Chinese Communism as the only possible one, in view of conditions at that time and in that place, one generation later and thousands of miles to the east and south.

The extension of the Marxist's faith to Asia was a foregone conclusion when the whole of Siberia and Russian Central Asia had fallen under the sway of Moscow. But the mere fact that Asia had been increasingly drawn into the vortex of Western politics before World War I was bound to alter the policy of the Marxists before they could even hope to gain power in Russia. Lenin had become interested in the fate of backward areas of the world shortly after Asian Japan had defeated Tzarist Russia. He even outlined a plan of action which would undoubtedly have been anathema to Marx, and in 1916 he wrote in the publication *Sozialdemocrat*: "We would at once systematically start to incite rebellion among the peoples now oppressed by the Great Russians—and all the colonies and dependent countries of Asia (India, China, Persia, etc. . . .)." From then onward, Lenin worked out gradually his entirely new "Theory of Imperialism," which he dedicated to Asia. Together with his theory of the peasantry's role during the dictatorship of the proletariat, it constitutes his great contribution to Marxist tradition and orthodoxy and was destined to bring a new and powerful message to an Orient already seething with hatred for the West.[16] Stalin, an Asian himself, described Lenin's farsighted and astute appraisal of the growing importance of Asia with a passion and fervor rare in so cool a man: "The scores and hundreds of millions of Asiatics and African peoples who are suffering national oppression in its most savage and cruel form usually remained outside their (*i.e.*, the Second International's) field of vision. They hesitated to put black and white, 'civilized' and 'uncivilized,' on the same plane . . . Leninism laid bare this crying incongruity, broke down the wall between whites and blacks, between Europeans and Asiatics, between the 'civilized' and 'uncivilized' slaves of imperialism and thus linked the national problem with the problem of the colonies." [17]

Soviet Russia now carried a new message to Asia, on Asian soil, a message which was no longer limited to the narrow field of mere nationalism with its restricted vision of local history, but was a much vaster, all-encompassing faith which "explained" the appalling predicament in which the Orient found itself at this juncture. It afforded an all-embracing explanation of the nature of scientific knowledge and the implications of the machine age in simple terms and based on a vast perspective of history which was not disparaging to Asia's past. It struck a prophetic note which impressed by its very assurance and certainty. The hated West was doomed according to this new message, doomed by the very nature of capitalism's cancerous growth and inner contradictions; and to an Asia which was still writhing under the implacable power of the West it was a moving message. The religious-like nature of this call to arms was bound to play on the emotions of those Asians who suffered from the destruction of all their traditional values, who therefore thirsted for suprarational and quasi-religious explanations and interpretations, who longed for faith and yet could not find it in Western Christianity.

The October Revolution, furthermore, was taken as a Russian withdrawal from the Western community in which Tzarist Russia had incorporated itself for more than two centuries. Sun Yat-sen, the founder of the Chinese Republic, pointed this out in his usual flat and pedestrian style: "At present, Russia is attempting to separate from the white peoples in Europe. Why? Because she insists on the rule of Right and denounces the rule of Might. She advocates the principle of benevolence and justice . . . Recent Russian civilization is similar to our ancient civilization. Therefore, she joins with the Orient and separates from the West." [18] Soviet Russia may have seemed more Asian and far more "benevolent" through the distorting prism of hatred. But there was no doubt as to her total and irremediable break with the West, and this alone was already a fabulous accretion to Chinese power.

part four

CHINA AND
THE WORLD

10

THE COLLAPSE OF
CHINESE CIVILIZATION

At the turn of our century, the fact that a geopolitical revolution had taken place was at last made dramatically plain to the Chinese: China was no longer an isolated, self-contained civilized world; she had acquired neighbors and was gradually becoming a *nation* in the midst of other nations. This fact alone was bound to put an end to her universalist vision of a self-enclosed world and induce the Chinese to seek for another, higher form of universalism. But it was inevitable that, in the process, her old, petrified civilization and the exclusivism which went with it would collapse.

China had acquired two main geographical neighbors: land-bound Russia, which had been slowly occupying the immense waterless oceans of steppes and deserts in central Asia and Siberia, and maritime Japan, beyond the seas, anchored off China toward the rising sun.

Japan's Moonlight Civilization had been able to carry out a complete metamorphosis in the last part of the nineteenth century, a startling achievement which few in China or in the West could understand and appreciate. Her psychological preparation for the Western onslaught was far greater than was commonly supposed in the West. Although the speed with which the nimble Japanese switched from the sword and the shield to the machine gun and the battleship was astounding, a great many favorable strains had actually been converging for more than a century, creating a frame of mind which made such a startling adaptation possible. Psychologically, the Japanese had already manifested many traits which appeared to be much more Western than Asian: a kinetic energy which was intensely dynamic whereas its Chinese counterpart was static, a mind directed solely toward the external world although the Japanese sensibility could penetrate intuitively into the essence of nature's reality, and a curiosity and a remarkable keenness for innovation.

To be more specific, Japan's historical evolution was chronologically more or less in step with that of the West. Even under the fossilized feudalism of the Tokugawas in the eighteenth and nineteenth centuries, a strong middle class had developed and the merchants and bankers of Osaka and Edo owned a large share of the national wealth. There was distinctly the beginning of a capitalist society, isolated though Japan was from the rest of the world. In many ways, Japan was going through the period through which the Chinese themselves had proceeded toward the close of the Spring and Autumn era, twenty-five hundred years before: the aristocratic military tradition, the feudal code of honor, the strong nationalistic feeling, the sturdy development and protection of property rights, the growth of a powerful entrepreneurial capitalism out of a decaying feudal structure, the social inequality entailed by primogeniture and the existence of a class of dynamic and audacious younger sons, all those features which recur with unfailing regularity at a certain stage of the historical cycle—the stage of China's Warring States era or of nine-teenth-century Europe. If nothing else, historical parallelism between Japan and the West was bound to make Japan's adaptation to the modern world easier than it was for any other Asian country.

Furthermore, the superpatriotism of the Japanese was the overriding psychological trait of this proud people, a feeling of such intensity that it includes not only the men and women of Japan and their imperial ruler as well as ancestors and yet unborn generations, but also the very soil and the delicate landscape of the Empire of the Rising Sun. The essential pur-suit of life which in other countries became the search for Transcendent Reality, for union with the Brāhman or a fatal-istic submission to the will of Allah, for Tao-like membership in the Universal Order or for mystical self-realization, became the relation of the Japanese to "Japan," the symbol of the all-embracing Divine Reality itself. To a stern and yet fervent stoicism the Japanese welded their incomparable technical skill and their acute sense of observation which enabled them to penetrate immediately into the "practical" essence of all concrete things and exploit them to their own advantage. The culture of Japan being one of *attitude* rather than of *expres-sion*, Westernization was far easier than it could possibly be for those profound civilizations rooted in the depths of a great cultural past such as the Chinese. All that was required of the Japanese was to assume a new attitude and emphasize certain traits of their character which had been kept in abey-ance by the cultural influence of China. As a skilled jiujitsu wrestler, Japan adapted its defensive moves and conditioned its soul to an entirely new cultural teacher and opponent, more dangerous by far than the Chinese had ever been since the days of Kublai Khan's armada.

Through her herculean metamorphosis, Japan was able to rid herself gradually of all the political fetters imposed by the West and, from her presumed "return" to a pre-feudalistic type of government, slowly evolve toward a Western-type political system. Extraterritoriality and privileges for Westerners were abolished on the initiative of the United States after Japan's victorious war against China in 1895—a strange reward for Japan's first aggressive military action. Her power grew by leaps and bounds, amazing an uncomprehending West. Japan was soon accused by the slightly alarmed Occidentals of being a freak, a mere copyist, an empty chameleon. The permutability of Japan was stressed in its flimsy constructions, burned and destroyed after each one of the numerous earthquakes which devastated the archipelago with dreaded frequency.

And yet it was quite obvious that the Japanese knew how to combine complete detachment from the dead, inert form, with fervent devotion to the living substance. The Shinto shrine dedicated to Ise, the sun-goddess who is alleged to have founded the imperial dynasty, remains intact in its venerable park although the same temple has been rebuilt every twenty years for the past fifteen centuries. Because of this essential and amazing immutability, Japan has been able to absorb alien forms and techniques without breaking with her past, without betraying herself. To each success in foreign policy, to each new victory, to each increase in international prestige, the Japanese reacted by reverting to their ancestral traditions and customs with progressively increasing reassurance. They had learned gradually how to dissociate Western forms from Western substance.

The Japanese population, rid of the limiting fetters of the Tokugawa regime, multiplied at a staggering rate. Industrialism invaded the entire archipelago, creating vast metropolises in Tokyo-Yokohama, Osaka, Nagoya and many more overcrowded centers surrounded by textile plants and steelworks. But the Japanese gradually reverted to their own costumes and their own traditions after the first Westernization frenzy had run its course. Shinto became more powerful than it had ever been in the past—in some ways, it was entirely re-created to suit the political purposes of the state, evolving into a national, patriotic code of ethics which was in step with the virulent nationalism prevailing in Europe. Japan kept her psychic balance by remaining in the constant center between the two mobile poles of Western and Eastern values, between swift industrialization and pure Japanese tradition. Each increase in outward Westernization called for an increase in inward Japanization.

All this, of course, reflected on the intellectual evolution of the Japanese after the Meiji Restoration, on the gradual detachment of Japanese thought from French and Anglo-Saxon liberalism in favor of German philosophy—a fatal change which was partly due to certain deep affinities between German thought and the general pattern of Asian thinking, but also to the unquestionable superiority of the Teutonic cogitations. Hegelian philosophy even invaded strongholds of Western influence such as the Christian Doshisha University, and it is interesting to note that many Japanese thinkers at the time claimed that Hegelian dialectics supported Buddhist thought whereas it conflicted with Christian doctrines and teaching. German political absolutism penetrated at first, shaping the political constitution of the empire, and German subjectivism came in later, in the twentieth century, to merge partly with the prevalent philosophy of Japanese Buddhism.[1]

This alteration in Japanese thinking remained almost unnoticed in the West. The importance of this change in Japanese thought lay in the fact that, quite apart from its impact on Japan's policy toward the West, Western thought was being introduced to the Chinese through the medium of Japanese translations. And the impact on China of such Japanese philosophers as Hiroyuki Kato, who rejected Locke, Hume and Mill, of Tetsujiro Inoue, who introduced German idealism and started Japan's Neo-Kantian school, was considerable. Western individualism could no more succeed in China than in Japan, and the thinking of the Japanese was a prefiguration of the coming evolution of Chinese thought. The urge toward synthesis which animated Kitaro Nishida, the marked Hegelianism of Shinichiro Nishi, or the more profound Hegelianism of Masayoshi Kihira, who blended Buddhist and German philosophies, all blazed the intellectual trail which the Chinese were to follow after the collapse of

the Celestial Empire.[2] In the end, they all reached the same
conclusion: A philosophy of history was the only intellectual
discipline which could possibly synthesize Asian and European
thought.[3]

Affinities with certain aspects of German thinking were
bound to crop up in a country where individualism is as nonexistent as it is in Japan. The Teutonic emphasis on collective
forces, collective souls, superego and suchlike, as well as its
irrational insistence on the impersonal or rather superpersonal
forces shaping history, its concept of entire nations constitut-
ing super-organisms to which the individual should be sacrificed without an afterthought, all this was bound to strike root
in Japan and become welded to the obscure forces of Shinto.
Here was the great challenge for the West—this amazing combination of tremendous technical power, industrial and military, with German philosophy and a dynamic will to expand,
which amounted to a staggering powerhouse in the Far East,
only too lightly despised and underestimated in the West.
Japan struck at Port Arthur with long-range artillery and
destroyed the Russian fleet in the Tsushima Straits with
powerful battleships—but the declaration of war against Russia
was communicated by a special envoy to the sun-goddess at
Ise.

Thus Japan's role in the contemporary Chinese revolution
was that of a *midwife*. Japan introduced Western thought to
China through her numerous translations, then contributed
to the destruction of the old Celestial Empire by raping it
through repeated aggressions, and finally was the main agent
in the downfall of European power in the Far East during
World War II. But the Japanese are insular people who, like
the British, are not attuned to universal ideas and values like
the Chinese or the French. They could never conquer China
because they could not conquer the Chinese mind and soul;
they live in the Far East and yet are not part of it. It is the
good fortune of the West—and perhaps of Russia too—that
there is a profound chasm between the Chinese and the
Japanese which is not likely to be bridged for a long time.

*   *   *

While the Asian world gazed admiringly at the swift metamorphosis of Japan's Moonlight Civilization, the older civilizations of Asia underwent a devastating transformation which threatened to wipe out thousands of years of cultural history. Those old countries in which the higher cultures and civilizations of Asia had found their birth and cradle could not tear out such immeasurably deep roots, and for them a "moonlight" metamorphosis was a sheer impossibility.

Of all these ancient civilizations and cultures, China's was by far the most vulnerable, not in a political sense—since the very vastness of the country and the fierce xenophobia of the inhabitants precluded any serious attempt at clamping direct colonial rule on them—but because of the very nature of an essentially worldly, utilitarian and unspiritual culture, and because of its immense pride. China had been more isolated than Islam or India behind the formidable barriers of Tibet and of the Central Asian wastes and had, as a result, developed a civilization which owed very little to foreign influence. Nowhere was the idea of totality, of universalism, more firmly rooted than in a China that was far more massive and compact than the Roman Empire and in no direct geographical contact with any other civilization. Armed with an amazing and proud self-assurance, the Chinese mandarins still looked upon all foreigners as hopeless barbarians, and—to quote it once more—Emperor Ch'ien Lung's reply to King George III of Britain throws a vivid light on this incredible vanity compounded of dangerous ignorance: "You, o king, live beyond the confines of many seas; nevertheless, impelled by your humble desire to partake of the benefits of our civilization, you have dispatched a mission respectfully bearing your memorial . . . To show your devotion, you have also sent offerings of your country's produce. I have read your memorial; the earnest terms in which it is cast reveal a respectful humility on your part, which is highly praiseworthy." [4] And only a few decades later one of history's most formidable collapses began. It became an awful agony, the withering away of an exceedingly brilliant civilization which had survived the test of thousands of years.

Molded before the birth of Christ and having passed into complete fixity shortly after, the Chinese world had gone on revolving on itself smoothly. All the compromises and blends had been made, the last synthesis of Confucianism, Taoism and Buddhism had been worked out to the benefit of Confucianism. The Sons of Heaven regulated the relations between Earth and Heaven, between the two mirrorlike halves of a universe of which they were the kingpin. Promising and ambitious intellectuals had sat on the benches of the Imperial Examinations for thousands of years, had become respected mandarins who wore with pride the jewels of their rank and who rose gradually according to their literary merit. A thorough permeation of Confucius' *Analects,* a good memorizing of the best T'ang poetry of Tu Fu or Po Chü-I were far more important for their career than knowledge of the workings of water mills or the constructions of durable bridges. The conformist mold was so implacable that at the triennial examinations the future mandarin was required to write his "Eight Legs" essay on a classical theme without expressing any opinion of his own which could conflict with Chu Hsi's philosophical school.[5] He was required to quote Confucius and other great classics according to prescribed rules, nothing more, nothing less, and only the best writers became government officials. The mandarin system had become completely fossilized, a gigantic, inhuman and inefficient machine corroded with rust. But this civilization could have gone on uninterruptedly for hundreds, thousands, even tens of thousands of years, on its momentum, like a dead planet revolving mechanically and smoothly until an unexpected comet comes along and explodes it. It was essentially satisfied, static, wedded to its belief in a historical recurrence of identical and endless cycles—completely opposed to the dynamic and linear concept of the Japanese.

The tragedy of the Western impact upon China was that its civilization was very much of this world and very little of the other. The Chinese had a worldly, humanistic, and not a spiritual culture like that of the Indians. They were too highly cultured, too steeped in mere literary intellectualism, too reasonable to be able to imitate the intuitive Japanese. Their power of ethnical absorption was and remains immense. But their power of cultural adaptation was nil. Because of its worldly, earth-bound character, Chinese civilization was vulnerable. Delicate and refined, contemptuous of the alien barbarians dwelling beyond their borders and even more disdainful of the *Yang Kwei Tzǔ*, the Ocean Devils who had been sailing up to their southern shores for centuries, the rationalist Chinese had no sense of reality whatsoever. The unerring instincts of the Japanese had made them raise the alarm signal decades before Commodore Perry put in an appearance with his squadron. But the Chinese mandarins repeatedly flew in the face of every evidence that their cherished civilization was being stabbed to death. It seemed utterly inconceivable to them that the immeasurably old civilization of China could fail to cope with any threat whatsoever, and most mandarins set themselves deliberately against modernization and reforms of any kind.

The last days of old China were entirely dominated by Dowager Empress Tzu-hsi, one of the most forceful and reactionary women known to history. She shared the contemptuous views of the mandarins toward the Western "barbarians" in spite of the obvious fact that their material superiority was devastating and that even the Japanese "monkeys" had been able, after a few years of Western schooling, to defeat gigantic China. She refused to listen to a few wise men such as Li Hung-chang who had traveled abroad and advocated a degree of Westernization. She destroyed another bright scholar by the name of K'ang Yu-wei who had submitted a memorandum in the last years of the nineteenth century and who had converted the emperor to his views. The emperor was imprisoned in his palace and all those who had attempted to carry out K'ang's reforms were exterminated. Old China was showing the last vigor and stiffening of the moribund, exhaling the last gasp of a corpselike civilization, attempting to intimidate the foreigners with the Boxer rebellion and floundering miserably.

The focus of discontent was located in the south of China, in the home of what might be termed the nonconformist Chinese. Southerners had been civilized by the cultured northerners at a relatively recent date (vast populations of aborigines are still left to be civilized as late as the middle of the twentieth century) and they had always retained a certain inferiority complex in their attitude toward the more refined and cultured northerners. There was not only a vast difference in speech—compensated by the universalism of the ideographic script—but even differences in racial constitution between the more Mongoloid northern Chinese and the dark-skinned southerners, who were a blend of Yao, Tai, Yueh and Miao aborigines and of pure Mongolian stock.

The northerner was more Confucianist, more devoted to cultural pursuits—and also more social-minded. He was a stickler for self-discipline, far more docile and respectful of authority than the perennially rebellious and individualistic southerner. Confucianism was a northern philosophy of life and also a code of ethics with a socialistic tinge, reflecting the northern yearning for schematic arrangement which was inspired by the unlimited spaces of the North China plains and Mongolian borderlands. In the concrete infinity of the Eurasian expanses, man's individuality was bound to wither away to a certain extent.

The south, broken up by innumerable mountains into small plains and valleys, was the home of individualism, anarchism and mystical introspection. But it was also—and became even more so as time passed—the home of the only important "bourgeois" middle class China has known in modern times, of traders and bankers, of men who valued self-interest far more than social or collective interests. All those Chinese who emigrated to Southeast Asia were southerners from Swatow or Canton, individualistic traders and merchants who rebelled against the Confucianist tradition which had despised them and placed them at the bottom of the social scale. To a certain extent, the position of the South Chinese was comparable to the position of the Indian untouchable: Both stood largely outside the pale of Chinese and Hindu civilizations, both were despised by the prevailing orthodoxy and both were potential recruits for a new civilization which would restore their dignity and find room for them. Islam captured a large share of the Indian untouchables, and the West had already captured, long before the downfall of the Manchus, a substantial part of the southern trading community.

So it was that at the turn of the century a formidable revolt was brewing in the south which would deal the first shattering blow to China's imperial structure and start the whole process of collapse. The standard-bearer of this southern movement of emancipation from the choking fetters of China's traditional culture was a young, Western-minded physician by the name of Sun Yat-sen, "Sun the Fairy of Tranquillity"—a misnomer if ever there was one. Sun had quickly understood from K'ang Yu-wei's experiences that reforms were utterly impossible, that the old massive tree would not bend and grow new twigs shooting out in new directions. It had to be entirely uprooted, whatever the consequences, and uprooted by the southern middle class, the only one in the Celestial Empire which could possibly rebuild a modern, Westernized structure in China over the wreckage of the old civilization.

Sun Yat-sen had lived in British Hong Kong and in American Hawaii, had become a Protestant Christian with vague socialistic yearnings. He had lived in Japan, where he felt great pride in the power of recuperation of fellow-Asians. But Japan had moved so fast toward Westernization that she had estranged herself from the slow-moving Asians on the mainland and especially from a China to which she could no longer be an example. The "sleeping giant" was being beaten, raped, parceled out among the foreign Powers, humiliated by the West. From 1898 onward, thousands of Western business concerns began to exploit China on a gigantic scale under the shield of extraterritoriality and leased territories, controlling the Chinese customs and finances, interfering in the local administrations and building up a new industrial world in the midst of a civilization which had nothing but contempt for the newcomers. While Shanghai raised its enormous buildings, its traffic-laden clattering Bund, its huge piers and docks, the same old intrigues and ceremonials went on in the Forbidden City of Peking as in the days of Kublai Khan and Marco Polo.

But the revolutionary movement was gaining momentum in the south. The wealthy Chinese merchants of Southeast Asia who had been in contact with the colonial West for decades gave financial support to Sun Yat-sen's revolutionary program: overthrow of the Manchus, establishment of a republic and the gradual evolution of China into a Westernized democracy. It had become so obvious, however, that the last days of the Manchus were at hand when the "Old Buddha" Tzu-hsi died in 1908, that a new and rival center of strength was created around an ambitious general by the name of Yüan Shih-k'ai, who mistook the approaching political storm for the habitual change of dynasty which had occurred so often when the Imperial House had forsaken the Mandate of Heaven. Clever and patient, Yüan waited quietly for the final disintegration of the imperial structure without realizing the gravity of the approaching collapse. The governors and viceroys in the provinces were gradually loosening their ties with Peking and slowly acquiring an autonomy they had not had since the breakdown of the T'ang era, negotiating directly with the Western Powers and with the Western business firms whose branches were beginning to penetrate into the remotest corners of the subcontinent.

The direct cause of the revolution of 1911 was odd, perhaps unique in contemporary history. The revolutionary movement in the south was centered around the wealthy, partly Westernized merchant class—the only class through which a modicum of Westernization had been able to penetrate into China, since the Confucianist barrier protected all the other social groups from barbaric pollution. Most of the university students in those days were sons of merchants and traders, and they formed the core of Sun Yat-sen's younger group. To put the whole problem in modern economic terminology, the revolution started as a capitalist revolt against the "socialistic" tendencies of the Peking government, which had taken the shape of a government bid to nationalize the newly built railroad running from Hankow into Szechwan province. The shareholders claimed that their financial compensation was inadequate, the entire trading corporation went on strike to protect the rights of the shareholders, and their student-sons started massive demonstrations against the moribund regime. Nothing more was needed to start the whole process of China's political and administrative disintegration.

One by one, the governors of provinces rose against Peking, wiped out the Manchu garrisons with the help of the local populations and proclaimed their autonomy. The mandarins quickly lost control of the administrative machinery, as earlier they had lost their prestige to Western technology. Panic-stricken, the Manchu government called in Yüan Shih-k'ai, whose small army was the only modernized body of troops in the whole empire. A quick calculation convinced Yüan that the time had come for bold decisions, and while he concluded an alliance with the Canton revolutionaries he persuaded the Peking Manchus that all was lost for them and that the only solution left was a peaceful abdication of the dynasty. The first "Republic of China" came into being in February 1912 and, fulfilling his share of the bargain, Sun Yat-sen recommended Yüan Shih-k'ai as its first president.

The old empire was now dead, and with its passing the disintegration of China, far from coming to a halt, merely increased its dizzy pace. Chinese "nationalism" had played its part in the overthrow and extermination of the Manchus. But, following a logic of nature which was beyond the understanding of the Chinese, the non-Chinese portions of the former empire sought immediately to free themselves from the authority of Peking. Tibet, Sinkiang and the Mongolias proclaimed their partial or total independence, while most provinces fell into the hands of ambitious or greedy war lords.

Yet traditional Chinese consciousness was still vivid in Peking, where the remains of imperial power lurked in the minds of ambitious men—as the dream of imperial Rome survived for centuries after its reality had totally disappeared. To Yüan Shih-k'ai, the whole process of revolution was nothing more than one of those changes of dynasty of which Chinese history is replete; in his view, the Chinese people had merely exercised Mencius' "sacred right to rebellion" because the Son of Heaven no longer knew how to maintain harmony between Heaven and Earth. The only problem left was to choose a new dynasty, and Yüan, who stood head and shoulders above any other northern Chinese, had no doubt as to who the choice of a suitable new ruler should be. Ignoring the gradual disintegration of the whole social fabric and the collapse of the very foundations of China's civilization, contemptuous of such war lords as general Chang Tso-lin, who had seized Manchuria, Ch'en Chiung-ming, war lord of Kwangtung, or the Mongol Hsiung-yün, who had seized Kansu and Shensi with the support of the Muslim Dungans, Yüan saw a unique opportunity in the outbreak of World War I and the subsequent concentration of Western attention on the European theater of operations.

But Japan, unencumbered by distant wars and floating on China's doorstep, saw the opportunity too. In 1915, Tokyo presented its Twenty-one Demands which, if accepted, would have amounted to a virtual protectorate over the whole of China. Expecting to be able to cope with the Japanese once his imperial power had been secured and once the Western Powers were back in the political field against Japan, Yüan accepted most of the demands over the violent opposition of the Cantonese republicans. As president, he held vast powers in his hands and used them with consummate skill to prepare his accession to the imperial throne. In the last days of 1915, he coerced the parliament into proclaiming him the first Chinese emperor since the passing of the Ming dynasty.

This imperial restoration was short-lived, caught as it was

between the southern republicans under Sun Yat-sen's leadership and the suspicious Japanese, to whom a reformed and united China was a deadly menace. Yet, no such danger existed and the process of Chinese disintegration went on unabated, provincial war lords and jealous rivals turning against Yüan and forcing him to abdicate a few months later. A short Manchu restoration followed and a new republic succeeded it. The conservative Chinese, still steeped in Confucianism, the last representatives of a dying civilization, were unable to cope with the growing anarchy and demoralization that soon engulfed them.

By and large, the Chinese had nothing left to believe in, no idea to hang on to, no moral and religious structure which could soften the impact of a disintegrating civilization such as the Roman world had possessed in the Christian Church. The destruction of the old moral and ethical codes went on pitilessly. The old mandarins, the most intelligent of whom now grasped the extent of the disaster, wept bitterly, but in vain; the past would never be resurrected. One Western philosopher who witnessed their downfall remarked that many preserved the typical stoicism of the Chinese sages of old and commented that "not long ago they were rich and mighty, now they are homeless and poor, and yet they bear their fate with equanimity. I have seen them in despair and even in tears: but it was out of sadness at the end of the great civilization of China which they saw approaching." [6] Blind as they might have been to the contemporary torrent of history, those were the best among the Chinese, stoics who remained faithful to the end to a civilized universe which was disintegrating under their very eyes.

Meanwhile, in the south a new world was taking shape. Sun Yat-sen had seen with impotent rage the betrayal of Yüan Shih-k'ai and with unmitigated pleasure his downfall. He watched with dismay the whole Chinese structure topple slowly and fall into chaos. He had long ago given up Western individualism as an ideal for China and had come to the conclusion that it was the family system and the lack of national consciousness which were responsible for the contemporary collapse. He began to see that it was not so much democratic freedom as a strong authoritarian state that was required as a substitute for the vanishing empire—until the remote, almost mythical day when the Chinese people would be ready for democracy.

He worked untiringly. He had the complete support of the middle class and the students but had to contend with undisguised hostility on the part of the Western Powers. Faced with this situation and with the unreliability of the various Peking regimes, conscious that China was floundering hopelessly because she lacked an ideology which might fill the vacuum, the "Father of the Chinese Republic" evolved his basic, simple and dry-as-dust gospel, the *San-min Chu-i*, the "Three Principles of the People," and laid down the three stages through which the republic would have to proceed: the struggle against the old system, the educative phase during which the people would be prepared for democratic rule, and in the end the truly democratic phase. Confucianism and all the ethical standards connected with it were largely rejected. Taoism was totally inadequate as a doctrine of political and social reconstruction, and as for Buddhism, it had been moribund for centuries. In fact and for the first time, the past was failing China, the historical mirror was forever blurred. A totally unknown and dangerous future faced the Chinese.

Sun Yat-sen had not really made up his mind which way he intended to go, although he swerved slowly to the left. His hesitancy found its expression in his vague pronouncements, in his "Tri-min-ism" or Three Principles of Race Determination, Democracy and Socialism which had become his political credo. In spite of everything, he remained overmuch Westernized, a member of the southern middle class, out of touch with the profound tremors coursing through the body of China. How blind he could have been to the real situation is proved by some of his writings: "China . . . owing to the backwardness of her industrial development, which is a blessing in disguise in this respect, has not yet entered into the class war. Our laboring class, commonly known as coolies, are living from hand to mouth and will, therefore, only be too glad to welcome any capitalist who would even put up a sweatshop to exploit them. The capitalist is a rare specimen in China and is only beginning to make his appearance in the treaty ports." [7] In view of subsequent events, it is almost inconceivable that he should have underestimated the growing agrarian problem, the only one in fact which could have shaken China to its very depths and could have started a class war. But it was typical of the middle-class viewpoint of a city dweller and explains much of what was to follow.

Torn and hesitant, tugged to the right by the bankers and traders who had financed his movement, lured toward the left by intellectuals and socialistic manual workers, Sun waited for inspiration. It came in the shape of the October Revolution in distant Petrograd and the subsequent change in the whole complexion of Asian problems. The new Soviet government manifested immense interest in the Chinese situation and great willingness to dispatch immediate help to Canton. Sun Yat-sen found his way at last. Turning deliberately away from his middle-class support and from the contemptuous West, he founded the revolutionary Kuomintang, the "People's Party." Bolstered almost immediately by Russian Communist advisers and funds, the Kuomintang started its historic career as an unholy and unstable coalition of suspicious "bourgeois" and daring revolutionaries, but promptly found itself without a leader through Sun's premature death.

Suffusing the quagmire of contemporary politics, the cultural disintegration of China was assuming disquieting proportions. Universities and colleges were engaged in political agitation, and the intelligentsia was too busy writing political pamphlets and making speeches to salvage anything from the wreckage. China's real, living cultural heritage was slowly vanishing with the gradual disappearance of the old-fashioned mandarins. What little was left was used by professors and students to promote the "literary revolution," an extension of the political revolution to the field of culture.

The old classical language of the mandarins was thrown out, to be replaced by the vernacular *pai-hua*. Professor Hu Shih, the leader of the movement, promoted the language of everyday life in literature and philosophy, or what was left of both. Newspapers, magazines, novels and technical books were now published in vernacular and the old classical language began to die out, like the old Egyptian language when the traditional hieroglyphics were replaced by the demotic script.

By promoting the vernacular, the reformers were merely carrying out the literary revolution advocated in the sixteenth century by Yüan Chung-lang, who had favored writing essays and novels by putting down words on the paper "as they flew from the wrist." This revolutionary suggestion had had a quick surge of favor but was soon drowned by the frigid hostility of the all-powerful mandarins, whose cultural privileges might have been seriously threatened. No such hostility existed at present and Hu Shih could write his *History of Chinese Philosophy* in popular language without having anything to fear. The forty thousand characters of former times were boiled down to the mere thirteen hundred needed for common, everyday use. But even so, the old literary style was not entirely given up because of the obvious danger of linguistic fragmentation and chaos. The vernacular of Peking is not that of Shanghai or Canton. The danger was great that local dialects would take precedence over the northern tongue and destroy China's cultural unity—the only real unity existing at the time in the whole subcontinent. This danger was even intensified by those who advocated abandoning ideograms altogether in favor of an ordinary alphabet with vowels and consonants. Since ideograms were the only link between all parts of China, were indeed the foundation of a Far Eastern civilization which included Japan and Korea as well as China, the risk of irreparable disruption was frightening.

A strong reaction set in and "High Chinese," a modernized version of the former Mandarin language, was adopted as the national tongue—a new medium of expression which was closer to the vernacular than the old literary language but also more concise and less long-winded than the popular tongues. Yet the problem presented by the use of ideograms in the modern life of an industrial world remains formidable. New technical terms cannot be created by the use of abstract symbols representing conventional sounds, but by the juxtaposition of ideas. A telegram, for instance, has to be depicted by the ideographic combination "not-have-wire-lightning-communication." Even boiled down to a few thousand, the characters present such hieroglyphic unwieldiness that they are an insuperable obstacle to technical efficiency. A script born out of aesthetic preoccupations cannot compete with a simple, logical and abstract alphabet. Even the Japanese have at times advocated the substitution of Romaji, a Western script, especially after the disastrous experiences of World War II, when the clumsiness of the ideograms slowed down communications to the extent of contributing to military defeats.

The language-script problem was only one facet of the tragic breakdown of the whole civilized structure. With that breakdown went the arts and crafts, now that the discriminating market for such refined products was doomed—except for Western collectors who disdained modern production anyway and persisted in searching for "antiques." Chinese wealth now went into manufactured products, machines from Japan or the West, American cars, refrigerators, plumbing, radios. The crafts of China were sacrificed, and old temples and palaces were burned to the ground, torn down, or left to rot away in disrepair. Painters and sculptors starved—old China was truly dying.

The collapse of a civilization is always accompanied by a social upheaval of volcanic proportions. The justification of a land-owning gentry living off the labor of tenant farmers lies in its being the warden of a precious cultural heritage which is at the disposal of all who care to master it. Providing many of the artists and most of the poets and philosophers; studying, preserving and annotating the great classics; bringing their teaching up to date; preserving the ethical values of the traditional philosophies, and serving the state in the capacity of ill-paid mandarins whose personal integrity was beyond question, in other words "living" China's traditional culture, the Chinese gentry had a moral right to its existence as the dominant social class. In Asia in general, where culture is not a mere matter of bookish, intellectual knowledge but of actual permeation of the scholar by all the ethical, artistic and poetic components of the culture, where true philosophic knowledge is not a mere matter of *knowing* with the mind but one of *altering* the whole human being, culture can be had only through long and hard work, and cannot be enclosed within the covers of abstract books. Such cultures have to be "lived," failing which they disappear from the surface of the earth— as Pharaonic Egypt disappeared before the birth of Confucius.

But when, for one reason or another, the culture embodied in this social class loses all validity and its correlative civilization perishes, this class itself is in danger of complete extermination—unless it can adapt itself instinctively to altered conditions, a remarkable feat accomplished by the Japanese ruling class in the nineteenth century. A refined mandarin or private scholar, poet or philosopher, well versed in Confucianism and in all the refinements of Chinese life, could always command the respect of his tenant farmers. He was, then, all of one piece, a harmonious representative of a great civilization, the essential although standardized cog in the huge mechanism which keeps the cosmic play of Yin and Yang within the bonds of Heavenly harmony. But the modernized and partly Westernized version of this landlord who has become totally uninterested in the culture which justified his social being, who brushes aside the old code of ethics and immorally squeezes extortionate rentals out of his hard-working tenants in order to purchase the newest type of Western-made gadget or spend fortunes on lavish entertainment which is not even in good artistic taste, such a landlord has no right whatsoever to his privileged status.

This change came over China in the early part of the twentieth century, and the consequent loss of moral standards and of a sense of responsibility by the landowning gentry prepared the ground for a cyclonic uprising of the agrarian masses. Overpopulation, economic depressions all over the world, disorganized markets and increasing rentals rendered the position of millions of Chinese farmers intolerable. And their main enemy was slowly becoming the new, modernized landlord who had abandoned the old-fashioned morality which went with a vanished culture but had failed to substitute another code. He was a fossil, a relic of a dying past whose parasitical existence could no longer be tolerated.

In post-Manchu China, the landlord problem was becoming acute, as it had become many times before in Chinese history but never with such fundamental gravity. Peasant revolts had occurred for three thousand years, but they had always been centered around economic problems: floods, famines or high rentals. Never before had such tragic and growing economic plight been welded to the complete collapse of a civilization. It was this, and this alone, which explained the subsequent agrarian typhoon and the ensuing atomization of the fabric of Chinese society.

General economic conditions enhanced the gravity of the situation. A substantial part of the gentry itself was being slowly ruined by the fall in value of the land and was being replaced by rapacious usurers and moneylenders. This "modernized" gentry, having thrown overboard the old moral code which was part and parcel of Confucianism, began to extract extortionate rentals with the help of corrupt authorities and local war lords. In the old days, the gentry would plot and scheme and struggle politely although ruthlessly within the limits of the imperial court and under the imperious arbitration of the Son of Heaven. But now court and ruler were gone and the field of intrigue was vast China herself. Cliques threw provinces and armies against each other. Taxes were collected by the war lords many years in advance to finance their internecine wars and private luxuries. Floods and famine devastated the Yellow River area while wholesale banditry and maritime piracy organized themselves on the large scale befitting such auspicious circumstances.

With the industrialization of Manchuria and of the coastal areas, the value of land began to change and rural estates became a mobile capital engulfed in all the fluctuations of a modern capitalist economy. Railroads, industries, public buildings started a fantastic land speculation which demoralized the old-fashioned gentry, who understood nothing about trade and capitalism and to whom private incomes had never been anything but the means to lead their cultured lives without having to worry about the future. Furthermore, agricultural prices fell disastrously under the impact of importation of cheaper rice and other primary produce while Japanese silk competed successfully with Chinese silk—increasing the plight of millions of tenant farmers who were no more able to grasp the essence of "productive money," of dynamic and functional money along Western lines, than were the landlords.

The old gentry of China fought tooth and nail a mysterious enemy they could not understand and were driven to fight their own people in the end—through intrigues with the ruthless war lords, through political pressure on the central government (which they finally captured for a brief, war-torn period in Chungking after having wrested control from the hands of the coastal capitalists [8]) and through private armies in the provinces. This agrarian problem was *the* great social problem of China, and for a long time none of the contending factions and leaders in China understood it—least of all Sun Yat-sen.

11

IN SEARCH OF
A NEW PHILOSOPHY

A great upheaval was brewing in China's immense countryside, the upheaval of elementary, instinctive, unintellectual
and totally primitive forces. Meanwhile, intellectual preoccupations provoked by the impact of the West and the subsequent collapse of the old civilization were monopolized by a
few large cities: Peking, Tientsin, Shanghai and Canton, the
various focuses of China's contemporary thinking. It was in
those urban settlements that the psychological impact of the
West was most strongly felt, where the Chinese intelligentsia
was searching for answers to the vast problems confronting the
Celestial Land and at the same time saw the old order pass
away forever without regret. It was in the cities that the true
impact of the industrial West was felt and that the intellectual framework of the Chinese revolution was worked out.

The revolution itself was the result of the interplay between
the intellectual doctrines elaborated in the cities by the respected scholars and the instinctive, primitive explosions of
rural anger; this was the beginning of the formidable alliance
between scholars and peasants before which everything with-
ers away in China. But even deeper than all these political,
social and philosophic problems, floating on the borderline
between consciousness and subconsciousness, was a profound
hatred of the West, of the humiliation it had imposed upon
China and of the stunning speed with which it had overthrown the mighty civilization of the Celestial Empire. Every
sacrifice which might restore China's collective "face" and
dignity would be worth while. Underlying all the changes, the
new doctrines, the peasant revolts, the war lords and the civil

and foreign wars, the old constants of China remained unimpaired. The old socialistic tendencies of Emperor Wang
Mang and of Wang An-shih, the ethics of Confucianism, the
sacred "Right of Rebellion" of Mencius and the constant reference to historical perspective, all came back to merge with
the new doctrines, because all were still alive in China's collective subconscious, because they were the very soul of China.

Beyond all this, a great need was felt for a complete overhauling of Chinese cosmic concepts, of a new metaphysical
system which alone could replace the old, discredited world-
outlook. Reasonable, humanistic and essentially utilitarian as
they were, the Chinese of the 1920's felt the religious urge
which every human being, individually or collectively, feels
in times of great stress and sorrow. They felt the need for a
new redemptive "faith," a new explanation of past history
which was being made clear to China by Western research,
now carried out along objective lines. This past they rejected
with bitter violence in the midst of their unlimited tragedy,
but they could not ignore it. As their ancestors had embraced
Buddhism with fervor after the T'ang collapse, so they now
embraced with equal frenzy any one of the innumerable religions or philosophies which were pouring into China's cultural void. They craved a new interpretation of human destiny
which Confucianism, Taoism and Buddhism no longer provided, new standards of belief which were compatible with
the new world emerging and which Christianity could not
give them. China's religious instincts had awakened, and few
among the influential foreigners understood this cardinal fact.

Chinese philosophical thought at the time of the empire's
breakdown was in a highly confused state, and the two decades
which followed aggravated its remarkable sterility. Compared
to the relative wealth of Japanese thinking, the Chinese appeared to be floundering around helplessly, floating indiscrimi-
nately from one extreme to another and totally unable to
evolve a constructive philosophy which might do justice to
the past as it did to the present and the future. Chinese thinking had always been noted for its total absence of discursive

logic—a glaring weakness when contrasted not only with Greek thought but even with Indian philosophy—and its unsystematic expression of intuitive understanding. Its main effort had always been directed along the lines of social philosophy, and as such it had surpassed in efficiency and profundity all other similar disciplines in the world. Yet many Chinese thinkers saw that the old systems were totally inadequate in view of the entirely new conditions created by the appearance of an industrial world. The result was that three main currents of thought emerged from China's cultural collapse: reaction toward the past, total rejection of the past welded to an unqualified worship of Western-type scientism, and, finally, historical materialism.

That the culture of the past still had a magnetic appeal for many Chinese thirsting for stability and a fixed system of ethical standards is proved by the fact that the constitution of the Republic of China proclaimed in 1917 that "Confucius is to be held in reverence," [1] and that as late as the middle of the century the Kuomintang still celebrated the Great Master's birthday with official fervor. A few old-fashioned philosophers—who, as human beings, stood head and shoulders above their modernistic, iconoclastic fellow-thinkers—still attempted to adapt China's traditional culture to the modern world.

The pitiable efforts of K'ang Yu-wei succeeded in extracting from Confucius' writings full justification for such incongruous notions as democracy, world federalism, communism and other contemporary doctrines, to end finally in the *Ta T'ung*, the Age of Great Peace of the Master's Record of Rites—which sounded even more mythically remote in K'ang's sketchy historical analysis than it could possibly have sounded in Confucius' days.[2]

Far superior was Ku Hung-ming's intensely conservative analysis of both Chinese and Western civilization, his understanding of the "terminated" character of Eastern evolution compared to the still unfinished Western process, his criticism of the West's lack of Tao and of its general mental confusion [3]

—a feeling undoubtedly produced by the lack of homogeneity in the Western message. The object of Ku's admiration, however, was by no means a contemporary China which he deemed decadent but the gracious China of the T'ang, and it was in contemporary Japan rather than in China that he found its best modern embodiment. As a staunch and irrepressible old conservative, Ku remained faithful to the fallen Manchus to the bitter end—not because they were Manchus but because they had upheld as long as possible the collapsing structure of China's great civilization. He might have been blind to the contemporary trends of history but his scathing criticism of Western civilization was often pertinent and found some powerful echoes in the West itself, especially after World War I. He denounced the West for having abandoned the grand unity of life which co-ordinates all of man's activities and gives purpose to his striving, but he put forth no remedy save an impossible return toward a dead past.

A last and interesting conservative was Liang Sou-ming, a professor of Indian philosophy at Peking University whose fervent admiration for Indian thought led him to believe that, ultimately, Western culture would gradually give way before a resurgence of Sino-Indian culture. Later he rejected Buddhism and, almost alone among his intellectual peers, embraced Confucianism. A few stragglers such as Chang Chün Li and Liang Ch'i Yüeh attacked the prevailing view of the omnipotence of scientific thought and attempted, but in vain, to preserve a few fragments of China's past wisdom.

A modernist flood led by Hu Shih drowned their quivering voices, and scientism was naïvely and enthusiastically adopted by the younger generations. This new school of thought had found its dry and pedantic inspiration in the pragmatism of John Dewey—who happened to be in Peking in the 1920's as visiting professor. Hu Shih's position was for a long time dominant in academic circles. Besides taking a large share in the literary revolution which reformed the whole structure of Chinese script, he used scientism as a weapon with which to destroy all those elements of a past which were dear to the

conservatives. He inveighed against the growing interest manifested by the West in the "spiritual values of the East,"
denounced Confucius as antiquated and out of date and suggested instead—with a sure but wholly unconscious feeling for
historical parallelism—studying the critical and speculative
philosophies of the fifth, fourth and third centuries B.C.,[4] the
chaotic, war-torn age of the Warring States and of the transition from Culture to Civilization, that very same age through
which the West itself was proceeding in the twentieth century.

Essentially irreligious, pragmatic Hu Shih led a group of
thinkers such as Wu Chih Hui who intended to base their
outlook on life exclusively on science, disregarding all the
other factors in China's past culture, or even those in Western
culture, which had gone into the actual building up of modern
science.[5] It is not for the first nor the last time that one can
observe this psychologically revealing phenomenon in the
contemporary thought of the East: a complete indifference in
regard to the mainspring of Western culture coupled with a
desperately passionate desire to annex, somehow or other, the
instrument of contemporary Western power, science. The
methods used by such worshipers of science—who one and all
misunderstand scientific thinking in the first place—take after
the old magic far more than after the dynamic and rigorous
experimental methods of the true scientists. The realistic
Japanese who actually "captured" the scientific thinking and
the applied sciences of the West and translated their thoughts
into acts, understood this perfectly and were mentally
equipped to uphold Kyoson Tsuchida's pertinent analysis that
"granting that the superiority of the Western civilization is in
its measurements and technique, that fact implies a spirit
underlying and characterizing it, which we may call the 'urge
toward civilization,' entirely different from the Oriental spirit
and when the two civilizations meet—no matter from what
angle—the real encounter is between these two spiritual elements of which the West has a special unity not found in the
Oriental." [6]

The dilemma between what might be termed the conservatives and the modernists, between the traditionalists and the scientists, could not be resolved on their level. But a third school was soon to take shape, the Marxist school of historical materialism, which went far beyond the second group by moving away from mere intellectualism and empty discussion to the higher spheres of religious fervor and emotion and, especially, action. In terms of Hegelian dialectics, the conservatives were the thesis, the modernists the antithesis and the Marxists-Leninists the synthesis. With the latter, we move away from the ineffectual worship of science and industrialism to the world of practical politics in which thought is transmuted into action.

But moving beyond the confines set by the second group implies unavoidably reverting to the past under disguise. And this is truly what the Chinese Marxists set out to do, although quite unconsciously. They closed China's first revolutionary cycle by incorporating in their modernized structure all those traditional elements and subconscious yearnings to which the Westernized "modernists" refused to render full justice.

The striking poverty of contemporary Chinese thinking goes a long way to explain both the temporary success of certain Western schools of thought, such as the pragmatists, utilitarians and positivists with their unmetaphysical and irreligious materialism—and also their static view of historical evolution—and the inability of the Chinese to penetrate deeply into the more profound and abstruse German philosophy of the nineteenth century. American pragmatism, English utilitarianism and French positivism dominated a large section of China's budding cultural institutions, colleges and universities. Had the Chinese been as alert as the Japanese, German thinking would have made its weight felt soon enough and would in all likelihood, in spite of the financial support of Western institutions, have captured the largest portion of the Chinese intelligentsia. But as events subsequently turned out, it was the cruder form of Hegelian dialectics as embodied in Marxism which captured a country seething with revolutionary elements.

What could the Westerners do if not help, unwittingly, in the destruction of China's culture, creating an emotional void which it was unable to fill? To a people thirsting for a new faith, they brought nothing but dry-as-dust pronouncements, uninspiring messages on the need for industrialization and economic productivity, and a typical Anglo-Saxon unconcern for metaphysical explanations. How were the Chinese expected to reconcile Dewey's pragmatism with the religious message of Christian missions when the West itself could not overcome its cultural atomism?

In the depth of despair and humiliation into which the people of China had fallen, there was no indigenous light to which they could turn. Sun Yat-sen himself was a practical idealist but an uninspiring leader whose Protestant Christianity did not compensate for his lack of dramatic appeal and could not make up for his being no prophet—such as the founder of the T'ai P'ing movement had been. His only faith was nationalism; but what could nationalism mean in a vast and complex subcontinent such as China, in which the people had always thirsted for universalism and could not develop an insular patriotism of the Japanese type?

In the midst of the postrevolution confusion, John Dewey and Bertrand Russell were invited in 1919–20 to lecture at Peking University in the hope that they might offer some striking solution to China's ills. Russell's influence was small and largely negative, Dewey's more important, more lasting and far more destructive. Nothing illustrates the incomprehension of the West more glaringly than the sight of two distinguished Western thinkers, of whom the Chinese expected some dramatic pronouncements befitting the momentous change of historical phase through which China was proceeding, and who merely advocated a slow, undramatic and painstaking effort to catch up with the West along democratic lines.

Bertrand Russell had correctly understood the psychological urge of the Chinese intellectuals: "The Chinese, even the most modern, look to the white nations, especially America,

for moral maxims to replace those of Confucius." But, confused by his own intellectual skepticism, he remained blind to
the depth and frenetic power of this psychological urge, and
he added: "They have not yet grasped that men's morals in
the mass are the same everywhere: they do as much harm as
they dare, and as much good as they must." [7] Nor are the
Chinese ever likely to grasp such a notion, because it is simply
not true; Bertrand Russell himself owed his freedom to ex-
pound his theories to a Christian code of ethics which he
despised and flouted. He then crowned an edifice of miscon-
ceptions by concluding: "What we have to teach the Chinese
is not morals, or ethical maxims about government, but science
and technical skill." This was the sure road to disaster for
Western influence. And when he concluded this masterpiece
of incomprehension by stating: "The hegemony of Russia in
Asia would not, to my mind, be in any way regrettable," [8] he
virtually abdicated in the name of Western civilization all
real influence on the course of China's future history.

Toward the end of 1920, Bertrand Russell took violent issue
with the habit of "empty discussions regarding this or that
ism," emphasizing again that the root of China's misfortunes
lay in her low productivity and lack of industries. A storm of
protest arose from the ranks of the young socialists in Shanghai, who maintained that whatever good capitalism may have
done to the West or to Japan, China sought a more ethical
system of production based on *co-operation* and not *competition*. The very notion of competition and everlasting struggle
—springing from the innermost depths of the Western soul
under the shape of the eternal duel between God and Satan
—was totally alien to the Chinese mind, which conceived only
of the rhythmic and complementary "co-operative" interplay
of Yin and Yang.

But the nub of the whole discussion was evidently that the
Chinese were not searching for merely intellectual explanation
but that, divested of all the trappings of their past civilization,
they were searching for a new emotional and all-embracing
creed. When, later on, the Russian Marxist Radek leveled the

same criticism at the young Chinese Marxists, the latter did not take issue with him but accepted the criticism meekly and mended their ways, proving beyond a shadow of doubt that they were quite prepared to discard empty theorizing and to act—provided the emotional stimulus of a new religion was forthcoming. Industrialization and economic productivity were meaningless terms in a country which was falling apart politically, without any deep national consciousness save its anti-Western xenophobia, and without any basic unity. The very representatives of the hated West now advocated slow, patient, progressive work and a pragmatic, utilitarian and positivist broad-mindedness to a people thirsting for heroic solutions, for a passionate belief that would dispel their mental chaos, that would put an end to the bitter humiliation of the recent past and the present.

The Chinese intelligentsia was still perusing the output of Western thinkers with diligence when the October Revolution broke out in Russia and dramatized Marxism, a doctrine which does not appear to have been examined at all in China before Lenin's rise to power. In an undeveloped country such as China, pure Marxism must have seemed completely inappropriate, its economic theories entirely out of place, and the fact that it was overlooked until the actual establishment of the Russian Soviets must have seemed entirely justifiable. And Marx, no doubt, would have wholeheartedly concurred.[9]

The result was that Marxism appeared in China through its Leninist adaptation—the "Marxism of the era of Imperialism" —as an entirely new doctrine in which Asia had a large part to play, an immense drama which was no longer restricted to the Western world according to strict Marxist orthodoxy. And to men already conscious of the notion of historical perspective— both in its purely Chinese form and in its Western shape— and largely indifferent to mere nationalism, Marxism-Leninism presented a doctrine that would satisfy both the Chinese yearning for unrestricted universalism—for doctrines applicable to all men Under Heaven, *T'ien Hsia*—and also satisfy their deep-rooted inclination toward some form of socialism. Freedom in the Western sense, and especially its Anglo-Saxon variety, they could never understand—nor could their future opponents of the Kuomintang grasp such a wholly un-Chinese concept. The few intellectuals and liberals inclined toward the Western viewpoint, followers of Dewey and similar Western thinkers, had no roots in the country and were bound to be crushed by the various contending forces with psychological roots in Chinese consciousness and social roots in China's Great Society.

The two founders of the Chinese Communist Party were Li Ta-chao and Ch'en Tu-hsiu, both of whom had great prestige in academic circles and great influence among their students at Peking University. And it is significant that none of the founders of the Communist Party were workers but that they were scholars, scions of mandarin families or well-to-do middle-class bourgeois or landlords. Still more significant—and this set them sharply apart from the more "southern" or coastal Kuomintang—they all came from Hupeh, Hunan and Szechwan, in central and western China.[10]

In all the main political events of China, university and college students were destined to play an important, almost essential part. A great deal of the academic power and prestige in China was based on the innate respect of every Chinese for mandarin-like scholarship. The mandarins were now gone, but the mandarin spirit was and still is too deep-rooted in Chinese consciousness to be easily eradicated. Furthermore, the prestige of the professors among the students was bolstered by the traditional Asian concept of teaching as being based on the *personal* relationship between professor and student far more than in the West, where the transmission of intellectual knowledge is largely impersonal. To this day, a subtle bond establishes itself between student and professor which is far closer to the disciple-master relationship of Confucianist days than to the merely intellectual and often mechanical transference of intellectual knowledge prevailing in the contemporary West. At a time of immense upheavals, the influence of intellectual leaders is therefore incomparably greater in a country such as China than it could ever be in the West or in the rest of Asia. In this sense, the Chinese university is closer to a church than to a Western institution of higher education.

Ch'en Tu-hsiu's intellectual development was in many ways typical of the befuddled thinking of many Chinese scholars. Having participated in the literary revolution alongside Hu Shih, his rejection of China's cultural past was total and was largely motivated by its "inefficiency" under the impact of the West. And it is extremely necessary at this point to keep in mind that the unspiritual and usually skeptical Chinese individual is one of the most superstitious of all human beings, a born utilitarian who has not much use for religion and metaphysics in times of happiness and prosperity but who is ever anxious to gain possession of magic charms and potent sorcery to ward off unpleasantness. So long as the Book of Rites and full observance of the Tao could regulate the world and put man in tune with Heaven, all was well. But once the whole ritual machinery had broken down, every bit of it, every cog, was thrown out.

Ch'en's attitude was that of most Chinese thinkers in the 1920's, but a certain yearning for final explanations impelled him to go beyond mere scientism and outpace Hu Shih. He perceived that the Western impact was mainly Protestant and Anglo-Saxon and, disregarding the real, profound basis of Western culture, he sought, like so many other Orientals, the short cut, the "secret" of Western power in its nineteenth-century development. He came out with "science and democracy" as his first, tentative answer. Democracy he conceived mainly as economic freedom for the individual, and science as a materialistic explanation of the workings of the universe which disposed of ancestor worship as well as of Buddhist or Taoist cosmology. In short, Ch'en was an agnostic materialist.

Li Ta-chao was a man of much deeper views whose main bent was metaphysical. A professor of history, he was among the few Chinese scholars who had been profoundly influenced by Hegel and by German philosophy of history. He had attempted to lay the basis of a philosophic system in his two famous essays, *Ch'ing Chun* ("Youth") and *Chin* ("Now"), in which Buddhist influence was noticeable and blended easily with German metaphysics.

Starting from the Yin and Yang dualism familiar to the traditional philosophy of China, he proceeded to sketch an evolutionary doctrine along Bergsonian lines, according to which Reality is an endless flux which relativity divides into innumerable perceptible phenomena, the *wan wu* of classical Chinese philosophy. Man is transient in the Buddhist sense but his inner ego is part of the cosmic flux and therefore part of Reality itself. However, instead of putting the Buddhist accent of pessimism on this evolution, Li adopted the boundless optimism of the Occident which he linked with the traditional optimism of China's full acceptance of the life-process. Furthermore, he remained faithful to the old Chinese conception which had justified all the distortions and rewriting of the historical past in the name of morality. He claimed that, in spite of the ceaseless flux, only the present exists, that the past is mere frozen memory and the future mere projection of the present; and he found no contradiction in his firm belief in progressive evolution—in a constant renewal of the universe on endlessly higher planes—presenting the whole evolution as a succession of connected "presents." From here on, Li swerved sharply again toward German philosophy in his denial of the individual's supremacy and claimed that the individual is significant only as part of the universal spirit.

Hegel was bound to strike an Asian echo in Li Ta-Chao with his unindividualistic attitude, with his negation of the individual's reality apart from the whole. Li, however, added to the Orient's traditional negation of individualism the dynamic, "linear" perspective of history opened to him by Hegel and his firm belief in the existence of vast, impersonal forces shaping historical evolution.

This general metaphysics laid the basis of his future conversion to Marxism, to which he would come from Hegel as early Russian Marxists had before him. Into this metaphysical structure Li injected his passionate conviction that the old China was not so much dead as undergoing a rejuvenating process: "What we must prove to the world is not that the old China is not dead but that a new youthful China is in the process of being born." [11] Confident in his belief that the process of contemporary history-in-the-making, rather than isolated individuals, would regenerate China, Li waited like Ch'en for the call of an epoch-making event.

Li Ta-chao was the first Chinese to seize eagerly the messianic message of the October Revolution and embrace Leninism wholeheartedly. Now at last, he was able to state his fundamental opposition to the narrow creed of nationalism and his faith in Bolshevism, the most potent destroyer of that false religion: "Henceforth all national boundaries, all differences of classes, all barriers to freedom will be swept away." [12] To Li and to numerous intellectuals who followed him gradually into Marxism, the October Revolution was the spark which would ignite, explode and destroy the Western world's imperial structure, and Leninism was the gospel of all those who sought to help in the destruction. Now the West could be attacked safely without having to sacrifice the "positive" acquisitions of Western culture: science and industrialism; they would simply become incorporated in a larger synthesis. Now at last, the main problem of dissociating the two apparently indissoluble components of the Western structure—its political imperialism and its scientific power—was solved.

Li went into action immediately and in the summer of 1918 founded the "Society for the Study of Marxism" at Peking University. Very soon its meetings were attended by a crowd of young and eager students, among whom we can already note the name of Mao Tse-tung, the assistant librarian. The upheaval produced by World War I, the tremendous loss of prestige to the entire Western world, the spread of militant Communism from Russia to Central Europe, fanned the curiosity of the thinking Chinese. Earnest students pored over

Marx and Engels—and then over Leninism as Moscow began to spread the new, more up-to-date version of old-fashioned Marxism.

Meanwhile, nationalism and xenophobia were once more on the rise as the continuous encroachments of the West and the manifestations of Japan's imperialism provoked violent reactions on the part of the students. Such nationalism was an explosion of anger rather than a real patriotism based on a simple "nationalistic" consciousness and was, in any case, completely alien to the concepts of Ch'en and Li, who stepped right out of Chinese culture's traditional universalism into Marxism-Leninism's broader internationalism. But the professors could not resist the passionate wave and were carried along, out of the sphere of intellectual speculation into the realm of practical, down-to-earth politics which contemporary circumstances fully warranted.

Still, before his total conversion to Marxism-Leninism, Ch'en made a last desperate attempt under Dewey's influence at finding a solid base for his democratic concepts. He turned for a last time toward China's past, discovering that below the mandarin bureaucracy a great many local institutions prospered in relative freedom, institutions which had survived the revolution and might form the framework of a new democracy. Here was the useful nucleus of a coming democracy which might be built up without ignoring all of China's traditional institutions.

But, strangely enough, something was yet lacking. Chen wanted to weld his actions and thoughts to an all-embracing formula, a philosophic panacea which would have universal value, susceptible of taking care of all future problems that might arise as a result of action. We know now that this psychological urge has been in evidence all through Chinese history; Confucius himself replied to a disciple who wondered whether the master had accumulated a vast fund of knowledge: "One single principle suffices to understand all." [13] Chinese philosophical doctrines had never elaborated logical structures in which parts could be detached from the whole, and those who sought to understand a particular doctrine had to disregard the articulations of the structure in favor of the one central idea, the magic formula and indispensable keystone without which the entire structure toppled to the ground. In order to grasp this central idea whose efficiency was always supposed to be universal, one had to go through a long initiation, replete with mental exercises, and a discipline which pervaded the student's life and which was concluded when this magic formula had at last pervaded his whole being. Mere intellectual effort conducted along logical lines could lead the disciple nowhere. The extraordinary feeling of appalling boredom and banality which appears to suffuse most Chinese classics is entirely due to this hermetic quality of all Chinese doctrines, all of which seek, not merely to *inform*, but to *transform* the student and, through the full, intuitive understanding of its central idea, put him in tune with the social, political and cosmic world—thereby acquiring the virtue of universal panacea which is claimed by one and all Chinese systems. To put forth a logical, discursive doctrine made of detachable parts and modestly claiming only a limited efficacy is the sure road to failure in China.

This basic trait of Chinese psychology was completely ignored by all those Westerners who attempted to influence the Chinese intelligentsia, and especially by John Dewey, whose failure—a mere reflection of the general failure of the West, of course—had catastrophic consequences. He insisted on rejecting universal solutions for mankind's ills. Ch'en, who sought the universalism of a redeeming faith, could not help turning to Marxism, like a drowning man clasping a floating snake. In 1920 his conversion to Leninism was total and irrevocable.

Li Ta-chao had preceded him, although with greater moral reservations. He was still an idealist but he slowly swerved away from his former spiritualism and gradually came to the conclusion that moral sense need not be connected with any supernatural agency but was in fact the outcome of a social Darwinism. The relativity inherent to any ethical system is due, in this light, to changes in the mode of production, each moral concept being tied to a definite economic system. Although he unorthodoxically substituted biological for social foundations, Li soon considered that his conversion to Leninism was complete. Diamat (Dialectical Materialism) became the new all-embracing, universal formula which now took into account all the contemporary phenomena of Western imperialism, scientific knowledge and industrialism.

Apart from intellectual considerations, the political circumstances of the postwar era might have driven both Li and Ch'en into Marxism anyway, in spite of their many mental reservations. The part they were constrained to play in the May Fourth movement, the incredible anarchy subsequent to Yüan Shih-k'ai's death and the total moral breakdown of the times forced this new creed upon them. Ch'en turned violently against Hu Shih, his former partner and still a faithful pragmatist, who criticized the Marxist catchall formula, its biased and one-sided view of history and especially its almost fatalistic predetermination—to which Ch'en replied that he insisted on retaining Marxism's synthetic monism in religion, economics, politics and morality.[14] It is clear now that it was Ch'en who was faithful to Chinese tradition and Hu Shih who was thoroughly blinded by an exaggerated Westernization that was gradually alienating him from the mainstream of Chinese intellectual life. It would not be an exaggeration to say, at this point, that Marxism restored China's traditional way of thinking and largely appealed to a cultural reactionary movement under a new guise—a movement against which Western influence, through sheer ignorance and lack of comprehension, was powerless.

The importance of the whole controversy lay in the fact that it was preparing China's future for generations to come. The two first groups of thinkers, the traditionalist and the modernist, and lastly the historical materialist—the group which was destined to overthrow the other two because it alone was able to fit new concepts borrowed from historical materialism into China's old traditional way of thinking—

these were the real protagonists whose thoughts, whose mental search and anguish determined China's future. The subsequent wars and upheavals were but the physical extensions of their cogitations, and the outcome of such struggles was largely predetermined by their philosophical conclusions. They alone were able to evolve a workable synthesis and strike the imagination of China's intelligentsia to the extent of capturing the larger portion of China's educated youth. The disaster was that Marxism should have been the synthetic agent, because of the very failure of the West to provide the necessary inspiration.

Both Li and Ch'en took with them a large number of enthusiastic students, among whom were most of the future leaders of the Chinese Communist Party. Many of them had tried other formulas: Tolstoyanism, guild socialism and even anarchism, which seduced Mao Tse-tung for some time and which had powerful roots in China's traditional Taoism. Ch'en promptly squelched all attempts made to organize an anarchist movement under the double inspiration of Bakounine and Taoism, and its speedy disappearance points to the enduring influence of Confucianism's spirit of discipline and authority.

At the same time, it became clear that there was little in common between the northern intelligentsia of Peking—who were slowly swerving to wholehearted Marxism with its universalism—and the southern groups in Canton with Sun Yat-sen's Kuomintang, its virulent nationalism which the northerners despised, and its commercial atmosphere which the northerners—heirs to both Confucianism and Marxism—despised even more.[15]

The relations between Ch'en and Sun Yat-sen were at all times cool, and long before the revolution Ch'en had been strongly disgusted by the Cantonese's crude anti-Manchu movement. Now, faithful to the old, traditional Chinese yearning for Totality and universalism, he poured all his scorn on a narrow-minded nationalism which could never satisfy the Sons of Han: "Chinese scholars in ancient times and our old-fashioned peasants only knew of the world and the universe and did not understand what a nation was. Now, however, we have a group of half-baked people who preen themselves on their modern learning and who are constantly prating about the 'nation' and 'patriotism.' Some of our students who are returning from Japan are also bringing back this shallow, selfish type of nationalism. At the present time when the cry is being raised in student circles to boycott Japanese goods, ought not our students to boycott this spiritual importation from Japan as well . . . an importation which is even more harmful?" [16] Now, however, the search for the all-embracing faith was ended and many among the best Chinese of the time turned toward Moscow, toward the new Mecca of the modern world where the Marxist religion had taken up its abode. Lenin was its prophet, and its dramatically apocalyptic vision of world history began to exercise a strange fascination on their minds.

Marxist orthodoxy had always prescribed a long capitalist stage—such as that of the "bourgeois" nineteenth-century West—before the socialist revolution could be consummated. Lenin had attempted to alter this proviso and almost without transition, save for the brief New Economic Policy concessions, threw a backward Russia directly into the socialistic stage, bypassing the truly capitalistic era which had never really started in Tzarist Russia. But he himself strongly implied that the small capitalistic framework which had existed hitherto was sufficient to justify Russia's immediate socialization. He would never have assimilated China's completely undeveloped structure to Russia's semideveloped economy.

But Ch'en Tu-hsiu was, in his profound ignorance, just as impatient as Lenin had been in Russia and he attempted to deny the necessity of a capitalist stage in China. Lenin himself, with his acute sense of political realities and his anxious search for allies in Asia—which ranged from such ruthlessly unprincipled war lords as Wu P'ei-fu to Sun Yat-sen's Kuomintang—was soon converted to Ch'en's views. He gradually worked out his famous doctrine according to which the

Comintern should adopt a special policy in "colonial" areas; this special policy consisted more or less in compressing the capitalist stage by uniting temporarily with democratic, bourgeois, nationalist and anti-imperialist movements, with the express proviso that the Communist Party would preserve its full independence.

The great problem at this stage was to translate all those brilliant theories into concrete actions, and it is still a great question whether the Chinese Communists would have ever been able to build a political machine without Russian help. However, help was forthcoming almost immediately and on an impressive scale. Gregory Voitinsky arrived in June 1920 as the first Comintern agent and settled down in Shanghai. The Russians had forty years of revolutionary experience behind them and they had acquired in the last few years a practical knowledge of government, administration and organization which was invaluable to the willing but totally inexperienced Chinese. Organization soon took shape: Creation of socialist youth corps, formation of a "Marxist Study Group," gradual elimination of all real or potential "deviationists" followed one another, and a full-fledged Communist Party materialized in the summer of 1921.

Many of the new converts were only tentatively committed, ignorant as they were of the rudiments of their new religion and totally unconscious of the profound and terrible implications of active Communism. Under the firm hand of Russian advisers, however, the party emerged and strengthened gradually and, following the orthodox Marxist dogma, undertook the first and elementary step of establishing contact with the small, scattered proletariat of China.

The growth of Chinese industry during World War I had considerably increased this proletariat, and large masses of cheap labor had agglomerated in densely crowded coastal areas. Western influence had already been strong enough to expose this proletariat to anarchist or socialist influences, but it seems that some profound Chinese instincts had deflected the energies of the newborn unions toward a purely utilitarian program of action, toward immediate betterment of their economic fate rather than devotion to any abstract political doctrine. The task of the Communist Party was therefore to alter that state of mind and inject a religious fervor into this small class of men who were historically predestined, according to Marxist-Leninist dogma, to lead China toward her Communist future. A "China Labor Union Secretariat" was created for this very purpose, and organizational work started almost immediately; railroad laborers, the workers of the Hanyehp'ing foundry, and dockyard workmen were soon organized and inspired.

The whole structure was vitiated from the start, however, by the very fact that the intellectuals who were the mainspring of the party were not able to establish more than a superficial contact with the working classes and failed to transmit their emotional message to the urban proletariat. Yet the workers followed them for a while, for as long as they could reasonably hope to better their living conditions under Communist leadership. But when it became clear that they were in for a bloody and hopeless struggle and that the aim of such sacrifices was not to improve a frightfully low standard of living but to further the "cause," they deserted *en masse* and by 1927 had abandoned Communism entirely.

But in 1922 the outward indications were that the Chinese proletariat was quite prepared to play its revolutionary role, and its eventual collapse was not foreseen. In Moscow, meanwhile, China was beginning to loom large, not only as a country ripe for Communism, but even more as a potential ally of immense strength against the West. Leninism pointed toward a close-knit alliance of all anti-Western elements, not toward an independent development of Chinese Communism as such. Besides, most Russian Communists—primitive, unintellectual and shrewd men of action—had a certain contempt for their Chinese coreligionists and for the bookish, intellectual instincts which they had inherited from the old mandarins. "Many of our comrades out there locked themselves up in their studies and studied Marx and Lenin as they had once studied Confucius," laughed Radek. Intensely practical and realistic, the Russians perceived that the immediate task was to develop political power by organizing the working class and to contract an alliance with the middle-class revolutionaries of the south in order to overthrow the remnants of the Peking regime—and eliminate Western influence. Communist control over China could be brought about only by organizing and leading an over-all coalition made up of all the anti-Western elements in the country.

To those impatient Chinese who expected Marxism to act with all the universal magic potency of the old formulas of their classical philosophies, who expected immediate and dramatic developments and effortless action, this Soviet decision acted as a cold shower. Moscow had to bring great pressure to bear on the Peking group as well as on many Communist sections inland before the Comintern decision was accepted and endorsed by the Chinese Communist Party as a whole. But it is unquestionably to the credit of the Russian power of persuasion that they were able to actually convert the Chinese to their long and painstaking program, where Western thinkers had failed.

It is interesting to note that idealistic Li Ta-chao had accepted Moscow's directives from the start whereas pragmatic Ch'en resisted stubbornly. He had not given up his previous "science and democracy" formula because of its slow, undramatic and largely ineffectual principle of action, to collaborate now undramatically and for a long time to come with the despised "commercial" nationalists of Canton. But he eventually submitted to party discipline and there gradually emerged the working theory that an alliance would be concluded with the Kuomintang—which had now become a "coalition party of all classes," in the Marxist jargon—in which the Communist Party would retain its full independence of action, not forgetting that it was the mouthpiece of the proletariat and the vanguard of the real revolution to come.

Party discipline was enforced with implacable rigor, and in August 1922 a special "Plenum of the Central Committee of the Chinese Communist Party" was called in Hangchow. The Russian Maring laid down the line of action while Dalin negotiated the Communist-Kuomintang alliance with Sun Yat-sen down in Canton. The naïve but also shrewd "Father of the Republic" forced the Russians to accept the principle, not of a mere external alliance, but of the obligation of all Communists to join the Kuomintang as "individuals," although he conceded that they could simultaneously retain their membership in the Communist Party.

To many Communists, the Maring decision was anathema. All of them, with Ch'en at their head, felt nothing but contempt for Sun Yat-sen's narrow nationalism, for his vague attempt to retain the traditional values of Chinese culture which they totally rejected—or so they believed at least—and for his diplomatic compromises with the hated war lords. But Moscow's decision was final and there was no appeal.

By now, the Russians had decided on a new, bold and, they thought, cleverer line of action: The Communists would infiltrate the badly organized and largely inefficient Kuomintang, gradually seize control of the party machinery and reorganize it along Leninist lines. In 1923, therefore, the Soviet agent Joffe and Sun Yat-sen issued a joint declaration sealing their alliance, and the foremost Russian envoy, Borodin, went to work on the complete overhauling of the Kuomintang machinery—without waiting for the expected Communist control to materialize. His considerable personal ascendancy over Sun Yat-sen enabled him to reorganize the Kuomintang along Leninist lines in a very short time, providing it with the best revolutionary structure conceivable in those days.[17]

The pattern of Communist action in China was now firmly set. Its main architect in Moscow had been Stalin, who was patiently working against Trotsky's virulent criticisms—and also against Ch'en's protestations, which resembled Trotsky's to an alarming extent. But Stalin's influence was fast becoming

paramount in the Marxist world and the coalition Kuomin-
tang-Communism, now centered in the south, endured until
1927—four fateful and illuminating years.

12

RISE AND FALL OF
THE KUOMINTANG

In 1923, anarchy and political chaos were supreme all over
China. Western business dominated the coastal areas, Japan
was biding her time and the war lords fought each other and
divided their spoils. The Peking regime had dwindled to a
shadow government and the new Comintern-Kuomintang
alliance was working methodically on its plan of action when
an unexpected disaster occurred: The northern war lord Wu
P'ei-fu crushed the strike of the Peking-Hankow railroad workers with bloody and decisive ruthlessness. This defeat dealt a
deathblow to the Communist labor unions from which they
never recovered. And at the same time it seriously undermined the proletarian base which is essential to any Communist movement even slightly respectful of Marxist orthodoxy.

The Communist leaders came slowly to the view that the
Chinese proletariat was immature and in no condition to lead
anything. Ch'en himself swung wholeheartedly toward the
view of firm and prolonged collaboration with the Kuomintang. He lent his full support to the gradual transformation
of Sun Yat-sen's party into a Leninist-type party with its iron
discipline, efficient organization and superb leadership, al-

though the agents of transformation were Sun Yat-sen himself, the Russian Borodin and doubtful Wang Ching-wei. Meanwhile, Borodin and his colleague Galen organized the Whampoa Military Academy with the help of Chiang Kaishek, a young, stern and promising officer.

But the gradual infiltration of the Communists into the Kuomintang aroused the keen suspicion of the underestimated right-wing, middle-class element, who went to work immediately and very effectively against the growth of Marxist-Leninist influence. In July 1924 several right-wing leaders, among them Chang Chi, Haieh Ch'ih and Feng Tzu-yu, violently attacked the Marxists in a striking pamphlet entitled "A Proposal for the Impeachment of the Communist Party." [1] And thereafter, growing suspicion of Communist motives went hand in hand with growing resistance to their infiltration —which finally led to the utilization of the Kuomintang's effectiveness and its monolithic structure, so painfully built up by the Soviet advisers, against the Communists themselves, a result hardly foreseen by either Borodin or Stalin in distant Moscow.

But before this came to pass, the alliance worked almost smoothly and Sun Yat-sen's successor, Hu Han-min, continued the policy of open collaboration with Russian advisers and Chinese Communists. And while their power within the party itself was being slowly undermined by right-wing intrigues, the Marxists went on organizing their mass action, regardless of the fact that there also their grasp was gradually slipping and that their proletarian base was slowly dwindling to nought.

On May 30, 1925, the British opened fire on a Shanghai crowd and anti-Western feeling reached a pitch of virulence. There followed a well-organized and effective boycott of British goods and, shortly afterward, a mammoth strike at the Japanese-owned textile mills of Tsingtao which raised the anti-Japanese furor to a new pitch of fanaticism. To the Kuomintang leaders who did not appreciate nor understand the importance of mass power, each new demonstration of the cunning utilization of profound social unrest by the Marxists was one more nail in the coffin of the Communist-Kuomintang alliance. This growing manifestation of right-wing anxiety and anti-Marxist feeling swelled slowly and finally broke out when Chiang Kai-shek made his famous coup of March 20, 1926, in which he seized full control of the Kuomintang machinery by removing the Communists from all prominent positions—a prelude to his weeding out every shred of Marxist influence, and to his transforming the monolithic party into his own personal tool.

To the Communists, this was an insulting blow and, in many ways, a disaster. But Chiang's prestige was considerable, and in faraway Moscow the insistence on preserving the alliance between the two parties remained as implacable as ever. A part of it was based on a natural reluctance to admit that they had been mistaken, but the main reason for this firm insistence on collaboration with virtual enemies was Chiang's plans for a northern expedition which should prove to be a devastating calamity for the West. On his part, Chiang was quite prepared to continue his alliance with the Communists, now that his freedom of action was complete and his bargaining position had improved a hundredfold. He even went as far as expelling the Kuomintang right wing, which thereupon held its own congress in Shanghai. Borodin kept on helping and advising Chiang as he had in the past, in the belief that the Northern Expedition would at last open a big field for Communist propaganda through the destruction of the war lords.

All through this period, from Lenin's death to Trotsky's expulsion from Soviet Russia, Stalin had to defend himself against bitter and often justified attacks by his mortal enemies in Moscow. These theological quarrels in the Mecca of Marxism found their reflection in the uncertain, wavering and often inconsistent policy of the Chinese Communists, whose position had already begun to deteriorate seriously. All this while Stalin pinned his hopes on the Northern Expedition, and when it started at last on its successful sweep through central

China, Moscow was firmly convinced that it would bring about
the utter destruction of Western influence in China, if not an
immediate Communization of the vast subcontinent. All those
Chinese Communists who balked at the Kuomintang alliance were expelled as Trotskyites and deviationists. But those
who were loyal were asked to remain in the Kuomintang and
simultaneously to infiltrate it and use it as a tool—by now a
sheer impossibility because of the monolithic perfection of its
structure, so fondly built by Mikhail Borodin. They were
asked, for instance, to start a radical agrarian program, but
through the Kuomintang and not independently. "The International asks us to implement our own policies. On the other
hand, it will not allow us to withdraw from the Kuomintang.
There is thus no way out," exclaimed Ch'en Tu-hsiu in
despair.[2]

The results of this confused and contradictory policy were
Chiang's victorious sweep to Shanghai and his complete and
final break with the Communists and the left wing on April
12, 1927. The steel trap now closed mercilessly on the Communists, and the carefully prepared rising of the general labor
unions was crushed and drowned in a blood bath by carefully
coached underworld gangs, whose leader Tu Yueh-sen was
rewarded by Chiang with the presidency of the Anti-Opium
League—which, in reality, gave him full legal control of the
profitable drug-smuggling business. Chinese Communism had
its back broken and lost its slender hold on the urban proletariat, while Chiang's exclusively nationalistic and anti-Com-
munist position provoked a remarkable inflow of Chinese
capital, and later on of foreign capital, which made him wholly
independent of Moscow.

This defeat was catastrophic for the Communists. They
had hoped to gain eventual control of the Kuomintang and
after the 1926 coup to base their power on the lower echelons
of the party, forgetting that they themselves had shaped the
Kuomintang in the hope of grasping its higher echelons, and
forgetting also that in a "democratic centralism" of that type
the top is dictator and the mass of the membership is power-

less and cowed into complete submission. Furthermore, they had lost all control of the weary labor unions, and the new Kuomintang swiftly built up a large number of "yellow" unions who were solely, if a little cynically, interested in the economic conditions of their worker members. These unions remained completely impervious to Communist propaganda while a gigantic "white terror" crushed anyone suspected of Marxist sympathies. Chiang Kai-shek became in fact a military dictator heading a party organized along Leninist lines, whose main purpose now was the utter destruction of his former allies and advisers.

While the Communists floundered around helplessly, Chiang consolidated his position by making peace with the banking and industrial groups on the one hand and by concluding a truce with the landowning gentry on the other. Land reform remained on the Kuomintang program, but no step was taken to implement it and, with the gentry completely reassured, Chiang was able to enter into negotiations with the northern war lords, taking up Sun Yat-sen's conciliation efforts where they had been left when the "Father of the Republic" died in 1925. Every sign pointed toward the complete destruction of the Communists. Russian advisers, formerly welcome by the Kuomintang, had to run for their lives, and Moscow lost all contact with the rising power of Chiang Kai-shek. But there still remained a separate left-wing Kuomintang to be disposed of. The anti-Chiang element had established a temporary capital in Hankow; it did not last long and had to give in under the combined pressure of the local gentry, the urban middle class and Chiang's military threat. As the Hankow government became mobile and took to the road, seeking refuge in Kiangsi, it finally shed its last "leftist coalition" taint and became purely Communist.

Chiang's diplomatic qualities sparkled brightly when dealing with and outwitting the northern war lords. The old traditional customs came back. Secret negotiations, shrewd bargaining, intrigues, poison and murder replaced actual military

combat. It was the old practical and utilitarian China all
over again, purely zoological events without historical significance whatsoever. The clock turned back thousands of years to
the days when falling and rising dynasties fought each other
with cunning duplicity.

For a time, Chiang had to recognize three main war lords
as supreme commanders: Feng Yü-hsiang, the so-called Christian general, Yen Hsi-shan, the very capable governor of
Shensi, and Li Tsung-jen. Further east, in Kansu and Sinkiang,
Chiang had to resign himself to watch, powerless, the growth
of an independent coalition of Chinese Muslim power directed
by the great Ma clan. Negotiations with all of them went on
until 1936, and although Chiang outsmarted his rivals he was
never able to abolish their power entirely. Manchuria had
long since become virtually independent under the authority
of its war lord Chang Tso-lin and, after his virtual murder
by the Japanese, under his son the "Young Marshal" Chang
Hsüeh-liang, whose violent anti-Japanese feelings did not
prevent the Empire of the Rising Sun from fastening its military and economic grip on the vast province. When Manchuria fell completely to the Japanese in 1931, the Young
Marshal had to withdraw while his overlord Chiang Kai-shek
remained impassive. Chiang had long ago given up this outlying territory which he could not possibly defend before
China proper was strong and united; and in each similar cir-
cumstance when, over the howls of anger of Chinese public
opinion, he had to give in, he was merely biding his time with
far greater realism than his critics gave him credit for.

The Generalissimo's regime appeared for a long time to be
an ideal compromise. His violent swing to the right had
reassured the West; the Kuomintang seemed to put an end
to revolution and anarchy, heralding a new constructive period in the history of China. Not only had the prewar idea of
partitioning China among the great Powers been completely
abandoned; the 1920 plan, which advocated financial control
through an international banking consortium, was shelved.
Chiang was able to do away with one capitulation after an-

other, recover the customs which had been previously alienated and, with his increased financial resources, build up a
small but excellent army on German lines. He had given up
Manchuria without striking a blow because he concentrated
on uniting China proper first and could not possibly tackle
every problem simultaneously. He was buying time, consolidating his hold on China, and was determined to avoid any
foreign involvement until such time as he felt that China's
power was sufficient to withstand the onslaught of Japan's
armed might.

All the while, Tokyo had watched the consolidating process within China with alarm. The Japanese were seized with
the same fear that had gripped them twenty years before
when Yüan Shih-k'ai attempted to retrieve the imperial crown
and reunite China. Time appeared to be working for Chiang
and, had it not been for his melodramatic capture by Chang
Hsüeh-liang at Sian, the Kuomintang might have continued
its retreat before Japan's thoroughly alarmed bellicosity. But
Chinese public opinion could not stand it any longer and a
wave of anti-Japanese emotionalism swept over China, en-
gulfing all parties and almost all personalities in its irresistible
sweep. When the Marco Polo Bridge "Incident" finally broke
out, war started between Japan and China—two years too
late for the Japanese, who had virtually united China against
them, and two years too soon for Chiang Kai-shek, who was
neither politically nor militarily ready. The stalemate which
ensued would be broken only by the intervention of an external agent: World War II and Japan's defeat in the Pacific.

From 1927 to 1937, it seemed that a coalition of China's
middle class, coastal capitalists and industrialists and provincial
gentry had at last coagulated for the good of the country, that
the left wing was decisively defeated and on the way out. But
no coalition of material interests has ever been able to maintain its supremacy for long without appealing to the higher
emotions of men, without a lofty ideal and a general philosophy of life. Chiang Kai-shek was intelligent enough to
grasp this fundamental fact and to understand that what was

needed above all else was a new faith, a new code of ethics to replace the appalling void created by the destruction of the old civilization's values. He was by no means blind to the vast potentialities of Communism and had long admired and feared the religious fervor with which the Communist leaders dedicated themselves to their political and social work. As a convert to Methodism, he himself was aware of the urgent, vital necessity of counteracting as speedily as possible the terrific inroads which Marxism was making among China's educated youth.

He therefore extracted out of his double personality as a Protestant Christian and a devoted Confucianist a strange idealistic blend which came to be called the "New Life Movement"—in fact an old revival of Confucianism with its four virtues of Etiquette, Justice, Integrity and Conscientiousness, to which he added Western "Clean Living." A few officials made it a point to follow the new code by mending their ways, giving up their family interests and forgoing luxurious living. But they were few and far between and the dry, static, undramatic New Life Movement finally died of sheer boredom, literally "laughed out of China." It never occurred to the Kuomintang leaders that there was a certain inconsistency in attempting to revive the dead and now meaningless virtues preached by Confucianism and at the same time to make the most outrageous political compromises, pronounce shameful and patent lies with a straight face and, on the whole, insult the intelligence of the educated twentieth-century Chinese with one of the most childish ideologies ever invented. A great deal of Chinese humor was spent on such Kuomintang creations as the Anti-Opium Bureau, the agrarian reform and even Sun Yat-sen's San-min doctrine [3]—and in China sarcastic wit can be as deadly as in France.

In the long run, no ethical system can survive without being rooted in philosophy or religion. Marxism's all-embracing, monistic interpretation of science, metaphysics, history, economics and politics, made the New Life's moralistic hodgepodge seem like a hypocritical compilation of contradictory notions, shallow and without the slightest intellectual or emotional appeal. Its Protestant morality itself fostered what seemed to be a thoroughly hypocritical spirit by divorcing economic and political behavior from an everyday morality which was good enough for the broad masses—and if there is one characteristic which the Chinese have hated at all times, it is dual standards and non-universal ethics. The Confucianist element sounded terribly old-fashioned, and by its sanction of family authority and solidarity it frustrated the increasing yearning of China's youth for complete and total emancipation. By encouraging family feeling, this modernized Confucianism automatically destroyed the prestige and authority of the state, placed family interests above national interests and was directly responsible for the alarming growth of a corruption and nepotism which had the sanction of the official code of ethics. Honest, sincere public servants who were personally disinterested and who lived frugally were at the same time wholly devoted to their large and clannish families and would sink without a qualm to any degree of corruption for the sake of their relatives. This ethical problem was solved by Marxism because it simply brushed aside Confucianism and atomized Chinese society by liberating at last its frustrated youngsters from parental authority, substituting Party and State for Family.

While this appalling failure developed like mortal cancer, the new Kuomintang's orientation toward the right had come as a bitter disappointment to the more "progressive" intelligentsia. A violent reaction ensued which for a time, out of sheer political impotence, assumed a purely intellectual aspect.[4] The great leaders of the 1917 literary revolution became old-fashioned overnight, and Hu Shih lost the major portion of his prestige when his mild conservatism and lack of constructive doctrine came at last to the fore.

An ancient trend began to reassert itself with the irresistible power of a torrentuous flood. There had always been great affinities between the Russian and the North Chinese mentality, a common way of thinking and feeling which might be termed Eurasian. The political position of Tzarist Russia as an imperialistic, pseudo-Western nation before World War I never really succeeded in destroying a certain affective kinship between the frustrated thinkers and novelists of both the youngest and the oldest people on earth. The younger members of the Chinese intelligentsia had already begun to emancipate themselves from the traditional cultural pattern of the mandarins; as early as the end of the nineteenth century, they had read voraciously Pushkin, Chekhov, Tolstoy, Dostoevsky and Turgenev. The two literatures had many psychological features in common, especially in the field of novels: the same intense realism, the same taste for an overabundance of detail and for startling lengths inspired by the common experience of the concrete infinity of Eurasia's geographical space, the same objective story-telling which sets them both apart from the literary subjectivity of the West, the same lack of individualism in the Western sense.[5] The resemblance of Russian novels to the great novels of China—to the historical *Three Kingdoms*, the tragic love story of *The Red Chamber Dream* or the famous adventure story, *All Men Are Brothers*—was immediately sensed and noted by the Chinese.

But now political conditions were so much more favorable that there was a resurgence of this pro-Russian sentiment, once purely literary and still largely distinct from pro-Marxist. In less than two years in the late twenties, more than a hundred literary works emanating from Russia were translated and published with frenetic speed, although most of them had no literary merit. Largely fostered by the virulent anti-Western atmosphere prevailing at the time, the powerful appeal of Gorki, Lunacharski, Fadeev, Semenov and countless others did a great deal to prepare the ground for vastly increased Marxist influence against which the repression of the Kuomintang's dreaded police was powerless.

The seemingly downcast Communists were far from being entirely wiped out by their disastrous defeats. For all their failures between 1923 and 1927, they had recorded a number of positive achievements which trial and error had served only to consolidate. The innumerable Russian advisers had given them a thorough training in the science of effective government and administration, in the technique of political sabotage, infiltration and subversion, in Leninistic party organization and in dissimulation. Furthermore, the Chinese leaders had shed their pure intellectualism and their taste for vacuous theorizing to come closer to the people, gradually realizing the importance of mass action and mass leadership—a switch which was partly forced upon them by their failure to retain leadership of the monolithic Kuomintang. They scrutinized with great keenness every possible angle of social discontent, in rural as well as in urban areas, learned how to build up their elites and how to harness the massive and formidable discontent of the peasants—although the net result of this new knowledge was to draw them away from orthodox Marxism, a result hardly anticipated by either Moscow or the actual founders of Chinese Communism.

The road leading out of the disaster of 1927 was steep and difficult. Moscow had blundered, but the Chinese leadership was made to pay the frightful cost. Determined to preserve all the appearances of infallibility, Stalin accused the Chinese leaders of "sabotage" and announced that he had been right all along: The recent phase of defeats had been an unavoidable historical stage and the Communists were now in the process of rising onto another, higher and more successful level. Utilizing the amazing Marxist jargon which puzzles the non-initiate but which always exercises a religious fascination over its devotees, the Comintern provided a Leninist explanation of succeeding historical stages, of the complex contents of a revolution and the structure of class forces. Lenin's theory of "Democratic Dictatorship" was put forth, preparing the way for the inclusion of the hitherto neglected peasants as a potential force, now that the proletariat had failed and the middle class had deserted. The peasant remained at all times an inveterate "bourgeois" but his massive discontent could provide a powerful vehicle for the coming revolution. However, even if the proletariat was not the sole revolutionary agent at this stage, it had to remain the preponderant one. It was the basic, incontrovertible dogma of the Marxist Church that a Communist revolution could be led only by the urban proletariat—and over the next few years countless Marxist leaders were destined to break their necks and careers, attempting to reconcile Moscow's instructions and the frustrating reality.

The present reality was plainly that Communism had lost all its hold on the proletariat (a hold that was destined not to be recovered until Mao Tse-tung's victory twenty-two years later). But Moscow maintained the outward appearances of a firm belief in Marxist dogma, whether it applied to China or to any other part of the world. Stalin insisted that revolutionary action went through the general process of history as waves through the ocean and that the fact of being in the trough should not blind one to the crest already looming overhead.

Following the "prophetic" views of Moscow, an entirely new leadership seized control of the Party in China. Ch'en Tu-hsiu was gently removed after having been loaded with the major blame for the recent failures, and Ch'ü Ch'iu-pai took his place. All his attempts at regaining control of the Shanghai proletariat through strikes and through the famous Autumn Harvest uprising failed miserably and bloodily. A November Plenum endorsed Stalin's view that a revolutionary wave—the Canton Commune—was to ignite the Chinese powder keg. It was another sanguinary and sensational failure. And so, out went Ch'ü Ch'u-pai. The sixth congress of the Chinese Communist Party took place in Moscow and laid down the new line. It was admitted that a revolutionary wave could not engulf the whole of China's immensity and that Communism would have to proceed piecemeal, province by province. Li Li-san became the new Communist leader and, following the new line, prepared for an "initial victory in one or several provinces." But he faced the same eternal problem:

the complete and total indifference of the "predestined" proletariat.

By then, a new danger was becoming evident: The center of Communist power was irresistibly shifting from the proletariat to the peasantry, from the urban to the rural areas against all the holy Marxist dogmas. The appalling danger was faced and the leaders recognized that the trend had to be fought at all costs. The Central Committee decided, once more, to concentrate all its efforts on the industrial centers: Nanking, Shanghai, Wuhan, Tientsin and the vast industrial areas of Manchuria. Li Li-san pointed out that the workers were not merely paralyzed by the Kuomintang's "white terror" but that the "yellow" unions were making great inroads and that Wang Ching-wei's "reorganizationists" were tempting the poverty-stricken proletariat with "false" promises. Struggling fiercely against overwhelming odds, he attempted at the same time to stem the rising tide of peasant guerrillas, only to end crushed between the two terms of Communism's basic contradiction, between dogma and reality, between proletarian sluggishness and rural revolutionary enthusiasm. When the time came to implement the "new line" and make a double-barreled assault on Changsha, combining for the first time the action of the proletariat and the rural guerrillas, the attempt failed and Li Li-san was thrown out.

A last attempt was made to rejuvenate the disintegrating urban leadership. The Russian authorities had founded several universities in Moscow dedicated to the careful preparation of new elites who would lead Asia toward revolutionary Marxism. They were and still are remarkable institutions with a great potential, in which the most highly competent technicians and experts in the world impart their vast knowledge of political organization and sabotage, social subversion and infiltration, Marxist theology and Communist science, the art of the *coup d'état*, of civil war and preparation of revolutions—in other words, the art and science of shaping "history in the making" and forcing it to conform to the prophecies of Marxism-Leninism and to the wishes of Moscow.

The Sun Yat-sen University, entirely concerned with the education and training of promising young Chinese, sent out an aggressive group of well-indoctrinated Chinese nicknamed the "returned student clique" under the direction of their teacher and Russian expert on Chinese affairs, Pavel Mif. They were all given important positions within the Party and in no time they had alienated a large section of the infuriated older revolutionaries. A paralyzing struggle for power among the various cliques ensued, destroying slowly but surely the entire Party machinery outside the rural areas; the disruption which followed ended in the creation by dissidents of an "Emergency Committee" in opposition to the regular Central Committee. The gradual recognition in Moscow that the peasant guerrillas were becoming the main support of the Party irritated the few old-fashioned Chinese proletarians left in the midst of a whirlwind of schisms and heresies. When the last maritime-union leaders were asked to organize the despised Yangtze boatmen to "support the Red Army in the Soviet Areas," the proletarians became thoroughly enraged at the prospect of playing second fiddle to the peasant guerrillas —and by all the canons of Marxist orthodoxy, they were absolutely right. But the withering away of the Party's proletarian base went on implacably and the leaders were soon left hanging in mid-air with no support whatsoever. And yet Moscow would not give in.

The Central Committee of the Party remained in Shanghai and control gravitated into the hands of the young returned students from Moscow, now nicknamed the "twenty-eight Bolsheviks." By this time, the dilemma was no longer connected with Marxist dogma. Trotsky had been eliminated and his criticisms were harmless, while Stalin remained sole master of world Communism. But it was precisely because he remained supreme head of the Marxist Church that he could not tolerate the growing power of rural guerrillas who drew all their prestige from local sources within the Soviet Areas, fully independent and financially self-supporting and relying not one whit on Moscow's help or advice. The Comintern no longer fought for dogma and orthodoxy but, desperately, for control. And, in the end, Moscow was defeated. The Russians had to cut down drastically their financial support and the Central Committee came to subsist entirely on the help and support provided by the Soviet Areas.

The last blow fell when the Kuomintang started a huge campaign of repression in 1931, in order to crush what was left of urban, proletarian Communism; several members of the Central Committee were arrested and shot. The end came during the 1932-33 period when conditions became unendurable and the temptation to move out of town became irresistible. Mao Tse-tung sent a number of telegrams to the Central Committee, urged the members to come over to the Soviet Areas, frightened them with accounts of the growing "white terror" which endangered their lives—and finally cut off all financial aid. Cowed into complete submission, the pitiable remains of the Central Committee left Shanghai forever and moved to Juichin under the protection of Mao's Red Army, now a formidable power.

Moscow was completely defeated, but Stalin's intense, inhuman realism made him accept the inevitable defeat with apparent good grace. With the full co-operation of Mao Tse-tung, Moscow's illusionary infallibility was safeguarded, the apparent continuity of Soviet policy was preserved and—in accordance with that very old Chinese tradition—past history was reshaped and streamlined to justify the present. The leaders of the agrarian revolution were themselves good and sincere Communists who were quite prepared to work with Moscow on an "official" history of Chinese Communism in which all the errors and disagreements of the past were wiped out.

The establishment of a Marxist-inspired agrarian movement occurred outside the regular framework of the Party. Its history and growth until 1931 lay entirely outside the scope of the urban proletariat and constituted a marginal development to which little attention was paid at first. Yet it began to loom large in 1927 when Mao sent his "Report on an Investigation of the Agrarian Movement in Hunan." [6] For all his peasant background, Mao drifted from the university to the countryside because of a deep feeling that the real power of China rested in the hands of its huge rural majority. His intellectual—and especially poetic—culture was already vast and, since he had worked for years as assistant librarian at the University of Peking, he was able to combine an impressive theoretical knowledge with a growing experience of the potentialities of mass power in the rural areas. Having decided to devote himself entirely to agrarian action, he acquired a passionate, almost mystical faith in the resilient strength of the Chinese peasant.

The immediate successes reaped by his astute handling of local problems inspired him further. His first report contains few Marxist references but a great deal of emotional feeling: "The force of the peasantry is like that of the raging winds and driving rain. It is rapidly increasing in violence. No force can stand in its way. The peasantry will tear apart all nets which bind it and hasten along the road to liberation. They will bury beneath them all forces of imperialism, militarism, corrupt officialdom, village bosses and evil gentry. Every revolutionary comrade will be subjected to their scrutiny and be accepted or rejected by them. Shall we stand in the vanguard and lead them, or stand behind them and oppose them?" [7] The gap between this threatening rural violence and the icy coldness of Leninism was immeasurable. The proletariat and the cities were brushed aside as unimportant and inconsequential.

Mao Tse-tung was to make quite plain that Chinese Communism would be, first of all, Chinese: "So-called 'wholesale Westernization' is a mistaken viewpoint. China has suffered a great deal in the past from the formalist adoption of foreign things. Likewise, in applying Marxism to China, the Chinese Communists must fully and properly unite the universal truth of Marxism with the specific practice of the Chinese revolution; that is to say, the truth of Marxism must be integrated with the characteristics of the nation and given a definite national form before it can be useful; it must not be applied subjectively as a mere formula. Formula Marxists are only fooling with Marxism and the Chinese revolution, and there is no place for them in the ranks of the Chinese revolution." [8]

But Mao remained a Marxist in every important respect and especially in the foremost one, in a definite feeling for *historical* materialism which rang clearly when he added that "the broad masses of the peasantry have arisen to fulfill their historic destiny." In the dramatic picture painted by Mao, there is no reference to mere economic needs, to starvation or to standards of living. But there is always that vision which stamps Marxism-Leninism, that irrepressible feeling of messianic destiny in which the economic causality of Marx himself has little part. It is in this inner feeling for historic destiny that the power of Communism—whether Russian or Chinese—lies. It is this innermost feeling of implacable determinism, of a predestined role for the "chosen" members of the Party, which wraps up all the apparent contradictions of Communism and makes it for a time into one homogeneous, disciplined, crusading Church.

There was in Mao's pronouncements a prophetic strain, an acute realism also, which made him size up a situation's far-reaching implications with almost unerring judgment. Criticizing the dreadful pessimism which had spread through the Communist Party, he wrote in January 1930: "Although the subjective forces of the revolution in China at present are still weak, yet so are all the organs . . . of the reactionary ruling classes . . . This explains why revolution cannot break out at present in the countries of Western Europe where, although the subjective forces of the revolution are perhaps stronger than those in China, the forces of the reactionary ruling classes are many times stronger than in our country. Although the subjective forces of the revolution in China at present are weak, yet because the forces of the counterrevolution are correspondingly weak, the revolution will certainly move toward an upsurge more quickly in China than in Western Europe." [9] One cannot but admit that this cool analysis was remarkably prophetic.

Many of the old, enduring traits of Chinese psychology are in evidence throughout his speeches and works: "When we study an event, we must examine its essence and treat its appearance merely as a guide to the threshold of essence; and once we cross the threshold we must grasp the essence." To this almost Buddhistic appreciation of things, Mao joined the skillful use of dialectics as a guiding thread through the complex maze of politics involving China and the whole world. His thinking was clear, disciplined, inhumanly realistic.

Faithful to the ancestral requirements of Chinese psychology, to the essence of Chinese thought which is not to *inform* the mind but *transform* the whole human being, Mao always clearly stated the need for religious-like conversion through re-education. Sensing the dynamic nature of Hegelian-Marxist dialectics and at the same time retrieving the old Chinese idea that thought was worthless unless aimed at action, Mao claimed tirelessly that "Marxism is not a dogma but a guide to action." [10] Compare this with the symbolic nature of Chinese script, numbers and other emblems which were all pointed at emotional impact and action rather than at abstract thought for its own sake, and it becomes plain that Mao's processes of thought conform to the traditional pattern.

And one by one, all the characteristics of Chinese thought process re-emerge in Marxist garb, among them contempt for mere empiricism: ". . . the vulgar plodders, respecting experience, yet despising theory, cannot take a comprehensive view of the entire objective process, lack clear direction and long-range perspective . . . were those persons to direct a revolution, they would lead it up a blind alley." [11] And Mao knew that he needed the scholars and intellectuals, the masters of theory, just as much as the harnessing of rural masses: "Without the participation of the intellectuals the revolution cannot achieve victory." [12] Also, the emphasis on the historical viewpoint: "Neither rationalism nor empiricism in philosophy recognizes the historical or dialectical nature of knowledge and . . . both are erroneous in the theory of knowledge as a whole." [13] Then, if we read the development of Mao's argument on the searing contradictions which tear the opponents of Communism apart, we can uncover the traditional pattern of Chinese logic: not structural with logical articulations, but converging inductions from the outlying periphery of perception and knowledge to the central, key formula, like the spokes of a wheel converging from the rim to the hub.[14] The new orthodox doctrine can be best studied in Mao's famous work, *On Practice*, which is now compulsory reading for China's Marxist elite.

Nor is the vision of cosmic totality lacking: "The Marxist recognizes that in the absolute, total process of the development of the universe, the development of each concrete process is relative; hence, in the great stream of absolute truth, man's knowledge of the concrete process at each given stage of development is only relatively true. The sum total of innumerable relative truths is the absolute truth" [15]—which is not such a bad description of the old, venerable Tao.

Mao was no enemy of violence, but his violence was passionate and primitive, not coldly ruthless on the pattern of Russian Marxism. It was a violence sucked from the very soil of traditional China and not from the Machine of the Industrial Age: "We must wipe out the political power of the gentry, throw them to the ground and even trample them underfoot." [16]

Mao's work was spectacular from the start. The agrarian discontent was growing by leaps and bounds, feeding not so much on the traditional oppression on the part of some landlords as on the general worsening of the peasant's fate. With falling agricultural prices, the landlords attempted to increase their rents and squeeze the marrow out of the farmers' bones. And yet landlordism was by no means a universal problem in a China in which the vast majority of the rural masses was made up of small landowners and where few large estates existed. But the growing pressure of overpopulation, the disorganization of the markets, the economic depression, the breakdown of communications and of flood control, the gradual demoralization of a soulless gentry with its traditional culture now lying in ruins and its code of ethics thrown overboard, everything combined to create a great revolutionary potential in some chosen areas.

Before 1910, farmers had to pay one half of their crops in rent. But after the revolution rates began to increase as fast as agricultural prices declined. And whereas the wealthiest landlords rarely owned more than three hundred acres before the revolution, some now began to accumulate enormous amounts of land. Rapacious usurers and moneylenders began to buy the land of bankrupt farmers, creating large estates which they fiercely defended against the traditional guerrillas, a recurrent phenomenon of rural life all through Chinese history. They built up their own private police, allied themselves with local war lords and forgot all about the old ethical standards of Confucianism: kindliness, tolerance, moderation and generosity. Corruption and greed overcame those landlords who formerly considered their estates as the hereditary, almost inalienable economic base of a cultured gentry. Now, victim of the general dislocation of China's economic structure, land became mere capital, transferable at will, gravitating into the hands of grasping moneylenders speculating on the ruin of Chinese agriculture. This dramatic agrarian problem was not essentially inherited from the past but was a recent, post-revolution creation, and to millions of farmers the resistance against this new type of modern landlordism became a life-and-death struggle.

In order to organize and control this revolutionary potential, an army was necessary. Mao went to work on the military problem at once but almost against the wishes of the Central Committee. All through the period of complex intrigues, of shifting Party line and waltzing leadership, the agrarian movement remained as aloof as possible, bent on its own tasks, avoiding systematically any involvement in the Party plots and cliques. It remained the "real power" faction, nicknamed thus by the frustrated and powerless big-city Communists who could sense the futility of their own proletarian work.

By late 1929 the achievements of "Soviet China" had become spectacular. They could no longer be ignored, either by Moscow or by the Chinese Central Committee. But for a long time the Chinese Soviets' actions, achievements and power remained bathed in a misty uncertainty and the Central Committee itself was almost as ignorant of the Soviet leaders' whereabouts as the Kuomintang—which was itself more powerful in the towns than in the countryside. Stalin himself had to confess his own ignorance and Trotsky once exclaimed with bitter sarcasm: "There is nothing surprising in the fact that in China a Soviet government was created about which the Chinese Communist Party knows nothing and about whose political physiognomy the highest leader of the Chinese revolution can give no information!" [17]

Mao went on quietly developing his power in Hunan and Kiangsi, building his own independent bases and his own army, which he provided with weapons taken from Kuomintang or war lord troops. A great deal of the history of those early days remains in the dark, however, and will probably never be known save through the "expurgated" official version which will come down to posterity. Mao had to establish his undisputed leadership over many rival guerrilla chiefs, weld all the guerrillas and all the Soviet territories into one solid striking force and one substantial geographical base, and regulate the relationship between military and civilian power by establishing once and for all the absolute dominance of the latter—which he took for himself. The over-all military command fell to Chu Teh after the long-standing dispute between Party faction and Red Army faction within the Soviet Areas had been resolved. Revolts were ruthlessly crushed—the Kiangsi Soviet in 1930, for instance. Attempts of Central Committee followers to carry out Li Li-san's instructions and establish collective farms in southern Kiangsi were violently opposed by the Maoists, who by now openly flouted the authority of the urban leadership. Mao's agrarian policy, for all its verbal violence, remained in fact extremely moderate; he always took the position that the fundamental claims of the peasants had to be satisfied and not frustrated so as to procure the indispensable "mass" base. But to start socializing agriculture at this stage was pure folly and could not be considered for a moment.

With the gradual disintegration of the proletarian leadership and its final absorption by the Soviet Areas government, Mao became the supreme head of Chinese Communism in 1933. Once the official investiture had been performed by Moscow, he reorganized the Party along strong Leninist lines, taking in such indispensable diplomats as Chou En-lai, who had worked with Li Li-san and the Central Committee, but rejecting systematically all those who were potential deviationists or possible rivals and purging all those who had no real ability or usefulness. With his reinforced Red Army, he now settled in "border areas," astride the frontiers of several provinces where the power of the Kuomintang's central authority was weakest and often in conflict with one or another war lord and where his own effectiveness was multiplied by his forays into several provinces all at once from one single base.

Then came the famous "Long March" across China and Central Asia and the establishment of the Chinese Soviets in the northwest. From its new capital at Yenan, the Communist leadership organized a regular government and administration and shifted its Party line from social issues to the more promising foreign-policy problem. Now that Chinese Communism had decided to base its action on the peasants, the approaching war with Japan was obviously a unique opportunity. By leading the anti-Japanese elements, the Marxists—rather than the meek nationalists of the Kuomintang—took full credit for rousing the xenophobia of all Chinese. While the prospects were that the Japanese would defeat the Kuomintang's field armies, the Communists could hope to organize behind-the-lines guerrillas and use their incomparable skill in local rural government without fear of intervention on the Kuomintang's part. Whatever happened could only be of benefit to them because the Japanese could never hope to occupy the country-side effectively and the Kuomintang could never hope to retain the large cities—and without its urban bases, the Kuomintang could never hope to prevent the Reds from organizing the peasants; the Japanese "occupation" would be the shield of the Communists. And when war with Japan broke out in 1937, the farsighted Communists could have known that an almost predetermined chain of events would give them virtual mastery of North China within a decade.

Meanwhile, all organic connection between the Communist Party and the proletariat had been severed, a devastating blow to Marxist orthodoxy. But reality was too compelling and overrode all doctrinal qualms. Orthodoxy could always be artificially re-established later on when power was seized through the action of the blind rural masses. Mao now felt strong enough and sure enough of himself to formulate the new version of applied Marxism, the "New Democracy" which success eventually glorified as being as sensational an adaptation of Marxism as Leninism had been twenty years earlier and which Stalin, the acute realist, sanctioned with his approval.

But to claim that the peasantry was the main factor in this vast revolution would be a gross distortion of the real, profound significance of the new adaptation, a twisting of reality as blatant as that produced by the Communist Party's own reshaping of history. Under Mao Tse-tung, the Chinese Communist Party was essentially a combination of a strong political elite "utilizing" the formidable but close-to-nature power of the discontented peasantry, primitive, instinctive and intellectually blind—"the pack-horse of civilization," according to Trotsky's lapidary formula. The leaders themselves were on the whole men of real intellectual stature.[18] A study of the background of seventy Communist leaders of the time revealed that 70 per cent came from decidedly "bourgeois" families: well-to-do farmers, members of the professions, merchants and gentry. Chu Teh, the son of a wealthy landowner in Yenan, had been led by dissolute habits to become an inveterate opium addict. His conversion to Marxism was powerful enough to regenerate him "morally" by curing him of his addiction, and his will power was such that he swiftly rose to the position of commander-in-chief of the Red Army. Mao Tse-tung's parents were wealthy farmers. Chou En-lai is the offspring of a great mandarin family. In fact, only 17 per cent of the leadership was proletarian.

The inescapable conclusion is that the new Chinese Communist movement was the product of the most realistically-minded portion of the Chinese intelligentsia, that it was a new, quasi-religious movement of the T'ai P'ing-rebellion type which gave meaning, cohesion and direction to a formidable but purely instinctive agrarian revolution which was bound to occur in any case. Its evolution proved beyond a shadow of doubt that such a party organized along Marxist-Leninist lines could exist—against every Marxist dogma—without any organic connection with the proletariat. But its leaders, realistic though they were, remained fanatically devoted to the Marxist creed and were to turn, in due course, against their former peasant allies—but only when, after power had been seized in the whole of China, they were able to build up a vast industrial proletariat onto which they could shift their mass base.

Using the subsequent atomization of a Chinese society which had hitherto remained faithful to Confucianist ethics in its family-based structure, the Communists encouraged a formidable revolt of the younger against the older generations —one which has been and still is taking place in many other parts of the world—and, by so doing, released a staggering amount of condensed and unused energy. Son against father, wife against husband, and so on all down the line until all the old family allegiances were transferred to the state. The release of the individual from all social fetters does not mean an increase but on the contrary a decrease in individualism. His former subordination to families, clans and traditional ethics is replaced by his total subordination to the sole state-church—as embodied in the Communist Party.

Such a revolution occurred once before in the history of China—twenty-two centuries ago. Besides re-editing the endless socialistic attempts made throughout Chinese history, the victory of Marxism-Leninism represents the victory of the authoritarian principle of "Ching," of a rigid, mechanistic system of impersonal government in which the state is supreme, the views on human nature basically—if not avowedly—cynical, and the strong social discipline enforced by law from the outside and no longer by an ethical code operating within the human being. The views of the anti-Confucianist Legalists, who built up the state of Ch'in and crystallized Chinese power as it never had been crystallized before, were identical. The Legalists attempted to destroy the principle of "Ch'uan," the more human and flexible idea of expediency, of the rule of morality and of moral individuals, of the organic pre-eminence of the family as being the main social cell—all the ideas which also were those of Chiang Kai-shek's Kuomintang but which were so ineptly applied. Twenty-four centuries ago, the great Legalist philosopher Han Fei-tzu had predicted all the weaknesses and attendant evils of the family system—the corruption, the nepotism and favoritism, and the resultant lack of what he called "public citizenship," [19] all of which filtered into the Kuomintang's last adaptation of Confucianism to the modern world. From the collapsing collectivism of Confucius' family system, China has now swerved to the state collectivism of the Legalists combined with the perennial socialism of the old reformers.

Mao Tse-tung, the "Saving Star of China," once told a foreign correspondent that Chinese Marxism is the "religion of the people." But it is even more the religion of the Marxist intelligentsia, from among whom the larger portion of the party's "elite" are recruited. To a people who have always been "history-conscious," Marxism has brought this invincible faith in the redemptive historic process underlining all those secular creeds which issued from Hegel's philosophy of history.

The belief that the Communist Party itself is the agent of such historic redemption is just as indestructible as the belief in the Roman Catholic Church's historic role, and it is this unshakable conviction that they are the "chosen," predestined leaders of the coming revolution which gave all its grave significance to Chinese Marxism.

In order to gain full control of China, the Communists had to dispose somehow of the urban elements. Even granted that they would seize control of the major part of the dissatisfied rural areas, they could not hope to rise to power by pitting rural China against urban China with its indifferent proletariat and hostile middle class. But fortunately for them, the eight-year war with Japan solved the problem by destroying the most vital element within the Kuomintang itself. While the Reds were highly successful in organizing the vast plains of North China behind the thin Japanese lines and in securing large areas in which they carried out their land reform, blind circumstances were working for them in another sector.

Under the waves of Japanese invasion penetrating ever deeper into China, the Kuomintang's central government was forced to retreat inland to Chungking and virtually sever its organic connection with the coastal capitalism, now largely under Japanese occupation. Once settled in the non-industrial heart of China, the leadership of the Kuomintang gravitated inevitably into the hands of landlord pressure groups and out of those of the coastal middle class, which had hitherto dominated the party.[20] This switch from the urban capitalists and the wealthy bourgeoisie to the landowning, "sedan-chair" gentry was fatal to the Kuomintang, since its leadership had fallen into the hands of that very social class which was bound to be destroyed by Mao's agrarian revolt. Powerless against an urban middle class because of the total indifference of the proletariat and its alienation from Marxism—which itself made a binding agreement between proletariat and industrial capitalism possible—the Communists were bound to achieve unquestioning victory once the Kuomintang had fallen into the hands of the landowning gentry.

When Japan was defeated in 1945 and the coastal areas were reoccupied by Nationalist troops, the double consequences of this disaster became obvious: On the one hand, the Communists, working behind Japanese lines, had been able to extend their control over more than a hundred million human beings; and on the other, the landlord-dominated Kuomintang back in Nanking, Shanghai, Peking and Canton became hostile to the middle class which had founded that very party and dominated it for so long. The Chiang Kai-shek government adopted a determined anticapitalist attitude—not according to the Marxist meaning of the word but in the sense of landowners' hostility and opposition to the urban, Westernized capitalist and bourgeois elements. Moving in *space* from the coastal east to the continental west, the Kuomintang had moved back in *time,* from the Industrial Age to the precapitalist.

Losing the middle-class support which was vital if it intended to rule at least part of China, the postwar Kuomintang was swamped by technical difficulties it could no longer solve. Inefficiency, corruption and nepotism riddled a party whose cynical neo-Confucianism was a debilitating factor of decisive importance. While runaway inflation ruined millions of middle-class men who might have provided the vital support needed, many capitalists and industrialists turned in disgust toward the Marxists, whose rising star seemed to be their only hope—one of those great but profound paradoxes of history. Put in Hegelian-Marxist terms, the dilemma resolved itself in a confrontation of the capitalist thesis with the precapitalist-Kuomintang antithesis—which would be solved by the postcapitalist Marxian synthesis. Their enemies were disintegrating through their own inner contradictions.

Whatever efforts the West could make to retrieve its position in the postwar period were now doomed. In China, those liberal and democratic converts to Western ideals were bound to be crushed between the old, strong landlord-dominated

Kuomintang and the new Communist faith, ruthless and determined to exploit all the weaknesses and blindness of Western-type liberalism. During and after World War II the intelligentsia, with very few exceptions, went over to the Communists, most of them out of bitter disappointment at the reaction of the Kuomintang toward a dead past; a smaller portion, and the only one that will eventually survive, went over already converted to the new faith. At least ten thousand students joined the Communists at Yenan during the war, and many more went over in the immediate postwar period. Many of those were and are bound to be sacrificed to the implacable Marxist-Maoist Juggernaut which uses cynically but soon discards mere discontented, embittered, self-seeking men.

Communism requires a strong, indestructible faith and, as coldly as early Buddhism, ignores or destroys all personal feelings of love, compassion, jealousy, pity, greed or anything which emphasizes the individualism of man. It uses cunningly and then slowly grinds to dust all those utopian liberals who do not understand that this is a new age requiring a reassessment of all philosophic concepts, an age in which mere pragmatism without faith leads to destruction.

13

RED CHINA

With the benefit of hindsight, we can see how psychologically predetermined was the unfolding of events in the Far East. They unrolled with the majestic sweep of a Greek tragedy whose outcome is preordained and known to all, but whose actors, caught in the fire and passion of action, are blind. Thousands of years of history on both sides had conditioned the Chinese and the Westerners each in their own ways; the Western comet, which had been in ascendancy for centuries at the other end of the world, finally tore into China's slow-moving star, exploded it and let loose a staggering amount of compressed energy. The irony was that, as the Western comet began to slow down, the devastating energy released by the explosion of China's crumbling civilization began to gather momentum.

Anyone who prods the depths of a problem looks upon surface events as mere reflections of powerful undercurrents. Western diplomatic activity in the first half of our century was nothing more than surface actions reflecting those undercurrents, and they must be looked upon as such. They reflected but did not determine the course of history.

It was not yet apparent at the turn of the century that Europe's imperial Powers were destined to crumble to pieces nor that the United States would become the ruling Power in the Pacific. Could the Greeks foresee, in the twilight of the Hellenistic Age, that Rome was destined to rule the civilized world and defend that civilization against the barbarians? But then, they had no historical perspective; we have. We can, today, see logic in the fact that Western civilization's center of gravity has been transferred from Europe to America, as it was transferred two thousand years ago from Greece to Italy. And we must look upon America's foreign policy—or the lack of it—as being the main agent of Western influence in the Far East.

American foreign policy was the product of American history and character: idealistic, yet unrealistic because it never seemed willing or able to relate policy with the effective power to enforce it. This was never so acutely felt as in the case of the Open Door policy, explicitly stated at the turn of the century when John Hay dispatched his notes to the world's Great Powers. The fear that China was about to be carved up by the Great Powers was not groundless, but unless the United States was prepared to back up this statement of policy with armed strength, it was bound to remain a mere proclamation. It was all very well to state that the cornerstone of America's foreign policy in the Far East was the preservation of China's territorial and administrative integrity. But China was a continent and not a nation on the Western model, an old civilization and not a full-fledged member of the industrial world which was coming into being. China's fundamental problems were not amenable to mere diplomatic statements. The coming conflicts of the twentieth century would soon transcend the traditional conflicts between nations, to become epoch-making clashes between alien civilizations and different ways of life. Sooner or later, America was bound to become the standard-bearer of Western Civilization, no longer one Power amongst others.

The Open Door declaration, high-minded as it was, had unfortunate repercussions. It lured the Americans into believing that the Chinese people would be forever grateful, which of course they had no intention of being. Too many other things stood in the way: the memory of the exclusion of Chinese immigrants from the West Coast in the 1880's, the patronizing attitude which Americans share with Europeans in their dealings with Asians, the lack of psychological understanding. The awakening came after World War II; it was rapid and brutal. And it was no accident of history; it was bound to happen, sooner or later.

After World War I, the power of the great European nations had begun to disintegrate visibly. Russia remained in the throes of civil war for a number of years and was presumed to be relatively harmless. Japan, with its industrial power, armed might and staggering overpopulation, became the villain. While the European Powers were slowly girding their loins for a second world war that would lay their continent in shambles, American foreign policy in the Far East became hypnotized by the danger of Japanese imperialism. There was no effort to look under the surface, to lay down long-range policies realistically geared to the relative powers and weaknesses existing in the Far East, to study earnestly the problem of Japanese overpopulation, to extend effective help to the Kuomintang in its efforts to reunite and rebuild China, to help in the *cultural* reconstruction of the Far Eastern nations and influence them *ideologically*. The rise of military extremists in Japan and of Red extremists in China, both fundamentally hostile to the West, was a foregone conclusion.

The West, caught in the tight web of its own Warring States era, was unable to influence the Far East in its favor. No one man or nation was particularly responsible for this sad state of affairs. It was largely preordained, although wise policies could postpone the day of reckoning. No day-to-day policy can compete with long-range plans operating in depth, and this is what the Russian Soviets had. They studied foreign policy as a clever chess player studies his chessboard and calculates twenty or thirty moves ahead, although there is plenty of evidence that they themselves were lost in the complex maze and did not foresee all the major consequences of their policy. But it did not matter too much. They had a serviceable instrument in their dialectical materialism; however hopelessly wrong it might be at times, it was bound to be right sometime; and, facing Western opponents who had no long-term policy, no over-all philosophy of action, no particular goal, no ideological aim, they were bound to win a great deal by default even if historical and psychological circumstances had not been as favorable as they were in China. They lived consciously in the stream of history, the West did not.

Those circumstances were, in fact, favorable to the Marxists, although for reasons which were beyond the limited reach of their historical materialism. And, waiting with great patience for the inevitable "inner contradictions" to set all their enemies fighting among themselves, bolstering those "contradictions" whenever possible, the Soviet Russians could afford to play a waiting game in the Far East while the world became engulfed in the Great Depression of the early thirties.

Japan's invasion of Manchuria was only one of the numerous political processes sparked or accelerated all over the world by this Great Depression. From then onward, Soviet Russia's primary aim was to safeguard her vital interests in the Far East against Japanese encroachments, and this at the cost of many humiliations and bitter retreats. Moscow feverishly rearmed Siberia's Far Eastern provinces, and her over-all policy became a blend of concession, such as the sale of the Russian-Chinese Eastern Railroad to Japan, and of stubborn resistance, displayed in hundreds of skirmishes and local battles waged all along the Manchurian border. The Soviets secretly favored a deepening of Japan's commitments in China as the best way of deflecting Tokyo's apparently inexhaustible energy, and the outbreak of the Sino-Japanese war in 1937 provoked sighs of relief in Moscow.

Russia began to send supplies and "volunteer" pilots to Chiang Kai-shek in the hope, fulfilled by later events, that Japan would become so deeply engaged in China that the war would drag on indefinitely, wrecking both Japan and the Kuomintang in the process. The Soviet "Far Eastern Army" itself had been trebled in size and firepower, and the "Special Red Banner Army of the Far East" had become entirely independent of western sources of supplies. Russian colonization was again frantically encouraged and slave labor was sent to the Maritime Province in increasing numbers. The Dalstroy agency of the N.K.V.D. handled hundreds of thousands of slave laborers spread out in camps between Khabarovsk and the Pacific, building railroads, airfields and military installations.

All this while the Chinese Communists were largely on their own, without any help from the Russians, who were too busy watching over their extensive possessions in the Far East. Chinese Marxism had developed its own doctrine and policy and had proved self-reliant. This was all right with Moscow, but the Chinese Communists would have to prove that they could grow and proliferate on their own without any real help from the Mecca of Communism.

Russia's policy in the Far East was brilliant. The situation, of course, was eminently favorable: The Germans and the Japanese, fundamentally split by searing suspicions, were unable to co-ordinate their Far Eastern policies;[1] the Japanese hated the Anglo-Saxon West even more than they hated the Russians; the Franco-German hatred was monumental and promised to wreck the heart of Europe itself; the colonial empires of Europe in India and Southeast Asia were seething with discontent.

With fundamental antagonisms splitting their foes, the Soviets could and did take full advantage of the situation. Not only did they neutralize Manchuria's Kwantung Army at a time when its intervention might have been decisive for all concerned, but they were able to deflect Japan's aggressiveness toward the hated Western Powers—and when Pearl Harbor's hour struck, Communism had accomplished its greatest task in the Far East. The mutual destruction of Western and Japanese imperialism, combined with the disintegration of Chiang Kai-shek's Kuomintang and the downfall of Western colonialism in Asia, was bound to lead to some form of Soviet domination in the Far East. Three years later the first results of this gigantic conflict began to appear.

Japan's unconditional surrender meant the total destruction of Japanese military might, power and influence, leading to the creation of huge power vacuums, none of which could be adequately filled by the improvident West. The Japanese lost all their overseas territories, investments, industries and sources of raw materials. Six and a half million Japanese were repatriated to the already overpopulated home islands, now under American occupation. The colonial domination of the European Powers was also wrecked forever. The Japanese had lost the war but had won it for colonial Asia. In Indo-China, Malaya, Indonesia and Burma they did not enhance their own popularity but they destroyed the last shreds of European power and lighted the spark of an immense awakening of the tropical Orient. And in the north the Soviet armies were poised for a quick dash which secured for them the great industrial power of Manchuria and North Korea. The Russo-

Japanese war lasted only one week but proved to be the most profitable military operation in history. Two billion dollars' worth of industrial equipment and machinery was either wrecked or removed to Siberia. In Manchuria and North Korea a highly valuable, strategic position had been won over for the expansion of Communism and for the eventual destruction of Western influence on the mainland.

Politics had played their part in the Far East as the handmaiden of Asian Communism, as they had simultaneously in Europe favored the expansion of Russian power. This was the grand result of intellectual confusion, conflicting philosophies of life, rationalism and skepticism; it was the inevitable outcome of Europe's "Warring States" era. Japan's eighty years of Westernized experiment had ended in total disaster—the penalty for having imitated too faithfully the nationalism and colonialism of European powers—and the Empire of the Rising Sun had now fallen into the orbit of America, a substantial but highly troublesome acquisition. On the mainland, a momentous change was taking place in which the substance of power slowly gravitated into the hands of those fanatics who believed that they were predestined to shape Asia's coming history and contribute to the doom of the West.

When the new policy of Kuomintang-Communist alliance against the Japanese had been decided upon in the late thirties, the Chinese Communists had evolved new social tactics to fit their latest political line. The "New Democracy" put a brake on agrarian reforms and increased its appeal by adopting a determined but economically liberal policy. With the war over, the Communists promptly enlarged their guerrilla territory so as to occupy most of the strategic North China plain, and strong contact was established with the Russian army of occupation in Manchuria. Because of international agreements with the Western Powers, the help afforded by Moscow was discreet but nonetheless effective.

The Russians prolonged their occupation as long as necessary so that the superb guerrilla organizations of the Chinese

Reds could effectively dominate the Manchurian countryside —but also cleverly handed back the ruined cities to the Kuomintang and thus induced the Nationalists to overextend themselves. Geographical distances, the inability of the Kuomintang armies to re-establish land communications with the Manchurian cities in the far north, everything pointed to Manchuria's becoming the grave of the Nationalists' military power.

Undoubtedly, Russian help to the Chinese Communists was extremely effective; but it would have been totally useless if the Chinese Reds had not developed their tremendous power on their own. And it is also quite plain that, having lost all control over Chinese Communism, the Russians had no idea as to its real strength. The Russians played their game with consummate skill. If Chiang Kai-shek was strong, nothing they could do would hand China over to their Chinese coreligionists; on the other hand, if Chiang was as weak as he proved to be subsequently, it was just as well to make the Chinese Communists more dependent on Russian help and power than they would have been if Manchuria had been handed intact to them on a silver platter.

As it was, Maoist troops penetrated into Manchuria disguised as civilian refugees and fanned out into the Manchurian countryside, an area hitherto closed to Communism by the efficiency of Japanese repression. Other Chinese troops trained and indoctrinated in Soviet Russia, many of them former Chinese soldiers who had been driven out of Manchuria by the Japanese in 1931, came back behind Marshal Malinovsky's Far Eastern Army. Hundreds of Chinese Red Army officers had been superbly trained, not only in military tactics and strategy but in Marxist history, mass psychology, civil and guerrilla warfare, propaganda and civil administration. Japanese arsenals and equipment were discreetly transferred by the Russians to Communist General Lin Piao, and the reoccupation of Manchuria by Nationalist troops proved to be virtually impossible.[2]

Also back came Mao Tse-tung's old rivals such as Li Li-san,

now a still-fervent but mature, circumspect Communist who had become an obedient tool of the Soviet Russians. He was typical of a great many Chinese Communists, young and old, who had been trained for many years in the Soviet Union and whose loyalty was first of all to the Marxist faith in its Russian incarnation. And with him came back Liu Shao-ch'i, who in July 1948 transmitted Stalin's imperious advice: Refrain from attempting to conquer the whole of China and continue the guerrilla war as long as possible so as to exhaust the Americans in their hopeless attempt to support the Kuomintang. But the Chinese Reds were past the stage where they were prepared to follow meekly the instructions of the Kremlin. Chou En-lai argued that China was now ripe for plucking and that an all-out effort was necessary. Mao upheld him—and the Russians had to accept his decision, which they did with more or less good grace.[3]

As their strategic position improved, the Chinese Communists had gradually switched from their formerly liberal policy to one of increasing, harrowing violence and radical ruthlessness. A revolutionary atmosphere had to be created, and from the end of 1946 onward the gradual atomization of China's social fabric proceeded at an increasingly fast pace wherever the Reds were in power. Landlords were ruined and murdered wholesale, women revolted hysterically against men, the younger generation—always naïve and idealistic—took command and destroyed the authority of the elders. The staggering amount of energy thus released was captured by the Reds because they, alone, had foreseen the inevitability of such social atomization; the Kuomintang, tied to its Confucian respect for traditional family authority and hierarchy, was blown to bits by this devastating explosion. The Communist Party extended its rule over increasingly vast areas of rural China while the Kuomintang armies gradually retreated behind the fortified walls of the cities—where, often deprived of the support of a large portion of the middle class and more often betrayed by demoralization, they surrendered wholesale.

The outcome of this vast movement could no longer be

doubted, and time and again a few clear-minded Nationalists attempted to displace Chiang Kai-shek—the Kwangsi generals Li Tsung-jen and Pai Chung-hsi, the "White Fox Alliance," especially—only to fail. Dispirited and without faith, without cohesion and loyalty since there was no ideal to be served and no faith to be inspired with, most Nationalist armies disintegrated at the summit. Some Nationalist leaders, war lords, generals such as Wei Li-huang and Fu Tso-yi (later minister of water conservation in Peking's Communist government), amazed at the consistency, determination and self-sacrifice of their Communist opponents, were considerably shaken in their former convictions—if they had any—and were sometimes converted to the new creed. Only in western China, in Kansu, Shansi and Tsinghai, did the Muslim Chinese fight with equal determination and fanaticism. But the time soon came when, victims of Chiang Kai-shek's hostile suspicions and stubborn narrow-mindedness, they ran out of supplies.[4]

The Red armies spread all over China, destroying the last shreds left of Western influence a century after the Western Powers had begun to blast their way into the Celestial Empire. The mammoth parades of the Reds in all conquered cities, their display of strength, iron discipline, rigid honesty and incorruptibility, the perfectly correct attitude of their battle-hardened veterans, their obvious selflessness and sincerity, everything pointed to an entirely new phenomenon in modern China. It was the final emergence of organized and messianic fanaticism, of a military religion which was taking over China's six hundred million people as Islam's armies had swept out of Arabia to Spain and India thirteen hundred years ago. And where had all this originated? In the minds and hearts of the Chinese intelligentsia of the 1920's. Narrow-minded and devout, endowed with an almost Biblical puritanism, those men were bound to make short shrift of their opponents. Once more, the capital of China was transferred to Peking, the ancient "Khan Baliq" of the Mongols and capital of the Manchus, and now, faithful to its destiny, once more the capital of an alien ruler from the north—but this time, of an alien philosophy blowing in from the vast spaces of Eurasia.

Unwelcome alike to Westerners and to Marxists, the basic fact was that the emergence of Red China closed a historical cycle which had started when Confucianist orthodoxy, and the great civilization that went with it, collapsed—long before the last Son of Heaven lost his throne in 1911. Under a new guise, often masquerading as a "progressive" movement in a modern sense, Mao's new up-to-date version of Marxism-Leninism was in fact a reaction toward the past. It conformed dramatically and often gruesomely to the basic urges of Chinese psychology which the West had chosen to ignore.

First of all, there was the urge toward a united world government, actual or potential, for all "civilized" mankind—that is, for the Communist world. The "barbarians," the non-Communists, are excluded from the pale but are destined to be eventually, forcibly or peacefully "civilized" as barbarians used to be in the old days. The old Celestial Empire collapsed; all right. All that had to be done was to find a broader unity, a larger framework more in line with a much broader and more compact world. The universalist pretensions of the old Sons of Heaven may have been misapplied, but in essence they were correct: the Chinese, Marxist or not, have to live according to a philosophy of life which is applicable to the whole of mankind.

This, then, was the second urge: the need for the supremacy of an orthodox philosophy, which harmonizes and synthesizes every thought and action of man with his destiny and with cosmic reality. This all-embracing philosophy encompasses ethics, politics, social life, economics, literature, art, science; it synthesizes perfectly theory and practice, thought and action. All that had to be done was to substitute Marx for Confucius.

The third requirement was that this new orthodoxy had to conform psychologically to Time-conscious people who had replaced the religious cults of former times by Confucianism and ancestor worship; it has to be a secular *philosophy of history* which seduces the historically minded Chinese and merely substitutes for the old Confucian, outdated explanation of the past. It takes the place of religion and emphasizes the Chinese contempt for "superstitious" explanations of cosmic reality. But it is, at the same time, the focus of all the emotional fervor and devotion usually granted to a religious faith. The Absolute cosmic Reality is a dynamic process unfolding dialectically in *time*, the process of history; it is not the Christian Almighty but a modernized version of the old, impersonal Tao. The Christian Almighty is conceived in the image of man, the unique incarnation of the Divine spark; He is the Almighty of individualistic men. The immanentist Chinese have displayed an opposite conception throughout history, in art, literature and philosophy, and to them the Absolute Reality is in the impersonal image of the whole of *nature*, not just *man*. It is bound to be less personal and less anthropomorphic.

The fourth requirement follows logically, echoed alike by Sun Yat-sen and the Reds, a rebirth of old yearnings welling up from the depths of the Chinese soul: the implacable reduction of the individual to his social function rather than the promotion of his full individuality, uniqueness and originality as in the West. This is to be achieved through the rigid enforcement of an almost "Confucian" conformism, through the *fan shen* process, the "change-over of the body" which amounts to a religious-like conversion euphemistically termed re-education, through Liu Shao-ch'i's "self-cultivation" which he specifically based on Confucius' philosophy,[5] through an almost traditional "brainwashing" which mutilates the individual's originality and idosyncrasy but transforms him into a smooth, well-designed cog fitting perfectly well into the intricate social machinery. The notion of *personal salvation* or self-realization, always dim in China, has been completely replaced by that of *collective progress*.

The fifth requirement springs naturally from the fourth: What is important in Marxist China, as it was in Confucian China, is the ethical standpoint. One of the contemporary thinkers, Ai Ssu-ch'i, makes it quite plain that conversion to the Communist world-outlook is primarily a moral problem; once that has been achieved, personal happiness follows inevitably, the happiness of mutilated men who have had their limbs cut off but who feel elated because they are permanently doped.

These requirements inevitably brought in their trail a massive effort at thought control, a modernized version of the old thought control which was so familiar to the Chinese at the close of the Warring States era: "All official histories . . . shall be burned; those who . . . permit themselves to hide the Shih-ching, the Shu-ching or the discourses of the hundred schools, must all go before the local civil and military authorities so that they may be burned. Those who shall dare to discuss among themselves the Shih-ching and the Shu-ching shall be put to death and their corpses exposed in a public place; those who shall make use of antiquity to belittle modern times shall be put to death with their relations. . . . Thirty days after the publication of this edict, those who have not burned their books shall be branded and sent to forced labor." [6]

This edict was promulgated by the First Universal Emperor more than two hundred years before Christ was born, when China became "modern." Twenty-two centuries later, Mao proclaimed in Yenan that literature and art must become "part of our revolutionary machinery" and, once in power, he put his theories into action in a way that the First Universal Emperor would have fully endorsed. Of the publications put out by the Commercial Press and the Chung Hua Book Company since the turn of our century, less than 14 per cent were approved and retained; the rest were destroyed: "From January to December 1951, in the Shanghai office alone, a total of 237 tons were destroyed for sale as waste paper." In Hsiangtan, the Hunan provincial government burned seventeen thousand cases of books belonging to a priceless collection. In Swatow, more than three hundred thousand volumes "were collected and burned in a bonfire which lasted from 22 to 25 May

1953" [7] . . . and so on. The wheel of history seems to have once again turned full circle.

Burning books is all very well, but it is not enough. The minds of living men have to be destroyed too, their memory obliterated, their personality blighted out of existence. The massive Ideological Remolding Movement, enforced in 1951, "brainwashed" what was left of independent minds in China and was described by a scholar as "probably one of the most spectacular events in human history. Tens of thousands of intellectuals . . . have been brought to their kness, accusing themselves relentlessly at tens of thousands of meetings and in tens of millions of written words." [8] A flood of abject confessions, denunciations of friendship, recantation and abjuration has drowned all expression of independent thought in China and has merged what is left of the Chinese mind into the structure of a monolithic state. And in May 1954 started the great reform movement which will so simplify the Chinese ideographic script that the past will be as effectively obliterated as Egypt's hieroglyphics once were. [9] Thought control will be made all the easier by this mutilation since there will not even be an instrument with which profound thought could be expressed if, by some odd chance, it should attempt to formulate itself. It will be so complete, so total and sweeping that Russian thought control will eventually seem childishly ineffective in comparison.

To those characteristics of Red China which brought out again in bold but different relief all the old constants of the Chinese temperament, we must add the socialization of all major economic activities, which has always been more or less congenial to the soul of China's inherent collectivism. Modern Marxism in China is almost a form of ancestor worship in favor of the ghosts of the great "socialists" of the past: Wu Ti, Wang Mang and Wang An-shih, and countless minor statesmen with a collectivist bent. It has brought back the old Confucian distrust of the profit motive, the contempt for individual economic pursuits, the triumph of the *co-operative* over the *competitive* spirit which has always been alien to the Chinese soul.

And, as a natural compensation, this new Marxist empire is hierarchic, ruled by an "elite" of chosen men who have mastered the new orthodoxy which has replaced the old one; they are the new Communist "mandarins," many of whom, like Chou En-lai himself, are the lineal descendants of great mandarin families. And under them the long-standing struggle against Mao's pet dislikes, "extreme democratization" and "absolute equalitarianism" [10] was intensified, bringing out the inevitable corollary of economic socialism: the creation of widespread social distinctions. For a vanishing economic incentive based on individual profit the Chinese Communists have substituted, as the Russians did before them, vast distinctions in wages, privileges, power and social status such as are unheard of in Western democracies. The profit motive is replaced by "prestige" and face-giving privileges. And when Li Li-san issued the Party's fiat in November 1949, "We oppose equalitarianism," [11] China could have known that the old days had come back in modern disguise.

Red China received its official birth certificate when the Central People's Government of the Chinese People's Republic was formally inaugurated in Peking on October 1, 1949. Lesser men would have been terrified by the crushing burden of having to rule one quarter of the human race after a half century of devastating foreign and civil wars. Mao Tse-tung and his lieutenants were only a few years away from their life in the caves of Yenan, and now they were masters of the fate of six hundred million Chinese. Yet they displayed from the start a remarkable political skill which puts to historical shame the crudeness and clumsiness of Lenin's Bolsheviks upon their own seizure of power in Russia. Mao Tse-tung did not proclaim the dictatorship of the proletariat; instead he proceeded to create a united front of "democratic elements" in which all approved "democratic" parties and individuals could find their appointed place. A large part of the Kuomintang's leadership had refused, for various reasons, to follow Chiang Kai-shek to Formosa—some emigrating to Hong Kong or the United States, some remaining on the mainland and more or less willing to collaborate with the new regime. The latter, an odd assortment of ex-warlords, army generals, diplomats, and businessmen, were put to full, if subordinate, use. Refusing to accept in the ranks of the Chinese Communist Party all those social elements that were hopelessly tainted by the past, the Communist leadership thus managed to preserve the ideological "purity" of its elite while disarming and utilizing many of its former opponents. This window dressing was not destined to last beyond the first stage of "socialist construction"; nor were these non-Communist elements naïve enough to believe that they had more than a short time span ahead of them.

No revolutionary regime has been as sure of itself from the start of its rule as the CCP. A close-knit organization, utterly disciplined and seasoned by thirty years of guerrilla warfare, it had known very few purges and no basic change of leadership. Coherent and stable, provided by Mao Tse-tung with a remarkable doctrinal corpus, the CCP fearlessly clamped its iron rule on China. Such iron rule had never been dreamed of in the old imperial days, even in the days of greatest tyranny, when, if only for lack of modern technical means to do so, mandarin authority never went below the county level (*hsien*). Now the Communist apparatus penetrated all the way down, through townships (*hsiang*), to the street and housing-block levels, tightening its relentless grip on all human beings without exception. This thorough organization was completed in 1954 when Red China's new constitution came into being.

The first phase, dedicated to "reconstruction," lasted three years. In Communist jargon reconstruction meant consolidation of Communist power. Land reform was carried out speedily and ruthlessly. Landlords were annihilated, rich farmers reduced to the level of poor peasants; in the process of this agrarian revolution, in which millions of men were slaughtered, the Communist regime fanned all the flames of social discontent, making the vast masses of Chinese peasants their ally and willing tool before turning against them and depriving them, in turn, of their landownership. In the short space of three years the entire "sedan-chair" gentry was liquidated, along with all its allies and subordinates. The New Democracy stage had come to an end.

Now came the "transition to socialism" phase, along with the first Five-Year Plan (1953–57). At no time, then or now, did Red China's leaders ever hide the fact that economic development was not meant to raise the low standard of living of China's population; they boldly proclaimed that it was aimed at increasing as rapidly as possible China's national power—which meant the maximum development of heavy industry at the expense of light industry and agriculture. However, in spite of wholesale expropriations of foreign assets and gradual socialization of all means of production, Red China had no available capital to invest in its economic development save some expected loans from the Soviet Union—no capital, that is, except the labor and sweat of its enormous peasant masses. Not only capital was in short supply; so were technical experts of all kinds, industrial managers, engineers. Undaunted, Red China's leaders went ahead, negotiated in 1950 and 1954 a total amount of 430 million dollars in Soviet long-term loans, and proceeded to launch the most ambitious project of industrial development ever conceived, believing that its "brain-washing" ability could dispense with economic incentives and rewards of any kind. Even in its first Five-Year Plan Soviet Russia never dared go that far. The Chinese people entered, in fact, a long nightmare during which every last ounce of energy was extracted from an underfed and exhausted population. Whipped into line by fanatical Communist cadres day in and day out, hundreds of millions of men and women scurried all over the Chinese landscape building dams, planting forests, digging irrigation canals, building rudimentary industrial plants—in fact, wasting a staggering amount of work through inefficiency, bad planning, lack of coordination, and absence of technical know-how.

The first grave signs of impending economic breakdown appeared in 1956, and Soviet Russia was called upon for additional assistance, both technical and financial. What remained of private industry was nationalized, and China's Communist leaders pushed and shoved an increasingly sluggish population into ever greater efforts. At the end of the Five-Year Plan, impressive progress had indeed been made in heavy industry; but largely at the expense of a lagging agricultural sector, now plagued as it was by the drive toward collectivization, which started in earnest in 1953. Food rationing was inaugurated in 1955, partly as a result of a shift from food to industrial crops, partly due to the fact that China could fulfill its external financial obligations only with agricultural produce. A considerable trade deficit was inaugurated in 1955; in 1956 Red China began to export more than it imported in order to start paying its external debts. Total trade dropped in 1956 and dropped further in 1957.

The general economic situation was becoming alarming, and China's Communist leaders realized that it was partly a consequence of profound political maladjustments. Not only the country's peasants and workers were unresponsive; even the intellectuals, many of whom had been their enthusiastic supporters for so long, had become antagonistic. Thinking over the old historical lessons of China's past, Mao Tse-tung decided that the time had come to reestablish a certain harmony in the relations between China's intellectual elite and the CCP. Besides, he took at face value all the recantations and abjurations that he had beaten out of them a few years earlier, believing his brain-washing to have been a success. In May 1956, he made a historical speech which he summed up in a now-famous slogan: "Let a hundred flowers bloom and a hundred schools of thought contend." It was as if the Legalists, masters of China twenty-two centuries earlier, had asked ancient China's cowed scholars to return to the famous era of the "Hundred Schools" of philosophy which they had just brought to a close. Lu Ting-yi, head of the propaganda department, developed his master's theme and proclaimed full freedom of expression for all intellectuals in all fields: literature, art, sociology, economics, politics.

At first nothing happened. China's intellectual elite had

learned to distrust all official pronouncements of this kind. The government, however, pressed its liberalization campaign in the spring of 1957 and prodded all non-Communist officials, independent personalities, and intellectuals into voicing out loud their innermost thoughts. Thus provoked, the Hundred Flowers began to bloom furiously in June 1957—and the result was devastating for the regime. The Hundred Flowers quickly metamorphosed themselves into millions of thorns in Communist flesh. A tidal wave of virulent criticism threatened to engulf the entire Communist leadership of China, catching it off balance. Its unexpected violence almost threatened, in fact, to put an end to the CCP's rule altogether, and a counter-offensive was immediately launched. Choosing to appear cleverly Machiavellian rather than naïvely sincere (which they were), the Communist leaders promptly proclaimed that their purpose had been all along to uncover the hidden "poisonous weeds." There followed a ruthless "weeding-out" process; critics were crushed, expelled from whatever official positions they occupied, jailed, or sent to distant concentration camps for "reeducation." This period of freedom of expression had lasted a mere six weeks; when it was all over, the Red leaders clamped down ferociously, but lost whatever confidence China's intellectual elite had ever put in them. Toward the end of 1957 a gigantic rectification campaign was undertaken and all hope of limited freedom of thought and expression was buried under a relentless avalanche of Communist propaganda and persecution.

The Hundred Flowers episode had revealed another dangerous source of opposition: the resurgent anti-Chinese nationalism of all the minorities. Red China had made it a point to recover all the territories that had belonged, at one time or another, to the deceased Manchu Empire (save Outer Mongolia, which had been firmly welded to the Soviet Union as a favored satellite since the early 1920's). In 1950 Red Chinese armies had overrun Tibet and had reestablished Chinese domination over the Rood of the World for the first time since the fall of the Manchu dynasty. In Sinkiang, as well as in Tibet, Red

Chinese rule was relatively mild during the first few years and, in words if not in deeds, respectful of minority nationalities. The government's propaganda steadily attacked "Great Han chauvinism," without, however, granting any substantial autonomy to Tibetans, Mongols, or Uighurs, without, in fact, being willing or able to curb the Chinese superiority complex vis-à-vis the "barbarian" minorities. In 1957 discontent reached a climax in Sinkiang and threatened to overthrow the rule of the Chinese minority in the immense Central Asian territory. Peking's patience came to an end. From December 1957 on, the attacks against "Great Han chauvinism" were halted, and in February 1958 the Nationalities Affairs Commission bluntly stated that all "local nationalisms" would be suppressed. Tibet's turn came in 1959 when the Dalai Lama fled to India and the Tibetan rebellion was ruthlessly crushed. The following years made it plain that Peking's solution to the problem was to drown all minority nationalities under an increasing flood of Chinese immigrants until such time as these nationalities would become small minorities in every district of their own homelands.

At the end of the first Five-Year Plan it became obvious that whereas the industrial and nonagricultural sectors had markedly improved, agriculture had failed to develop to any appreciable extent. On his second pilgrimage to Moscow (November 1957), ostensibly to attend the fortieth anniversary of the Bolshevik Revolution, Mao Tse-tung applied again for greater Soviet economic and technical assistance; he was turned down and came back to Peking empty-handed. Following a secret struggle between moderates and radicals in the higher echelons of the CCP, Mao Tse-tung decided to embark on the boldest but most precarious adventure of his remarkable career: at the February 1958 meeting of the National People's Congress, he proclaimed the inauguration of the "Great Leap Forward," a headlong rush, without any external assistance, into a staggering rate of economic development that would startle the world. What followed deepened the nightmare in which the Chinese people had now been living for years. Agriculture had already become fully collectivized, but that was only the first step. In April the first "commune" appeared, and soon hundreds of thousands of collective farms were merged into the most monstrous socio-political invention of modern man: husbands and wives lost their homes and children, and often one another as well, were sent to separate dormitories, ate in mess halls while the children were attended to in nurseries. Organized along paramilitary lines, the communes turned out to be vast concentration camps in which hundreds of millions of Chinese led a spartan life under harsh discipline. Collective farms lost all their property, which became the property of the "whole people." What the Legalists had advocated but never dared apply twenty-two centuries earlier had now come to pass. More than seven hundred thousand collective farms were amalgamated into twenty-four thousand communes—and now Peking's Red leaders could boast that China was bypassing the socialist stage and entering into full Communism way ahead of Soviet Russia.

Flogged into frenzied action by the fully mobilized party cadres, hundreds of millions of Chinese men, women, and children worked fourteen to sixteen hours a day tilling fields, digging canals, building backyard furnaces; peasants by day, most Chinese became industrial workers at night. Enfeebled by lack of food and sleep, hundreds of millions of blue ants scurried hither and thither at the whistled command of party cadres, but in fact accomplishing far less than they would have under normal humane conditions. Spontaneous resistance started building up when the attempt to destroy family life became apparent to all and the "Great Leap Forward" began to collapse slowly, irresistibly, like a disintegrating plaster giant. The utter confusion and inefficiency generated by this incredible revolution threatened to turn to chaos. The Communist leaders faced the appalling situation and reacted quickly; in December the Wuhan Resolution confirmed a discreet shift away from the commune back to the collective and a more pronounced shift toward personal incentives: money wages were again emphasized as against free supplies; homes, agricultural implements, savings, and small plots of land were returned to the peasant owners, who were again allowed to sell their private produce in a free market; mess halls were no longer compulsory, and private dwellings were no longer torn down to make room for huge dormitories. Having for a while stood on the threshold of true Communism (as the Russians never had), the great bulk of the Chinese population shrank back in horror and returned to socialism with a sigh of relief.

The communes did not disappear altogether but were integrated in a more complex structure based on the "three levels of ownership": commune (*hsiang*, or township), production brigade (collective), and production team (cooperative, which coincided more or less with the old agricultural village). However, the economic consequences of the disaster were felt for years to come. Hunger and sometimes starvation stalked the land. In 1960 China had to ask the Soviet Union for permission to postpone payment of 300 million dollars due on its debt; in 1961 China was compelled to buy ten million tons of food grain abroad. The entire economic structure of Red China was temporarily dislocated by this experiment. A grandiose export scheme launched in 1958 whereby Chinese goods would swamp the Far East with cheap goods also collapsed. China defaulted on many of its foreign-trade commitments and saw its economic influence abroad decline drastically. But the worst part of Red China's economic dislocation was yet to come. As a result of smoldering differences with the Soviet Union, the thousands of Soviet technicians and engineers who were working in China left for their country in 1960, taking their skills and blueprints with them. Red China was left alone, to get out of its gigantic predicament all by itself. And by now the most important element in China's relations with the outer world echoed around our planet like a clap of thunder: Red China and the Soviet Union had reached a parting of the ways.

Red China's foreign policy was inscribed in the context of China's past, both remote and recent. The only country left with significant privileges in China when Mao Tse-tung took

over was Soviet Russia—and in spite of its being the acknowledged leader of the "socialist" brotherhood, it was promptly
asked to liquidate all such privileges. In the early to middle
1950's all Soviet rights to the joint operation of the Manchurian railway system were abandoned without compensation; so were Port Arthur and Dairen. Every other foreign
privilege or asset that had not already been liquidated before
(extraterritoriality had been abolished in 1943) was taken over
and confiscated. But all that was child's play. China's Communist masters had barely established their rule in Peking
when they rushed headlong into a military intervention in
Korea, where, with merely their raw manpower in unlimited
supply, they boldly took on simultaneously the United Nations and the United States. It became apparent then, and
was steadily confirmed later on, that Red China's aggressive
involvements in foreign affairs were more than a display of its
obvious imperialism: it was also a convenient way for its leaders to tighten up their political control of the country and
of whipping up the ever-present xenophobia of the Chinese.

Red China's aggressiveness had, and has, many targets: first
and foremost, of course, was Formosa and the remnants of
Chinese Nationalists who had sought refuge on the island.
Right next to it was the protecting power whose umbrella
covers the entire Far East: the United States, whose strategic
interests range from Japan and South Korea to South Vietnam.
More remotely but still definitely were all those foreign countries that had been tributaries of the Chinese Empire at one
time or another—which includes all of Mongolia (Inner and
Outer), all the Himalayan states, and the entire Indochinese
peninsula. Chinese maps display other potential targets, such
as the Soviet Union's Far Eastern Province and most of Soviet
Central Asia as far as the Caspian Sea. Last but not least, Red
China's leaders made it plain that they expect the rest of Asia
to revolt and go over to the Communist camp in the near
future.

Red China's accomplishments in foreign affairs during the

first fifteen years of its existence are truly spectacular, considering the weakened state of its economy: paralyzing American power in Korea and then gradually in Laos and Vietnam, blocking Nationalist power during the Formosa Strait Crisis, neutralizing Burma, Nepal, and Pakistan, thus isolating India diplomatically prior to attacking it and seizing large slices of Himalayan territory. However, these were more specifically *Chinese* than *Communist* actions: Red China gradually proved to be more Chinese than Red, more able to depend on its enormous manpower than on the ideological spread of its doctrine—the only exception being the remarkable mastery of protracted guerrilla, warfare, which is Mao Tse-tung's great contribution to Communist doctrine and which is highly exportable, as can be seen in Southeast Asia. It was, and is, this fundamental cleavage in the Red Chinese package that had to lead, eventually, to a loosening of its ties with its Soviet ally and to a dramatic break in 1960. This break was a few years in the making, and only a combination of Soviet diplomacy, overwhelming economic superiority, and Chinese economic bungling prevented it from taking place earlier. But as years went by and as the Chinese asserted with increasing forcefulness their belief that Mao Tse-tung's gospel was the more valid form of Marxism-Leninism, and criticized the Soviet Russians for sliding into a thaw in the Cold War, the break became inevitable. The chasm between the Communist giants opened wide after Khrushchev's blasting speech at the June meeting of the Rumanian Communist Party Congress, and was formalized at the December meeting of eighty-one Communist parties when Soviet Russia's position received an overwhelming endorsement by most of the delegations. From then on, until Khrushchev's fall from power in 1964, the debate between the two Red powers became increasingly acrimonious. Nor did Khrushchev's departure imply any real reconciliation.

It is quite clear that behind the ideological arguments and counter-arguments lies a whole body of national and cultural reality that cannot be ignored—the reality of conflicting national interests and ambitions along a five-thousand-mile common border, the giant stature of the contenders, which makes it impossible for the one to overpower the other, the great disparity in economic development and technological know-how, the profound differences in their psychological and cultural outlooks. These basic elements of the Russia-China reality will remain in the future regardless of whether the two Red giants appear to paper them over or not. Wringing out of its hundreds of millions of sweating subjects a modest amount of ecnomic power, the Red Chinese leaders have been able to "go it alone"; sustained by their great sense of national pride, they have overcome all obstacles to develop and explode their first crude nuclear device in the fall of 1964, establish Red China as the successful model for, and leader of, all present and future revolutions and protracted guerrilla warfare in the underdeveloped countries of the world—without or, on occasion, even against Soviet Russian assistance. The Red Chinese have begun to split many of the world's Communist parties right down the middle into pro-Moscow and pro-Peking wings (notably in India). Red China's more violent attitude toward the West is bound to appeal to those impatient elements in Asia, Africa, and Latin America that are disappointed at Soviet Russia's increasingly "bourgeois" outlook. It is, however, a plain fact that Red China has not been able to develop all the sinews of a modern industrial economy compatible with its ambitions, and is not likely to do so in the near future; its main element of power is the gigantic size of its population and territory. Largely paralyzed by Marxist socialism and its clumsy application, China's rate of economic development cannot compare, even when due allowance is made for its more backward starting point, with Japan's miraculous recovery in a climate of relatively free enterprise. And the fact that Japan, with hardly any natural resources, finds itself in the position of being a world power in every sense of the word except the military is an important fact to bear in mind: as so often in the recent past, a great deal of the future history of China will depend, in the long run, on Japan's attitude toward the mainland. Right now it looks as if Japan is getting into the postion of being able to play off (at least economically) against one another the United States, Soviet Russia, and Red China and may end up being a natural ally of the weakest contender against the strongest.

There is no blinking the fact that regardless of all its internal weaknesses, Red China is a world power today. This it owes, more than anything else, to its size and new-found unity and to its vigorous, if fanatical, leadership. It is also clear that so long as it remains faithful to Marxist economics and sociology in its most extreme form, its internal weakness is not likely to be overcome. It is only to the extent that, like Soviet Russia, it modifies and adapts its doctrine to basic human nature that it can truly become a formidable power. But this is a long way off. It can never do so abruptly, even if it so wished, for fear of losing the all-embracing magic recipe that is psychologically introducing it to the mysteries of the modern world. To that extent Red China finds its limitations at the heart of the very philosophy that has made it again into a great power.

14

TODAY AND TOMORROW

Red China is a more up-to-date, more ruthless, more efficient version of what the Celestial Empire had been for thousands of years. The forms have changed, drab caps and standardized tunics have replaced the glittering apparel, peacock feathers, jewels and silk brocades of former times; but the contents are the same. From the depths of the Chinese soul, there welled up an irresistible urge to revert to familiar patterns, an urge to retrieve a monistic view of things while adapting this view to a new and revolutionary world. Now that the blinding dust raised by the thunderous collapse of China's civilization is beginning to settle in blood and tears, this is becoming increasingly evident.

But besides this almost cyclical recurrence, there are some fundamental changes. The universalism is now world-wide, and the urge to "civilize" the non-Marxist "barbarians" makes imperialism an inevitable by-product of the Communist revolution in China. It has given to Chinese consciousness a "messianic" striving which was totally lacking in Confucian orthodoxy. The former stability, having been shattered by the impact of the West, is replaced by a dynamic striving toward some apocalyptic goal. The static cycle of Confucianism has become a spiral in which the cycles themselves are in motion and tend toward a goal: Yin and Yang have become Marx's thesis and antithesis, and the Tao has been metamorphosed into an explosive "Diamat." Everything now is in movement, tending toward Communism in China, then Communism in Asia and finally in the whole world—and then, at last, the golden age of world peace and world-wide classless society.

Chinese Communism has fully adopted Lenin's revision of original Marxism which added the world-wide struggle between capitalist and proletarian *nations* to the orthodox *class* struggle. As such, world Communism in its Chinese incarnation now assumes the significance it had always meant to assume: It is a struggle between wholly alien civilizations, a gigantic protest against the dominant civilization of the West, an exasperated reaction such as the Classical world of Greece and Rome faced when the Parthians invaded Persia and Mesopotamia and destroyed Greek culture and influence, which had dominated the Orient for centuries.

This is the great Far Eastern problem today. It is difficult to foresee to what extent the endemic inertia of a vast population of earth-bound peasants and the inherent economic weaknesses of collectivism can brake this messianic imperialism; in any case, they are not likely to deflect it in the near future. It is symptomatic that, true to their basic Marxist orthodoxy which had been so badly mauled during their rise to power, the Red Chinese decided in March 1949—as soon as victory was in sight—to shift the Party's "center of activity from rural to urban districts." [12] The peasants, on whose angry discontent the Communists had rolled to power, are now discarded and relegated to an inferior status, behind the urban proletariat which had contributed next to nothing to their victory. And, from then on, a gigantic propaganda campaign has been seeking to raise the prestige of the urban and industrial worker to the detriment of the "less civilized" peasant. Industrialization and the creation of a vast, mobile, dynamic, urban proletariat will tend to overshadow the hitherto irrepressible power of the earth-bound peasant.

At this point, it is essential to take into account the physical environment. The biological vitality and colonizing ability of the Chinese are truly fabulous. Overpopulation threatens to add its weight to Chinese imperialism and make full use of a power of expansion unmatched by any other race. The nature of this threat is quite plain if one remembers that the Chinese can live at ease in the arctic climate of Manchuria as well as in the tropical and equatorial heat of Southeast Asia. They have, in our century, swamped the native Manchus. Fifty years after having been allowed to settle in the northern land, the Chinese number more than forty million and all signs point to a population of over a hundred million Chinese in Manchuria before the century is over. They outnumber the Mongols three to one in Inner Mongolia. Fifteen million of them live in Southeast Asia; they almost outnumber the Malays in Malaya (ten to one in Singapore). They constitute at least one fifth of the population of Thailand. And they are all backed by the formidable power of seven hundred million compatriots in China proper.

This threat is plain but the way it is being blunted is just as plain. Not only are the Southeast Asians aware of this threat, but the Russians themselves can live in holy terror of seeing their almost empty Far Eastern possessions drowned by a staggering influx of Chinese. This biological vitality is bound to become part and parcel of Chinese Communism, bound to favor its expansion or, on the contrary, arouse such resistance along its borders that the Marxist expansion will slow down. In any case, it is well to keep in mind a cardinal fact: the growing weight of the entire Far Eastern people—seven hundred million Chinese, Koreans and Japanese—an energetic group of technically skilled populations, living in the invigorating climate of temperate or cold areas. This fact stands out in bold relief when the Far Easterners are compared with the nations of tropical Asia or the Middle East. The Far East is the only non-Western area of the world, with the exception of Russia, that can possibly challenge the power of the West.

There is something almost terrifying, for us Westerners, in this recurrence of old Chinese themes in a new dress—terrifying because it shows the amazing superficiality of our impact, which has been mostly negative, and also terrifying because, somehow, we ourselves begin to doubt our own values if they are rejected with such violence by a large part of the human race.[13] To these two types of fear correspond two independent problems, two ways of looking at the Chinese revolution; the first one revolves around the Chinese themselves, the second concerns the West and its own future evolution.

If we uncover the deep-rooted feelings which the Chinese concealed for so long under layers of urbane courtesy, we find an immense hatred for the West which has been constantly swelling for generations. This hatred was based on a multiplicity of sentiments: the despair of a collapsed civilization, the inability to adapt the broken fragments of this former civilization to a Western-type structure as Japan had been able to, the mental frustration imputable to the West's inadequate message in religion and philosophy, the bitter humiliation of a proud people who had become second-class citizens in their own land, the frenetic anger at the hypocrisy of the globe's new overlords. In short, a hatred which had reached such pathological proportions that whatever new creed would seize hold in China was bound to be basically anti-Western. It was even made plain in the old days of Kuomintang supremacy when the right-wing "C.C. Clique" made no secret of its virulent anti-Western feeling, in Chiang Kai-shek's own book, *China's Destiny*.[14]

A great deal of ground is cleared once this fundamental truth is faced and accepted. It is not pleasant nor flattering to ourselves, but the facts glare at us. This is also the way the West had instinctively felt it although the West could not understand it quite clearly. On the Western side a psychological reaction set in, and it was discovered with amazement that the Chinese, after all, were capable of a number of things for which few Westerners had credited them: individual abnegation and religious-like fervor for an idealistic cause, extreme discipline and rigid honesty, great fighting potential and remarkable political efficiency. But by the time these unexpected psychological treasures had been uncovered in the Chinese soul, it was too late for the West; it had not read the lessons of history in time because it had not sought for any.

Had it read those lessons correctly, the West would have understood the real, *symbolic* meaning of Marxism. At this stage of history, the Chinese simply do not *understand* economics, productivity or social relations, in the Western sense. To them, capitalism and socialism in our sense of the words mean nothing, evoke no inward response. Economics is the artificial world in which the West moves, the hermetic, esoteric phraseology which it uses, the *emblem* which the Communists have to grasp and possess if they are to accomplish their main purpose, defeat of the overpowering West. The Marxist-Leninist doctrine is filled with social and economic theories, most of which have been proved blatantly false. But no matter; what is objectively false can be subjectively true; Marxism affords its devotees a psychological satisfaction of a religious nature. When Kuo Mo-jo, the "Cultural Commissar" of Red China, applies the exceedingly narrow Marxist terminology to an interpretation of Chinese history,[15] he gratifies the sentiments of his coreligionists. Narrow as it is, his interpretation is still more satisfying emotionally than the conflicting interpretations of Western and Western-oriented Chinese scholars—and it is far more gratifying to the pride of the offsprings of the old mandarins.

What the West has hitherto refused to see is that the falsity of Marxism's economic thesis is quite immaterial and simply does not touch the vital core of Marxism's historical significance. "Scientific" Marxism is in fact based on primitive but powerful *magic*, on the desire to overpower a mysterious foe (the technological power of the West) by *duplicating* it artificially and destroying it by ritual reproduction. In adopting the Marxist philosophy, Red China is in fact reverting to a more primitive outlook than that offered by the contemporary West—but one that is more congenial to China's traditional culture.

Magic is the response of people who face an external challenge but who cannot understand the logical articulations of this challenge. This irrational response is based, as Chinese culture was, on the presumed laws of correspondence of natural sympathy and antipathy: like attracts like. Ritual reproduction will *constrain* and bind these occult forces that cannot be faced rationally. Five-year plans, socialistic reforms, elimination of nonproductive elements, labor reform, production targets, all these are very real. They take place in the world of concrete facts. But what is usually overlooked is that they also represent magic spells, incantations, and that this is perhaps the most important point. Magic is highly effective, but its impact hits the practitioner rather than the object; its impact is *subjective*, not objective. Those Chinese Communists who live consciously and completely in a world of economic statistics, norms and production targets really do believe that they become superior to those Westerners who taught them this mysterious language to start with. But whereas the Westerner understands this economic world which he created rationally, and takes it casually, the Chinese Communist will embrace it with religious fervor and all the ruthless excesses of unbounded passion. Westerners have not yet been willing to understand this psychological element in the tremendous appeal of Marxism in Russia and Asia.

Even the style of Red China is in the tradition of Old China. History is rewritten to conform to the moral norms of the (Marxist) present, and is not meant to present an objective picture of the past as it really was. Official statistics published by the government no more conform to objective reality than Marxist historiography—they are meant to have an emotional impact at the time of publication. Marxist jargon often gives way before classical Chinese proverbs and sayings or before modern aphorisms expressed in the traditional style: "The East wind prevails over the West wind," "paper tigers," "Hundred Flowers," concrete and vivid expressions that have no counterpart in Soviet Russia. Just as traditional is the love of the Red Chinese for numerology, with all its implicit magic appeal: Five-Antis, Three-Strengths, Four Pests, Five Daggers, and so on, which enclose in striking fashion all the main Commandments of the Chinese Communist bible. Communism in Red China is more than anything else a tremendous moral experience (in spite of its built-in inhumanity): central to its creed is Mao Tse-tung's profound conviction that human nature can and must be radically altered in order to build the Communist "paradise on earth" of the future.

Communism in China is a means to an end, not the end itself. It triumphed because it was congenial to some parts of the Chinese soul—and also because no other philosophy was available. Europe and America were far too engrossed in their own economic development to bother about philosophic and religious reconstruction. What picture of itself did the West present in China? As anywhere else in Asia, it was a discordant conflux of religious missionaries who were often divided by profound and bitter rivalries and who exported a bewildering variety of conflicting teachings; of philosophers who contra-dicted the teachings of the missionaries; of businessmen who cared neither for religion nor philosophy but were solely bent on extracting the maximum of commercial profits; and of a variety of other Westerners who seemed imbued with a pre-posterous superiority complex for which there was no apparent justification, either in their religions or in their philosophies. How could such a civilization impress the Chinese, who spent four thousand years of their long history searching for the all-embracing system which explains and co-ordinates everything?

We are irretrievably bound to past and future, whether we like it or not. We are made to pay in every way for our fore-fathers' errors and we must consciously work, not for ourselves, but for our children and for their descendants. We must have a *philosophy of history* because we must have a philosophy of life, because we must know who we are, where we come from and where we are going—because, as the example of China has dramatically demonstrated, if we do not provide such a philosophy for the rest of mankind, others will; and their crude philosophy will not be to our liking. The beginning of wisdom would perhaps be to meditate Sir Walter Raleigh's incisive remark that "councils to which Time hath not been called, Time will not ratify."

NOTES
AND REFERENCES

Introduction

1 Even without the benefit of a comprehensive philosophy of history, many experts on Chinese history have been struck by those cyclical recurrences. One of them claims that "In some cases similarities between the experiences in China during the Spring and Autumn period and events at later times in the West are unbelievably precise" (see Walker, *The Multi-State System of Ancient China*, pp. xi, 124, 129). The same is true of all other civilizations, India for example (see Law, *Interstate Relations in Ancient India*).

Chapter 1

1 Coulborn, *Feudalism in History*, pp. 188, 189.
2 Lin Yutang, *My Country and My People*, p. 277.
3 Needham, *Science and Civilization in China*, i, p. 87. See also Maspero, *La Chine Antique*, p. 103.
4 Needham, *Science and Civilization in China*, i, p. 88.
5 *I-Ching*, i, p. 1.
6 Ibid., i, p. 3.
7 Ibid., i, p. 5.
8 Competition can oppose only elements that are identical and comparable. The Chinese, with their emphasis on the sexual co-operation of the complementary Yang and Yin had an *organic*

outlook on life which emphasized the fundamental *differences* in Being rather than their identity. Co-operation, rather than competition, presides over the association of elements which are wholly incomparable—the co-operation established by the various organs of a living body because each one of them performs a different function.

9   *I-Ching*, i, p. 9.
10 Needham, *Science and Civilization in China*, ii, p. 286.

Chapter 2

1   This is a typical phenomenon of "mimetic" magic which is perfectly in tune with the requirements of Chinese psychology. But it is also an example of what Arnold Toynbee calls the "mechanicalness of Mimesis," the disease which sets in at the dawn of Civilization when trail-blazing cultural growth comes to an end: "Just because mimesis is a kind of drill, it is a kind of mechanization of human life and movement. . . . The condition required for effective mimesis . . . is a considerable degree of machine-like automatism" (Toynbee, *A Study of History*, pp. 276–78).

2   Needham, *Science and Civilization in China*, ii, p. 13.

3   Thomas, *Chinese Political Thought*, p. 5.

4   The truly colossal number of historians in China has struck every thoughtful observer. But it was probably the philosopher Hegel who perceived for the first time the glaring contrast between the Chinese feeling for history and the complete absence of any such feeling among the Indians. In his *Philosophy of History*, he remarks: "It strikes everyone in beginning to form an acquaintance with the treasures of Indian literature, that a land so rich in intellectual products and those of the profoundest order of thought, has no History; and in this respect contrasts most strongly with China—an empire possessing one going back to the most ancient times" (*op. cit.*, p. 61). And the Indians themselves have been at a loss to explain this contrast. A contemporary Indian historian states: "The almost utter lack of historical texts certainly appears as a somewhat strange phenomenon . . . We have therefore to admit that the literary genius of India, so fertile and active in almost all conceivable branches of study, was not applied to chronicling the records of kings and the rise and fall of states and

nations. It is difficult to give a rational explanation for this deficiency but the fact admits of no doubt." (Majumdar, *The Vedic Age*, p. 47.) We know, of course, that there is a perfectly rational explanation: a different attitude as regards Time and Space, a world-outlook which conceived Time to be an illusion and made the Indians live in a permanent "present."

5   Hughes, *Chinese Philosophy in Classical Times*, p. 28.

6   Ibid., p. 157.

7   The Chinese discovered the "conditioned reflex" long before Pavlov.

8   Keyserling, *The Travel Diary of a Philosopher*, ii, p. 41.

9   Ibid., p. 40.

10   David Riesman's sociological studies point out this basic difference between what he terms the "inner-directed" man who is a product of the individualism of post-Renaissance Europe (and who was still the dominant type in the China of the Spring and Autumn era), the "tradition-directed" man who preceded him and the "other-directed" man of our days who is now replacing him. But in fact, historical perspective shows us that the "other-directed" man (who needs approval and direction from others, but "contemporary" others rather than ancestors) slowly metamorphoses himself back into a tradition-directed man when cultural growth comes to an end and unadulterated Civilization takes over. Thus there are only two basic types: the Culture man and the Civilization man, the "other-directed" man of our days being only a temporary phenomenon in the transition from one to the other. The Chinese became briefly "other-directed" in the Warring States period, and eventually became "tradition-directed" for thousands of years thereafter. (See Riesman, *The Lonely Crowd*, p. 38.)

11   Needham, *Science and Civilization in China*, ii, p. 109.

12   *Tao Te Ching*, chap. 48.

13   Ibid., chap. 25.

14   Indian (Hindu and Buddhist) art, however great in its own right, never reaches the extreme spiritual quality of Chinese art because it insists only too often on remaining on a lower level where materialistic elements predominate. The true parallel is between the profound Hindu mystic who is not artistically creative and the profound Chinese artist who "spiritualizes" coarse matter.

15   Lin Yutang, *My Country and My People*, p. 296.

Chapter 3

1   Hughes, *Chinese Philosophy in Classical Times*, p. 28.

2   Ibid., p. 43.

3   It was to China the equivalent of what the philosophies of Adam Smith and Stuart Mill were to the West in the nineteenth century—practical, mostly concerned with economics and ethics, basically utilitarian.

4   Hughes, *Chinese Philosophy in Classical Times*, p. 151.

5   Ibid., p. xviii.

6   Hu Shih, *Development of the Logical Method in Ancient China*, p. 152. It is interesting to note that Hsün-tzu (the counterpart of Hobbes in our Western philosophy) was a pessimist who thought that man's fundamental nature is bad and has to be regulated by law, whereas his opponent Mencius thought (like Jean-Jacques Rousseau in the West) that man is basically good (see Walker, *The Multi-State System of Ancient China*, p. 119).

7   Hughes, *Chinese Philosophy in Classical Times*, p. 106.

8   Walker, *The Multi-State System of Ancient China*, p. 35.

9   Ibid., p. 15.

10 Ibid., p. 16. The growth and proliferation of the middle class was due, and is always due, to the growth of cities and urban living, expanding trade and commerce, technical improvements and the development of industry, however rudimentary by our standards. It is part and parcel of the "modernization" which heralds the approach of Civilization, democracy (in the sense of social equality) and the predominance of economic thinking. The rise in influence of the upper middle class and of capitalists reached its peak during the subsequent period of the Warring States (see Walker, *op. cit.*, p. 126, note 18).

11 Ibid., p. 18.

12 Ibid., pp. 37, 38.

13 Ibid., p. 33.

14 Needham, *Science and Civilization in China*, ii, p. 212.

15 Hughes, *Chinese Philosophy in Classical Times*, p. 258.

16 Ibid., p. 266.

17 Ibid., p. 77.

18 Coulborn, *Feudalism in History*, p. 67.

19 Grousset, *The Rise and Splendor of the Chinese Empire*, p. 39.

20 Walker, *The Multi-State System of Ancient China*, p. 74.
21 Ibid., pp. 35, 36.
22 Ibid., p. 78.
23 Grousset, *The Rise and Splendor of the Chinese Empire*, p. 44.

Chapter 4

1 It was about this time that the Chinese gave up the old aristocratic institution of primogeniture whereby the eldest son inherited all the property of his father. From then on, the land was equally divided among the sons. This democratic reform has tended to equalize landholding and prevent the creation of big landed estates. But it might also have contributed to slow down the growth of China's population for fifteen hundred years, as it seems to have slowed down the growth of France's population during the past hundred years (see Fairbank, *The United States and China*, pp. 37, 38, 139).

2 Grousset, *The Rise and Splendor of the Chinese Empire*, p. 44.
3 Granet, *Chinese Civilization*, p. 38.
4 Hughes, *Chinese Philosophy in Classical Times*, p. 293.
5 Walker, *The Multi-State System of Ancient China*, p. 126.
6 Lin Yutang, *My Country and My People*, p. 182.
7 Keyserling, *The Travel Diary of a Philosopher*, ii, p. 116.
8 Ibid., ii, p. 117.
9 Karl A. Wittfogel has explained a great deal of the history of past civilizations in China, India, Mesopotamia, Egypt and pre-Columbian America, by pointing out that they were endowed with centralized bureaucratic systems, this being made necessary by the need to maintain government supervision over water control in the "key economic areas." He claims that the "Oriental" type of society is basically different from our own in that their governments maintained a thorough monopoly over large-scale economic activity.

Actually, the difference seems to be one of degree rather than of kind. Although the scale is different, it does not seem that economic activity in the "Oriental" types of society was much more monopolized by the state than in the type of semisocialist bureaucratic organization which is beginning to prevail in our own day in Europe and America. It might be that the type of private enterprise enjoyed in the nineteenth and early twentieth centuries will prove to be as transitory as it was in China during the Warring States era as described by the great historian Szuma Ch'ien in chapter 129 of his *Shih-chi* (see Walker, *op. cit.*, p. 126, note 18).

In the specific case of Chinese society, we can do no better than quote a summary of Wolfram Eberhard's pertinent criticism: "(1) Irrigation was not vital to the wheat and millet culture of North China (where Chinese civilization had its start), but assumed real importance only in connection with the later rice culture of the South; (2) Chinese political interest in water-control works cannot be traced with assurance far back into the feudal period, and became conspicuous only during the imperial epoch, when, moreover, it centered more around canal-building activities (themselves but one aspect of the rising interest of the time in improved communications), than it did around irrigation projects per se; (3) when, as we sometimes read in the literature, purely irrigation projects were undertaken, their initiative usually came from the local populace and not the central government." (Coulborn, *Feudalism in History*, p. 79.) A valid interpretation of history requires valid parallels. Those monolithic "Oriental" societies should be compared in the West to the Roman Empire in the days of Diocletian, not to the Greek city-states or to Renaissance Europe, which were the counterparts of the multi-state system in the China of the Spring and Autumn period.

10   Granet, *Chinese Civilization*, p. 113.

Chapter 5

1   Granet, *La Pensée Chinoise*, p. 37.
2   Ibid., p. 16.
3   Hughes, *Chinese Philosophy in Classical Times*, p. 89.
4   This was in evidence as early as eleven hundred years B.C., when the Chou rulers allowed the defeated Shang dynasty to continue ruling the diminutive feudal state of Sung rather than destroy it altogether, and as late as 1912 when the Chinese republic was inaugurated. The revolutionists offered the boy emperor "splendid treatment and glorious honors" (Sharman, *Sun Yat-sen*, p. 136); he was allowed to retain his imperial dignity, a miniature court and the privileges of the palaces in Peking's Forbidden City, while Sun Yat-sen formally closed the Manchu cycle by paying

formal homage at the foot of the Ming tombs, where the members of the preceding dynasty were buried. It was only in 1924 that General Feng Yü-hsiang brought the miniature Manchu court to an end by expelling the boy emperor from his palace and taking it over in the name of the people.

5   Granet, La Pensée Chinoise, p. 37.
6   Hughes, op. cit., p. 89.
7   I-Ching, vol. I, p. xxxv. Introduction, Carl Jung.
8   Needham, Science and Civilization in China, ii, p. 209.
9   Granet, La Pensée Chinoise, p. 273.
10 Needham, Science and Civilization in China, ii, p. 29.
11 Ibid., p. 28.
12 Strausz-Hupé, The Zone of Indifference, p. 62.
13 Needham, Science and Civilization in China, ii, p. 502.
14 Barnett, The Universe and Dr. Einstein, p. 126.
15 Granet, La Pensée Chinoise, p. 338.
16 Ibid., p. 409.
17 Hughes, Chinese Philosophy in Classical Times, p. 249.
18 Ibid., p. 277.
19 Granet, La Pensée Chinoise, p. 412.
20 Lin Yutang, My Country and My People, p. 85.

Chapter 6

1   Needham, Science and Civilization in China, ii, pp. 518–83.
2   Ibid., ii, p. 391.
3   Gautama's doctrine was a purely practical, utilitarian but negative and agnostic expression of an exhausted Culture, under the spell of a pessimistic world-sentiment. It was the Indian counterpart of Classical Stoicism, centered around man's suffering, aiming at putting an end to that suffering through voluntary annihilation in a voidlike Nirvāna: he taught that there was no Brāhman, no Godhead, no Atman, and made no room in his doctrine for love, pity or mercy. His philosophical doctrine was essentially a rebellion against the profound metaphysics of the Brāhmins. The transformation of his philosophy into the Mahāyāna's optimistic Greater Vehicle was so complete that it amounted to the creation of a new religion, emotional and positive, endowed with a deep metaphysical doctrine elaborated by Nāgārjuna and

Asvaghosa, which could not compete with a rejuvenated Hinduism but filled a gap in China.

4 Needham, *Science and Civilization in China*, ii, p. 401.

5 In one of the wisest and most farsighted books ever written on China, Thomas T. Meadows remarked (more than a century ago): "All cultivated Chinese are—intellectually at least—strict and conscientious atheists. But however consistent in their views, as taken by the bare understanding, it is impossible for them practically to repress the action of their naturally inherent religious faculties. Argue with them, and you find them unmistakably atheists. Let them talk themselves about the vicissitudes of human affairs and about their own lot in life, and you find them influenced by a belief in Teen (*T'ien*) as a supreme, intelligent, rewarding and punishing power, with more or less of will and personality. Theoretically they are atheists; practically they are pantheists or even deists." (Meadows, *The Chinese and Their Rebellions*, p. 361.)

6 Needham, *Science and Civilization in China*, ii, p. 491.

7 Keyserling, *The Travel Diary of a Philosopher*, ii, p. 55.

Chapter 7

1 Fitzgerald, *China*, p. 303.

2 Murdoch, *History of Japan*, iii, p. 491.

3 Keyserling, *The Travel Diary of a Philosopher*, ii, p. 159.

4 Nitobe, *Le Bushido*, p. 39.

5 Sansom, *The Western World and Japan*, p. 199.

6 Keyserling, *The Travel Diary of a Philosopher*, ii, p. 228.

7 Nitobe, *Le Bushido*, p. 41.

8 Many neighboring nations were still considered tributaries as late as the twentieth century (Vietnam, Burma, Bhutan, Nepal). These claims were never formally abandoned, regardless of the regime in power in China.

9 Lin Yutang, *My Country and My People*, p. 328.

Chapter 8

1 The greatest failure of the Jesuits (as well as of all other Roman Catholics and Protestants) was their inability to explain logically the connection between their religious beliefs and their

scientific knowledge. Under these circumstances, it was inevitable that the pragmatic Chinese would make use of their scientific ability without embracing a faith which had no apparent connection with it.

2   Morand, *L'Epopée des Jésuites Français en Chine*, p. 89.

3   Ibid., p. 29.

4   Ibid., p. 196.

5   Ibid., p. 214.

6   Ibid., p. 219.

7   Ibid., p. 127.

8   Wells, *The Outline of History*, p. 793.

9   Devilliers, *Histoire du Vietnam*, p. 17.

10 Thomas T. Meadows, who lived in China during the rebellion and saw it at first hand, had clearly seen this. ". . . my knowledge of the Chinese mind, joined to the dejected admissions that Protestant missionaries of many years' standing occasionally made of the fruitlessness of their labors, had convinced me that Christianity, as hardened into our sectarian creeds, could not possibly find converts among the Chinese. . . . Consequently when it was once or twice rumoured that the large body of men who were setting Imperial armies at defiance 'were Christians,' I refused to give the rumour credence. It did not occur to me that the Chinese convert . . . might either fail to see, or (if he saw them) might spontaneously eliminate the dogmas and congealed forms of merely sectarian Christianity, and then by preaching simply the great religious truth of a One God, and the pure morality of Christ's Sermon on the Mount, obtain numbers of followers . . ." (Meadows, *The Chinese and Their Rebellions*, p. 193.)

Chapter 9

1   Pringle, *China Struggles for Unity*, p. 20.

2   Walsh, *Introduction to Philosophy of History*, p. 123.

3   The intellectual argument of Kant was based on his famous Categorical Imperative, which is essentially an *a priori* concept, unprovable by reason but felt intuitively. Because of its universal character, which is also postulated *a priori*, the Categorical Imperative is one and the same at all times and in all places, and is applicable to all human beings. Such *a priori* knowledge is

therefore not dependent on the whim or passions of individuals but on the general public mind. Kant dismisses the "ego" as the knowing self and replaces it with the "transcendental ego," which is essentially collective and unindividualistic (see Northrop, *The Meeting of East and West*, pp. 198–202).

4   Needham, *Science and Civilization in China*, ii, p. 454.
5   Russell, *History of Western Philosophy*, p. 735.
6   Needham, *Science and Civilization in China*, ii, pp. 499–505.
7   Marx, *Capital*, p. xii.
8   Ibid., p. xxi.
9   Ibid., p. xxi.
10 Russell, *History of Western Philosophy*, p. 811.
11 Ibid., p. 816.
12 Hook, *From Hegel to Marx*, p. 36.
13 Stalin, *Leninism*, p. 2.
14 Ibid., p. 595.
15 Ibid., p. 596.
16 Peasants, being bound to the local soil, are always the mainstay of national feeling and local patriotism—which is not necessarily the case with industrial proletariats. Their inevitable and massive participation in the revolutions of Russia and Asia has had a profound impact on the "international" character of Communism; it has made a telling contribution to its transformation into an "oriental" way of life. As a socialist Premier of France once remarked, Communism is not so much a political *left* as a geopolitical *east*.
17 Stalin, *Leninism*, p. 50.
18 Dallin, *The Rise of Russia in Asia*, p. 208.

Chapter 10

1   Tsuchida, *Contemporary Thought in Japan and China*, p. 64.
2   Ibid., p. 63.
3   Masayoshi Kihira derived his philosophy from Fichte and Hegel. In order to understand the intellectual background of Japan's dynamic imperialism in our century, we need only read his following statement: "Necessity by means of 'values' creates history just as 'causal' necessity creates the natural sciences. Then history is a self that has been extended in time; and conversely I am now here as one who has unified some material transformed into his-

tory. The State is the self extended in space . . . which demands our absolute submission." (Tsuchida, *Contemporary Thought in Japan and China*, p. 112). Most Japanese thinkers were haunted by the necessity of a synthesis of Eastern and Western thought. And as one of their articulate spokesmen explained, men like Nishida, Nishi and Kihira ultimately "all in the same way arrived at historism" (Ibid., p. 113).

4 Pringle, *China Struggles for Unity*, p. 20.
5 Russell, *The Problem of China*, p. 46.
6 Keyserling, *The Travel Diary of a Philosopher*, ii, p. 82.
7 Sun Yat-sen, *The International Development of China*, p. 161.
8 Fairbank, *The United States and China*, p. 209.

Chapter 11

1 Tsuchida, *Contemporary Thought in Japan and China*, p. 143.
2 In his book, *Confucius as a Reformer*, K'ang Yu-wei attempted to break down the orthodox interpretation of the great Master. Although he correctly pointed out the fact that Confucius had falsified history for ethical purposes, he stretched his material too far in trying to read into the Master's work notions that could never have entered his head twenty-five hundred years ago (see Sharman, *Sun Yat-sen*, p. 52).
3 Tsuchida, *Contemporary Thought in Japan and China*, p. 204.
4 Ibid., p. 207.
5 Ibid., p. 217.
6 Ibid., p. 202.
7 Russell, *The Problem of China*, p. 81.
8 Ibid., p. 177.
9 Karl A. Wittfogel has pointed this out in his article, "The Historical Position of Communist China: Doctrine and Reality" (*Review of Politics*, October 1954). He argues, extending his thesis on oriental despotism, that in China as well as in Russia, the Communists have substituted a completely managerial state instead of the traditional semi-managerial.
10 Most of the great leaders in Chinese history, including all the imperial dynasties, had hitherto come from the area which lies north of the Yangtze.
11 Schwartz, *Chinese Communism and the Rise of Mao*, p. 12.
12 Ibid., p. 14.

13 Granet, *La Pensée Chinoise*, p. 15.

14 Tsuchida, *Contemporary Thought in Japan and China*, p. 220.

15 Schwartz, *Chinese Communism and the Rise of Mao*, p. 42.

16 Ibid., p. 214.

17 Disgust with the failure of the parliamentary republic set up in Peking partly accounted for this sharp swing toward a disciplined and monolithic structure. But it was pointed out at the time, with great discernment, that the Kuomintang was just as much patterned after the traditional committee administration of China's trade guilds as it was after the Soviet Russian. Similarly, Sun Yat-sen's insistence on adding two independent governmental "powers" to the three powers familiar to the West (legislative, executive and judicial) harked back to the old imperial system: a Department of Examinations for the recruitment of the bureaucracy and a Department of Control with censorial powers. In fact, a thorough study of Sun Yat-sen's biography reveals that the main theme of his life was an unconscious overcoming of the pro-Western feelings of his youth; even his nationalism slowly gave way to the traditional Chinese yearning for participation in a world order—and Borodin was quick to notice it (see Sharman, *Sun Yat-sen*, pp. 262, 269). Shortly before his death, he even turned against his spiritual parents and denounced foreign missionaries as "running-dogs of imperialism" (Ibid., p. 304). There can be no mistaking in Sun Yat-sen's own evolution a prefiguration of the coming evolution of China.

Chapter 12

1 Schwartz, *Chinese Communism and the Rise of Mao*, p. 51.

2 Ibid., p. 67.

3 Lin Yutang, *My Country and My People*, p. 65.

4 Ibid., p. 268.

5 Ibid., p. 263.

6 Schwartz, *Chinese Communism and the Rise of Mao*, p. 73.

7 Ibid., p. 74.

8 Mao Tse-tung, *Selected Works*, iii, p. 154.

9 Ibid., i, p. 118.

10 Ibid., i, p. 282.

11 Ibid, i, p. 292.

12 Ibid., iii, p. 69.

13   Ibid., i, p. 292.
14   Ibid., i, p. 120.
15   Ibid., i, p. 296.
16   Schwartz, *Chinese Communism and the Rise of Mao*, p. 75.
17   Ibid., p. 136.
18   Ibid., p. 199.
19   Lin Yutang, *My Country and My People*, p. 170.
20   Fairbank, *The United States and China*, p. 209.

Chapter 13

1   Dallin, *Soviet Russia and the Far East*, p. 150.
2   Ibid., p. 323.
3   Fitzgerald, *Revolution in China*, p. 172.
4   Relations between the Chinese Muslims and the Kuomintang
    were always strained. I had several interviews in Taiwan (June
    1951) with leading Chinese Muslims who confirmed this hostility
    of the central government and its failure to support them.
    Earlier, my own observations in Tibet and Central Asia (1947)
    had led me to believe that there was a deep-seated antagonism
    between the Kuomintang and the Muslim governors of Tsinghai
    and Kansu. (For details of Chiang Kai-shek's policy in Central
    Asia, see my *Roof of the World*, pp. 207, 209, 304.)
5   Liu Shao-chi'i, *How to Be a Good Communist*.
6   Fitzgerald, *China: A Short Cultural History*, p. 145.
7   Walker, *China Under Communism*, p. 193.
8   Ibid., p. 206.
9   On January 1, 1956, the entire Chinese press adopted the
    horizontal, instead of the traditional vertical, system of type-
    setting. The Hsinhua (New China) news agency then announced
    in February that this was only a preliminary move pointing toward
    the eventual destruction of the ideographic script altogether. It
    will eventually be replaced by a Latinized alphabet. Wu Yu-
    chang, chairman of the Chinese Written Language Reform
    Committee, had already announced in April 1955 that the ideo-
    graphic script would be gradually abolished in favor of an alpha-
    betical system—and simultaneously, in order to avoid any local
    separatism, the Peking dialect is being compulsorily extended to
    the whole of China. However, early in 1957, the Chinese Commu-
    nist authorities decided to postpone this reform because of the

immense difficulties entailed and the opposition of many scholars. But the fundamental problem is still there and remains to be solved.

10 Mao Tse-tung, *Selected Works*, i, pp. 108, 111.

11 Walker, *China Under Communism*, p. 161.

12 Ibid., p. 160.

13 The bafflement and anxiety of sincere Westerners has rarely been expressed with such eloquent humility as it was by Sun Yat-sen's biographer, Lyon Sharman: "But where is our own boasted occidental intelligence that we should have been party to the muddling of social changes in this horrible fashion? . . . We have been impelling China toward changes so drastic that we have got her into a maze of confusion in which she seems incapable of understanding herself. . . . We make sad failures in attempting very much smaller problems of our own. But to confess this is not going to save ourselves, much less another people. Where are there resources of intelligence able to make headway against the disaster that has come upon China?" (Sharman, *Sun Yat-sen*, pp. 344, 345.)

14 In his *China's Destiny*, Chiang Kai-shek blames almost all of China's misfortunes on the West with a remarkable lack of discrimination. The similarities between his program and Mao Tse-tung's are remarkable, and they suggest that their foreign policies would not have been too different. He even makes it quite plain, in an additional work entitled *Chinese Economic Theory*, that his views on economics are much closer to Marxism than to the Western system of free enterprise: China's economic policy should aim at strengthening the state rather than promoting individual welfare and should aim at state socialism; he clearly advocates state ownership of the major means of production and goes so far as to advocate collective farms in order to train farmer-soldiers.

But Chiang Kai-shek misread the significance of China's historical past. It is not Confucianism that he should have revived but the Legalist tradition. Neo-Confucianism was bound to destroy the power of the state instead of bolstering it, and his narrow nationalism had far less appeal in China than some form of universalism such as Marxism-Leninism. Back of him were the heads of the C.C. Clique, Ch'en Kuo-fu and Ch'en Li-fu, whose ardent feelings against the West would have prompted them to promote a foreign policy which would have been very similar to the Communist. The ideological difference between them was significantly small: Ch'en Li-fu had elaborated a complex philosophy whose cornerstone, "vitalism" (*wei-sheng chu-i*), he opposed to the Marxist "materialism" (*wei-wu chu-i*). Unfortunately, he did not possess the mental qualifications of a Karl Marx and could not compete with his Communist opponents (see Fairbank, *The United States and China*, pp. 253–56).

All this suggests that, basically, the Chinese Marxists are able to do more efficiently what the Kuomintang wanted to do all along—that, in fact, regardless who ruled China in the second half of the twentieth century, Western influence and prestige were bound to decline.

15 Walker, *The Multi-State System of Ancient China*, p. 10.

BIBLIOGRAPHY

Since this volume is intended for the general reader, the bibliography which follows is rudimentary. I have merely listed those works which I have quoted directly or on which I have relied heavily. Most of them carry extensive bibliographies of their own which make it unnecessary to extend this short list. I hope to be forgiven for having omitted many major works on China and I can only advise the reader who wishes to pursue his studies to refer to the extensive bibliographies that are included in some of the works listed below. I would like to point out that I have been compelled by the nature of this work to add a number of books which are not concerned with China but which I have quoted directly.

Barnett, L., *The Universe and Dr. Einstein*, New York, 1952.
Berdyaev, N., *The Russian Idea*, London, 1947.
———, *The Beginning and the End*, London, 1952.
Bodard, L., *La Chine du Cauchemar*, Paris, 1961.
Bodde, D., *China's First Unifier*, Leiden, 1938.
———, *Tolstoy and China*, Princeton, 1950.
Chiang Kai-shek, *China's Destiny*, New York, 1947.
Clubb, O. E., *Twentieth Century China*, New York, 1964.
Coomaraswamy, A., *Buddha and the Gospel of Buddhism*, London, 1928.
Coulborn, R., *Feudalism in History*, Princeton, 1956.
Crankshaw, E., *The New Cold War*, Harmondsworth, 1963.
Creel, H. G., *Chinese Thought from Confucius to Mao*, Chicago, 1953.
Dallin, D. J., *The Rise of Russia in Asia*, Yale, 1949.
———, *Soviet Russia and the Far East*, London, 1949.
Eberhard, W., *A History of China*, London, 1950.
———, *Conquerors and Rulers. Social Forces in Medieval China*, Leiden, 1952.
Escarra, J., *Le Droit Chinois*, Peking, 1936.
Fairbank, J. K., *The United States and China*, Harvard, 1948.
Fitzgerald, C. P., *Revolution in China*, London, 1952.
———, *China: A Short Cultural History*, London, 1954.

Frazer, J., *The Golden Bough*, London, 1950.

Goodrich, L. C., *Scientific Developments in China*, Santiniketan, West Bengal, 1954.

Granet, M., *Chinese Civilization*, New York, 1930.

——, *La Pensée Chinoise*, Paris, 1950.

Grousset, R., *L'Empire des Steppes*, Paris, 1939.

——, *The Rise and Splendor of the Chinese Empire*, London, 1952.

Hegel, G. W. F., *The Philosophy of History*, New York, 1944.

Hook, S., *From Hegel to Marx*, New York, 1944.

Hughes, E. R., *The Invasion of China by the Western World*, London, 1937.

——, *The Great Learning and the Mean in Action*, New York, 1943.

——, *Chinese Philosophy in Classical Times*, London, 1950.

Hu Shih, *Development of the Logical Method in Ancient China*, Shanghai, 1922.

——, *The Chinese Renaissance*, Chicago, 1934.

I-Ching, 2 vol., London, 1951, translated by Richard Wilhelm.

Keyserling, H., *The Travel Diary of a Philosopher*, 2 vol., New York, 1942.

Kohn, H., *Orient and Occident*, New York, 1934.

Landon, K., *South East Asia*, Chicago, 1949.

Latourette, K. S., *The Chinese, Their History and Culture*, 2 vol., New York, 1946.

Law, N. N., *Interstate Relations in Ancient India*, London, 1920.

Legge, J. *The Chinese Classics*, 7 vol., Oxford, 1895.

Linebarger, P., *The Political Doctrines of Sun Yat-sen*, Baltimore, 1937.

——, *The China of Chiang Kai-shek*, Boston, 1941.

Lin Yutang, *My Country and My People*, London, 1948.

Majumdar, R. C., *The Vedic Age*, London, 1951.

Maspero, H., *La Chine Antique*, Paris, 1955.

Mao Tse-tung, *Selected Works*, 3 vol., London, 1954.

Marx, K., *Capital*, New York, 1932.

McGovern, W. M., *Early Empires of Central Asia*, North Carolina, 1939.

Meadows, T. T., *The Chinese and Their Rebellions*, Stanford, California, n.d.

Mehnert, K., *Peking and Moscow*, London, 1963.

Murdoch, J., *History of Japan*, London, 1925.

Mure, G. R. G., *An Introduction to Hegel*, Oxford, 1940.

Needham, J., *Science and Civilization in China*, 2 vol., Cambridge, 1954–1956.

Nitobe, I., *Le Bushido*, Paris, 1927.

Northrop, F. S. C., *The Meeting of East and West*, New York, 1946.

Okakura, K., *Les Idéaux de l'Orient et le Réveil du Japon*, Paris, 1917.

Ortega y Gasset, J., *Toward a Philosophy of History*, New York, 1941.

Pringle, J. M. D., *China Struggles for Unity*, Harmondsworth, Middlesex, 1939.

Radhakrishnan, S., *Eastern Religions and Western Thought*, Oxford, 1940.

Reischauer, E. O., *The United States and Japan*, Harvard, 1950.

Riencourt, A. de, *Roof of the World*, New York, 1950.

———, *The Coming Caesars*, New York, 1957.

Riesman, D., *The Lonely Crowd*, New York, 1955.

Russell, B., *The Problem of China*, London, 1922.

———, *History of Western Philosophy*, London, 1948.

Sansom, G. B., *The Western World and Japan*, London, 1950.

Schwab, R., *La Renaissance Orientale*, Paris, 1950.

Schwartz, B., *Chinese Communism and the Rise of Mao*, Harvard, 1951.

Sharman, L., *Sun Yat-sen*, New York, 1934.

Soulie de Morand, G., *L'Epopée des Jésuites Français en Chine*, Paris, 1933.

Stalin, J., *Leninism*, London, 1940.

Strausz-Hupé, R., *The Zone of Indifference*, New York, 1952.

Sun Yat-sen, *The International Development of China*, London, 1926.

Thomas, E. D., *Chinese Political Thought*, New York, 1927.

Tsuchida, K., *Contemporary Thought in Japan and China*, London, 1927.

Waley, A., *The Way and Its Power*, London, 1934.

———, *The Analects of Confucius*, London, 1938.

———, *Three Ways of Thought in Ancient China*, New York, 1956.

Walker, R. C., *The Multi-State System of Ancient China*, Hamden, Connecticut, 1953.

———, *China Under Communism*, Yale, 1955.

Walsh, W. H., *Introduction to Philosophy of History*, London, 1951.

Wells, H. G., *The Outline of History*, London, 1951.

Wittfogel, K. A., *Oriental Despotism*, Yale, 1957.

INDEX

ABOUT THE AUTHOR

Amaury de Riencourt was born in Orléans, France, in 1918 and was educated in France, Switzerland, and North Africa. He received his B.A. from the Sorbonne and his M.A. from the University of Algiers. During the war he spent three and one-half years in the French Navy. Mr. de Riencourt has traveled extensively throughout the world, including most of the states in this country. He has lived for four years in Africa, one year in the Balkans, two years in Asia, and ten years in North America. He has written political articles for various publications and news agencies and has lectured extensively all over the United States. Mr. de Riencourt is the author of *Roof of the World*, *The Coming Caesars*, *The Soul of China*, and *The Soul of India*.

COLOPHON BOOKS ON EUROPEAN HISTORY